D0565704

AP EUROPEAN HISTORY FLASHCARDS

Premium Edition with CD-ROM

Test-Readiness Quizzes
with Instant Scoring

PLUS European History
Timeline & Charts
For Windows®

Mark Bach
AP European History Teacher
Apex Learning
Seattle, Washington

Research & Education Association
Visit our website at: www.rea.com

Research & Education Association
61 Ethel Road West
Piscataway, New Jersey 08854
E-mail: info@rea.com

REA's Flashcard Book for the AP European History Exam Premium Edition with CD-ROM

Published 2014

Copyright © 2009 by Research & Education Association, Inc. All rights reserved. No part of this book may be reproduced in any form without permission of the publisher.

Printed in the United States of America

Library of Congress Control Number 2008940107

ISBN-13: 978-0-7386-0508-1
ISBN-10: 0-7386-0508-5

About This Premium Edition with CD-ROM

REA's unique Premium Edition Flashcard Book features questions and answers to help you study for the Advanced Placement European History Exam. This book, enhanced with an interactive CD-ROM, is designed to fit conveniently into your study schedule for AP European History. You'll find it's an especially effective study tool when paired with REA's *AP European History All Access*, our comprehensive review and practice-exam book, or our *AP European History Crash Course*.

This handy volume is filled with 500 must-study AP European History questions and detailed answers. The questions are chronologically ordered and cover all topics found on the AP European History exam from the Renaissance to the present. The full index makes it easy to look up a particular subject and review a specific historical time period.

Unlike most flashcards that come loose in a box, these flashcards are bound in an easy-to-use, organized book. This innovative Flashcard Book lets you write your answer to a question on the front of the card, and then compare it to the answer on the back of the card. REA's flashcards are a great way to boost your test-readiness and are perfect for studying on the go.

The interactive CD-ROM includes four test-readiness quizzes, timelines of all chronological periods covered on the actual AP test, and a concise European History review.

This Premium Edition Flashcard Book has been carefully developed with REA's customary concern for excellence. We believe you will find it an outstanding addition to your AP European History prep.

Larry B. Kling
Chief Editor

A Note from the Author

Purchasing this book means you have undertaken the challenge of studying AP European History and taking the AP European History exam. I congratulate you on this decision. It shows you are not afraid to work hard and learn about the world around you. AP History courses give you a taste of college level work and academic expectations. Experiencing these more rigorous standards now will prepare you well for what comes next in your education.

AP exams cover a lot of material, which can be an overwhelming experience. You will not be expected to know everything, but you will be challenged to demonstrate your knowledge of trends in the human experience.

This book is purposely designed to give you practice with the multiple-choice section of the AP European History exam. The more you practice these questions and answers, the greater your confidence will be when taking the exam. Study the questions and answers in this book to review and expand your knowledge of European history.

AP European History is a college survey course and divides history into three main categories:

1. Intellectual and Cultural History covers ideologies, the arts and religious trends;
2. Political and Diplomatic History has to do with political movements, international relations and wars;
3. Social and Economic History deal with industrialization, social structures and class hierarchies.

Based on my experience as an AP History teacher, this book gives you a broad sampling of the types of questions you will see on the test. I wish you well on the exam, and hope that your understanding of the 21st century will be enhanced by what you learn in your AP course. Our lives connect with the past constantly—we have to know how to see the connections.

Best of luck with your studies and the exam!

Mark Bach

Table of Contents

Test-Readiness Quizzes on CD

After studying questions 1 through 125, take Quiz 1.
Take Quiz 2 after studying questions 126 through 251.
After studying questions 252 through 375, take Quiz 3.
Quiz 4 starts after question 500.

About the Author

Mark Bach has been teaching European History since 1983 and is currently an online instructor for AP History at Apex Learning in Seattle, Washington. He is also on the history and drama faculty at the International Community School in Kirkland, Washington.

Mr. Bach received his B.A. in History, German and Religion from St. Olaf College in Minnesota and his M.A. from Michigan State University.

About Research & Education Association

Founded in 1959, Research & Education Association (REA) is dedicated to publishing the finest and most effective educational materials—including software, study guides, and test preps—for students in middle school, high school, college, graduate school, and beyond.

Today, REA's wide-ranging catalog is a leading resource for teachers, students, and professionals.

Visit *www.rea.com* to see a complete listing of all our titles.

Acknowledgments

In addition to our author, we would like to thank Larry B. Kling, Vice President, Editorial, for his overall guidance, which brought this publication to completion; Pam Weston, Publisher, for setting the quality standards for production integrity and managing the publication to completion; John Cording, Vice President, Technology, for coordinating the design and development of REA's TestWare®; Diane Goldschmidt, Senior Editor, for editorial project management; Alice Leonard and Kathleen Casey, Senior Editors, for preflight editorial review; Heena Patel and Amy Jamison, Technology Project Managers, for their design contributions and software testing efforts; and Christine Saul, Senior Graphic Designer, for designing our cover.

We also extend special thanks to Jeanne Bowlan for her technical review, Marianne L'Abbate for copyediting, Carolyn Duffy for proofreading, Terry Casey for indexing, and Kathy Caratozzolo of Caragraphics for typesetting this edition.

Questions

Q–1

The Hundred Years' War was fought between which of the following kingdoms?

(A) Germany and France

(B) Russia and Poland

(C) France and England

(D) Denmark and Prussia

(E) Holland and England

Your Answer _____ C

Q–2

The rise of France as a distinct nation in the late Middle Ages can be credited to the

(A) chaos following the Black Death

(B) Hundred Years' War

(C) Protestant Reformation

(D) Great Schism

(E) civil war

Your Answer _____ B

Correct Answers

A–1

(C) The Hundred Years' War was an on-again, off-again conflict that carried into the 1400s. It was fought over territory in southwestern France that England claimed. The fighting took place in France, where great destruction ensued. Mercenaries, nobles, and freemen fought in the war, but there were deep class divisions on both sides. After initial victories, the British were put on the defensive and eventually lost to the French.

A–2

(B) The Hundred Years' War helped forge French nationalism in the face of foreign invasion. English armies pillaged and laid waste to large sections of France after 1350. Savage guerilla wars were fought by the French to harass the English while they controlled pieces of the continent. The hope of divine intervention and the need for national leadership helped establish a viable monarchy in France. Finally, military victories bolstered the French cause and brought the French to victory.

Questions

Q–3

The Hundred Years' War ended in 1453. Which of the following were outcomes of this war?

(A) France was ravaged by both the conflict and diseases.

(B) The French monarchy was strengthened.

(C) European banks were weakened by the conflict.

(D) Papal authority continued to be disputed.

(E) All of the above

Your Answer ___E_____

Q–4

The term *mercenary* refers to a

(A) cleric

(B) priest who repents

(C) noble at war

(D) soldier for pay

(E) merchant who makes a profit

Your Answer ___D_____

Correct Answers

A–3

(E) The Hundred Years' War had political, economic, and ecclesiastical outcomes. French territory was destroyed, and some banks that financed the war failed when loans could not be repaid. The eventual victory by France created a cohesive kingdom in western Europe that changed the balance of power in the region. The split in the church over different popes also lingered because the nations involved in the fighting did not come to terms with the divisive issues of the church until after the war.

A–4

(D) At the end of the Middle Ages, warfare was changing as more and more men were needed for fighting. Larger armies took more and more men, often from the lower classes. These men would fight for money. Eventually, certain soldiers began to fight for the best-paying kings or princes. The mercenary could be from any class and eventually became the prototype of the modern paid professional soldier.

Q–5

By the year 1400, the Holy Roman Empire was

(A) the most powerful political entity in Europe

(B) split between the French and German nobility

(C) under the influence of the Moors

(D) located in eastern Europe

(E) unified in name only

Your Answer _____ E _____

_____

Q–6

Successful popular uprisings after 1350 in the central Alpine region led to the creation of

(A) the Swiss Confederation

(B) a unified Italy

(C) a more powerful Lithuania

(D) the Knights Templar

(E) the Hapsburg dynasty

Your Answer _____

_____

Correct Answers

A–5

(E)   While western European monarchies were growing stronger, central Europe remained a patchwork of many smaller kingdoms supposedly united under the Holy Roman Emperor. But princes and dukes who wanted more autonomy often challenged the emperor's authority—and were successful. Peasant revolts were also successful in undermining the power of the Holy Roman Emperor.

A–6

(A)   During the Middle Ages, towns and communes were created in the high Alpine valleys of present-day Switzerland. Free peasants became more powerful over time and challenged the power of the Hapsburg monarchy. The peasants eventually raised their own armies, defeated the Hapsburgs, and created an alliance of cantons that eventually formed a confederation. This loose association of member states still exists today.

Q–7

Which of the following is another name for the Iberian Muslims?

(A) Basques

(B) Moors

(C) Ottomans

(D) Janissaries

(E) Sephardim

Your Answer _____

_____

Q–8

The word *schism* can best be described as which of the following?

(A) An extension of more rights for the peasantry

(B) The acquisition of dual nationality

(C) Church unity under the papacy

(D) Disagreement leading to an organizational split or divide

(E) Church councils that lead to standard doctrine

Your Answer _____

_____

Correct Answers

A–7

(B) Islam had spread into southwestern Europe for many centuries after 700. Christian lords pushed back the Muslim incursion and by 1400, Muslims remained only in the southern part of the Iberian peninsula. As Christian power increased in Iberia, the Moors were either captured and converted or forced to retreat to North Africa.

A–8

(D) A schism is a split within a body or organization leading to two factions. The Christian church experienced one such schism when it split into the western Roman church and the eastern Orthodox faith. Later, rival popes fought for authority and created a temporary schism within the Roman Catholic Church in the medieval period. Islam is also divided into the Shia and Sunni traditions.

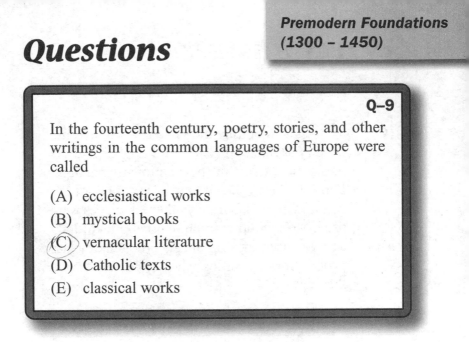

Q–9

In the fourteenth century, poetry, stories, and other writings in the common languages of Europe were called

(A) ecclesiastical works

(B) mystical books

(C) vernacular literature

(D) Catholic texts

(E) classical works

Your Answer _____

_____

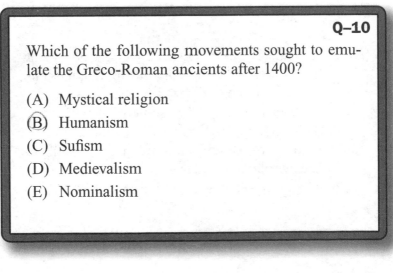

Q–10

Which of the following movements sought to emulate the Greco-Roman ancients after 1400?

(A) Mystical religion

(B) Humanism

(C) Sufism

(D) Medievalism

(E) Nominalism

Your Answer _____

_____

Correct Answers

A–9

(C)   Vernacular literature bloomed in the fourteenth century as Italian, French, and English authors wrote more often in their national languages. Latin had been the dominant language of the medieval period, but now other languages were used. Most authors, including Petrarch of Italy and Chaucer of England, were middle-class people from the cities who wrote about what they saw.

A–10

(B)   Humanism was a new intellectual movement that flowered as early as the fourteenth century in Europe. Centered in the cities, scholars began to rediscover some of the works of the Greek and Roman world of the past. The writings of Aristotle and other great thinkers became popular, and the study of the Greek language enjoyed new attention in universities.

Q–11

In late medieval Europe, a woman's rights depended on both her

(A) dowry and parish

(B) marriage and religion

(C) landownership and standing in the church

(D) class and region

(E) parental support and the church's blessing

Your Answer _____

_____

Q–12

Which of the following is true about medieval prostitution?

(A) It was increasingly managed by other women.

(B) All prostitutes were captured slaves.

(C) Prostitution was banned in every kingdom.

(D) It was condemned by the church but widely tolerated in many cities.

(E) It was thoroughly regulated by local governments.

Your Answer _____

_____

Correct Answers

A–11

(D) Women in northern Europe enjoyed more basic legal rights than their southern counterparts. In the north, women could testify in court and even own property. Southern European women were more bound to their fathers and husbands and could not manage their property without male oversight.

A–12

(D) Women have been denied direct access to economic activity throughout most of human history. In medieval times, many poor women found prostitution to be the only way to support themselves. Though deplored by polite society and the church, prostitution thrived in most urban areas and was sometimes regulated by local codes.

Questions

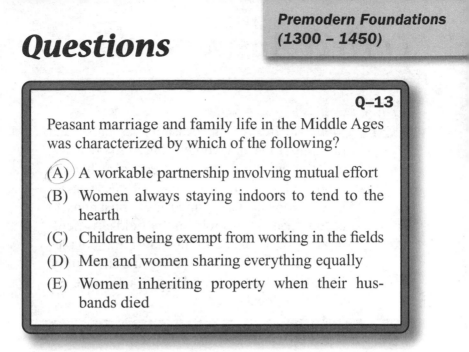

Q–13

Peasant marriage and family life in the Middle Ages was characterized by which of the following?

(A) A workable partnership involving mutual effort

(B) Women always staying indoors to tend to the hearth

(C) Children being exempt from working in the fields

(D) Men and women sharing everything equally

(E) Women inheriting property when their husbands died

Your Answer _____

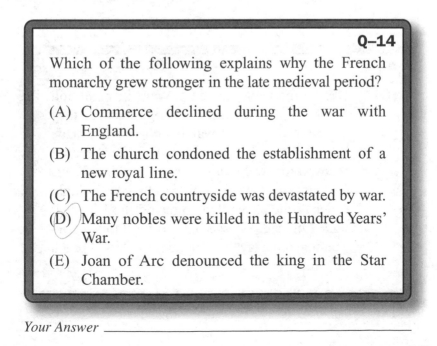

Q–14

Which of the following explains why the French monarchy grew stronger in the late medieval period?

(A) Commerce declined during the war with England.

(B) The church condoned the establishment of a new royal line.

(C) The French countryside was devastated by war.

(D) Many nobles were killed in the Hundred Years' War.

(E) Joan of Arc denounced the king in the Star Chamber.

Your Answer _____

Correct Answers

A–13

(A) Medieval life for the peasant was harsh and grueling. Men and women shared many tasks, and the entire family was needed at harvest time. While men did some of the heavier work, women often joined their husbands to accomplish various jobs in the fields. Agricultural work dominated their days, and couples shared the burdens of farming and the family. Peasants owned little and would not move beyond their locale.

A–14

(D) During the Hundred Years' War, the death toll among the nobles was very high because they were the traditional warrior class. This made consolidation by a royal family easier because there were fewer rivals to oppose a king. Louis XI was one of the first monarchs who brought order to the chaos that followed the long war with England. He was able to reestablish government and lay the foundations for French absolutism.

Questions

Q–15

Until the *reconquista* (reconquering) of Spain, Iberia remained a

(A) unified Christian kingdom under one family

(B) loose confederation of Muslim domains

(C) mix of Jewish and Christian states

(D) dual monarchy

(E) collection of disparate and disconnected kingdoms

Your Answer _____

_____

Q–16

The great storyteller and chronicler of English life in the late Middle Ages was

(A) William Shakespeare

(B) Geoffrey Chaucer

(C) John Boleyn

(D) Henry Tudor

(E) Jean Froissart

Your Answer _____

_____

Correct Answers

A–15

(E) Iberia, or Spain, was a mix of Muslim and Christian domains until the *reconquista* by the Christians in the late 1400s. The large kingdoms of Castile and Aragon were important, but other smaller kingdoms also existed. By the fifteenth century, the Moors (Spanish Muslims) retained some control of southern Iberia until they were expelled or converted.

A–16

(B) Geoffrey Chaucer created short vignettes of medieval life in England in his *Canterbury Tales*. He showed ordinary people in real-life and humorous situations. His characters included many of the archetypal medieval people, such as yeomen, local bureaucrats, farmers, and priests. Chaucer's works give us some of the best views of English life from the time period. Popular in his own day, Chaucer served the crown as a civil servant and traveled widely.

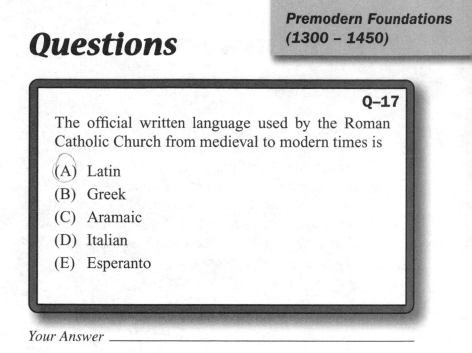

Q–17

The official written language used by the Roman Catholic Church from medieval to modern times is

(A) Latin

(B) Greek

(C) Aramaic

(D) Italian

(E) Esperanto

Your Answer _____

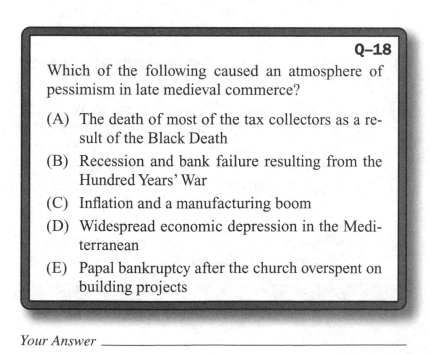

Q–18

Which of the following caused an atmosphere of pessimism in late medieval commerce?

(A) The death of most of the tax collectors as a result of the Black Death

(B) Recession and bank failure resulting from the Hundred Years' War

(C) Inflation and a manufacturing boom

(D) Widespread economic depression in the Mediterranean

(E) Papal bankruptcy after the church overspent on building projects

Your Answer _____

Correct Answers

A–17

(A)   Since the fall of the Roman Empire, Latin has been the prominent language of learning and scholarship. The popes in Rome wrote their proclamations in Latin, and almost all Holy Scripture had been translated into Latin. In medieval times, most people were illiterate, but they still heard the church services and pronouncements in Latin.

A–18

(B)   The mid- to late 1400s saw a slowdown of the economy of Europe because financial institutions were in distress. The war in northern Europe caused leading Italian banks to fail after England defaulted on some large loans. Merchants became cautious and investment was rerouted to local projects. As continental trade slowed down, many moneychangers from Florence to Amsterdam went out of business.

Q–19

The most important trade axis in the late medieval period was between

(A) Holland and Germany

(B) England and France

(C) the Holy Roman Empire and Italy

(D) France and Spain

(E) Italy and the Low Countries

Your Answer _____

Q–20

Which of the following characterizes the living spaces of European peasants and artisans over four hundred years ago?

(A) Privacy was ensured by separate quarters for the children.

(B) Large rooms were available for family members.

(C) Humans and animals often shared the same spaces to keep warm.

(D) Bathrooms were common in most homes.

(E) Sanitary kitchen areas were the center of family life.

Your Answer _____

Correct Answers

A–19

(E) Italy was a major producer of certain luxury products that northern Europeans wished to buy. Items such as silverware and jewelry were brought to Ghent or Bruges, in present-day Belgium, where they were resold in Scandinavia, Poland, or England. The Low Countries also had well-established banks to handle business financing.

A–20

(C) Most families kept chickens or cows to provide eggs and milk for the family. While these animals were placed outside for part of the year, during the harsh winters, rooms existed inside the homes for a variety of animals, even pigs. Wild dogs and feral cats were in abundance, and humans shared their lives with an array of animals. Hay was kept to feed the animals and used as bedding material for children.

Q–21

Religious dissent in the late Middle Ages took which of the following forms?

(A) Mystics asserted that the sacraments were unnecessary.

(B) Pious laypeople created communes.

(C) People set up independent convents outside church control.

(D) Intellectuals challenged church traditions not found in the Bible.

(E) All of the above

Your Answer _____

_____

Q–22

The claim of papal authority in Rome has always been based on

(A) the riches of the church

(B) the apostolic succession traced back to Saint Peter

(C) political sponsorship of the kings of Europe

(D) secular political support

(E) the power of the College of Cardinals

Your Answer _____

_____

Correct Answers

A–21

(E) Church authority had been eroding in the Middle Ages as the church became more and more political. Some believers saw the contradictions between church practice and the Holy Scripture. Common priests sometimes struggled to survive, and the people saw their plight in contrast to the wealth of high-ranking church officials. The dual rival papacy (the Great Schism) in the 1300s also undermined church authority.

A–22

(B) The papal claim to authority dates back to the Roman period when the Apostle Peter was believed to have been the first bishop of Rome. After the Romans martyred Peter, all succeeding bishops of Rome claimed the authority of the apostle who had learned from Jesus himself. After that, all popes were believed to be inheritors of God's authority through Jesus.

Questions

Q–23

Upon the death of the pope, a new Holy Father is selected by

(A) a conference of the laity

(B) the bishops of the Catholic Church

(C) the College of Cardinals

(D) the Swiss Guard of the Vatican

(E) the Holy Roman Emperor

Your Answer _____

Q–24

In 1417, the Great Schism ended with the election of Pope Martin V at

(A) a church council in Constance

(B) the palace in Avignon

(C) the council of Pisa

(D) the Diet of Worms

(E) the University of Paris

Your Answer _____

Correct Answers

A–23

(C) The College of Cardinals serves as an electing body when the papacy, or Holy See, is vacant. This happens when the existing pope dies and must be replaced. The College of Cardinals first met in 1059 to assert that the church needed to select its own leader. Since then, when a pope dies the College assembles in Rome to select the next leader of the Roman Catholic Church.

A–24

(A) At one point during the Great Schism in the 1400s, there were three popes vying for the leadership of the Roman Catholic Church. This cast much doubt on church authority and encouraged critics of the papal monarchy. In the end, this and other challenges to the church led to the council in Constance. This council deposed the rival popes and elected Martin V to the Holy See.

Q–25

Roman Catholic parish priests interfaced with the common people through the

(A) appointments they received by the bishops

(B) bans from Rome

(C) baptism they received as infants

(D) sacraments of the church

(E) bidding of the congregation

Your Answer _____

_____

Q–26

Though women could not join guilds, they were often

(A) able to own their own businesses

(B) de facto business partners with their husbands

(C) able to inherit a husband's estate when he died

(D) allowed to hold political office

(E) leaders in the retail business

Your Answer _____

_____

Correct Answers

A–25

(D) Priests were the only ones who could administer the sacraments of the church to the common people. Without these, believers were thought to be deprived of salvation and condemned to eternal damnation. There are seven sacraments recognized in the Catholic Church. These include ordination, which consecrates priests for God's service. This meant that the church selected its own, and only they could oversee the holy rituals needed for eternal salvation. The Roman Catholic Church alone could deliver these sacraments that were administered to believers from infancy to death.

A–26

(B) Although women were excluded from all professional associations, they were crucial helpmates to their husbands. Often they ran stores informally and sold items in the marketplace. They helped make beverages; spin cloth; and sell extra food items, such as eggs or milk, when they had them. Their role in the economy was crucial because they bought and sold goods.

Questions

Q–27

What effect did the bubonic plague, or Black Death, have on the European population?

(A) Scapegoats were persecuted and terrorized.

(B) Wages rose for the working classes.

(C) Prices fell for agricultural goods.

(D) Religious fanaticism offered escape for some.

(E) All of the above

Your Answer _____

_____

Q–28

While western Europe formed stronger kingdoms in the fourteenth century, central and southern Europe remained

(A) united under the pope

(B) fragmented and unconsolidated

(C) under the domination of the Muslims

(D) under the control of the Holy Roman Emperor

(E) peaceful and prosperous

Your Answer _____

_____

Correct Answers

A–27

(E) The widespread death that occurred during the Black Death had multiple outcomes in Europe. Demand for workers rose and surviving craftsmen were able to ask for more money. As the population plummeted, so did demand for food, which caused prices to fall. The church's power was undermined as people lost faith in God to save them from the plague. Religious cults flourished because people believed that new rituals might save them.

A–28

(B) In the late Middle Ages, Italy was not united but consisted of city-states and territory under the pope. Central Europe was a patchwork of many domains that were supposedly united under a Holy Roman Emperor. This was mainly a fiction because the princes often defied the emperor and maintained local control. This disunity had the effect of delaying the political evolution of the Germanic and Italian peoples while the French and English were building powerful kingdoms.

Questions

Q–29

Which of the following were regions under Muslim control in the 1400s?

(A) Sicily and Portugal

(B) Granada and the Balkans

(C) The Baltic States and Hungary

(D) Aragon and Naples

(E) Germany and the Low Countries

Your Answer _____

_____

Q–30

The term *pogrom* means

(A) a rebellion by peasants

(B) a church meeting on doctrine

(C) riots that target minorities

(D) a list of cultural achievements

(E) a military venture

Your Answer _____

_____

Correct Answers

A–29

(B) Islam spread rapidly after 700. The parts of Europe that Islam most affected were Spain and the southeastern Balkans. The Moors stayed in Spain for centuries until they were expelled by the Christian kingdoms. The Ottomans from Turkey remained in the Balkans for many years. A strong Muslim presence in that part of Europe remains to this day.

A–30

(C) A pogrom is a riot in which a majority religious or ethnic group attacks a minority living among them. Jews have been targets of pogroms by the Christian majority in Russia, Germany, and elsewhere. Similarly, throughout history, the Romanian and Armenian peoples have been persecuted by intolerant majorities.

Questions

The fall of Byzantium in the 1400s marked the rise of the last great Muslim world empire, which was created by the

(A) Dalmatians

(B) Seljuk Turks

(C) Abbisids

(D) Moors

(E) Ottoman Turks

Your Answer _____

_____

By the 1350s, parts of Greece had been taken by Muslims from what area?

(A) Mongolia

(B) Syria

(C) Egypt

(D) Asia Minor

(E) Hungary

Your Answer _____

_____

Correct Answers

A–31

(E) A Turkic military had been in existence for many years in Asia Minor and developed into a larger fighting force by 1400. This army became the vanguard of the Ottoman Empire as it grew in west Asia. In 1453, they besieged and took the great Christian capital of Constantinople, bringing to an end the last vestiges of the Roman Empire. From there, the Turks spread into parts of southern Europe and created a Muslim presence in the Balkans.

A–32

(D) Out of the collapse of the Seljuk kingdom arose another Turkic group called the Ottomans who began to expand their domains. These Turks came from central Asia Minor to become one of the longest lasting and largest empires in world history. In the fourteenth century, they initially bypassed Byzantium, invading Europe and taking pieces of northern Greece. Later they took all of Asia Minor and the Balkans to create a strong Muslim region in southeastern Europe.

Q–33

Which of the following tactics and technology benefited the Ottoman Turks in their fifteenth-century expansion?

(A) Bronze cannons and massed cavalry

(B) Use of the trebuchet and siege warfare

(C) Gatling guns and railroad-borne artillery

(D) Mass assaults by infantry and grenadiers

(E) Flame throwers and large infantry brigades

Your Answer _____

_____

Q–34

The spirit of pessimism that predominated the late Middle Ages was partly due to widespread death from

(A) parasites and spoiled food

(B) marauding bandits

(C) disease and war

(D) suicide and domestic violence

(E) holy wars and accidents

Your Answer _____

_____

Correct Answers

A–33

(A) The Ottoman Turks were skilled horsemen, and their cavalry was a potent weapon in their military campaigns. They learned how to make bronze cannons from the Europeans. Cannon fire aided their attacks on cities in the Balkans. This combination of rapidly deployed cavalry on horseback and artillery firepower led to many victories over their enemies.

A–34

(C) Two great calamities of the fourteenth century were the Black Death/bubonic plague and the Hundred Years' War. The death toll from the plague left whole towns and villages empty. Fields were left to grow wild and homes were left vacant. The Hundred Years' War between France and England also left parts of Europe devastated and ruined. These two devastating events created their own responses to God and the political order. Church authority was more fragile and led to a crisis of faith for many.

Q–35

Whoever wishes to be a member (of a baker's guild) must bring proof to the councilors and the guildsmen that he is born of legitimate, upright German folk.

Brandenburg, 1432

Which of the following sums up the limitation expressed in the quotation above?

(A) Only Teutonic Knights could be bakers.

(B) Membership in professional associations was based on ethnicity.

(C) Guildsmen were often illegitimate.

(D) Craft organizations recruited many people in Danzig.

(E) The church was involved in enrolling guild members.

Your Answer _____

_____

Correct Answers

A–35

(B) Ethnic groups had begun to form in Europe by the late Middle Ages. In northern Europe, enclaves of Germans settled along the Baltic coasts. They created their own communities and resisted mixing with other groups around them. The quote shows that guilds had begun to limit membership to those of certain ethnic and social backgrounds. One had to be both German and "legitimate," which meant coming from a known family.

Q–36

Which of the following was an important result of the Muslim and Mongol invasions of Europe during the Middle Ages?

(A) The eastern expansion of Christianity was ended.

(B) Turks began to intermarry with Slavs in eastern Europe.

(C) The political development of Russia was accelerated.

(D) The Byzantine Empire was strengthened.

(E) Europeans sought escape in cults and witchcraft.

Your Answer _____

_____

Correct Answers

A–36

(A)   Christianity had expanded for centuries after the fall of the Roman Empire. Missionaries had gone north and east to spread the Christian religion into Scandinavia and eastern Europe. The arrival of the Mongols, and later the Muslims, put Christian Europe on the defensive in the face of these large-scale invasions. Christianity did not penetrate beyond central Eurasia, and Russian political development slowed down during the Mongol occupation.

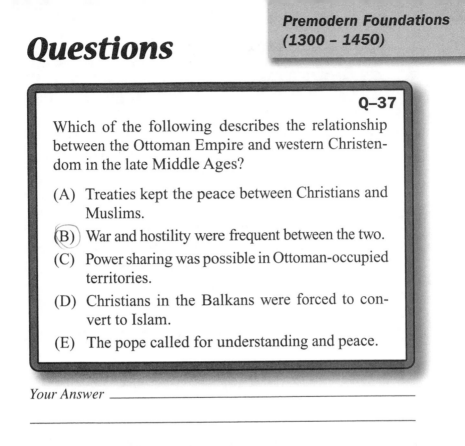

Q–37

Which of the following describes the relationship between the Ottoman Empire and western Christendom in the late Middle Ages?

(A) Treaties kept the peace between Christians and Muslims.

(B) War and hostility were frequent between the two.

(C) Power sharing was possible in Ottoman-occupied territories.

(D) Christians in the Balkans were forced to convert to Islam.

(E) The pope called for understanding and peace.

Your Answer _____

_____

Q–38

The failure to establish a strong German monarchy in the Middle Ages was caused by

(A) a disorganized Roman church

(B) nobles who chose weak kings so they could retain their own autonomy

(C) an attempted coup by bishops in northern Europe

(D) constant invasions by Vikings from the north

(E) interference by the Hungarian princes

Your Answer _____

_____

Correct Answers

A–37

(B) The dramatic expansion of the Ottoman Turks had an electrifying impact on Christians in Europe. The fall of Constantinople was a dramatic military defeat in the 1400s, and central Europe prepared to do battle with the Muslim invaders. Christians viewed Muslims as unbelievers, and Muslims saw Christians as infidels. The climate of hostility led to many military campaigns between the two different cultures.

A–38

(B) Some German nobles served as electors who chose the Holy Roman Emperor. These electors would sometimes select weak leaders to oversee the fragmented Holy Roman Empire, leaving the electors to rule their domains as they saw fit. This meant that central Europe remained decentralized and fragmented politically.

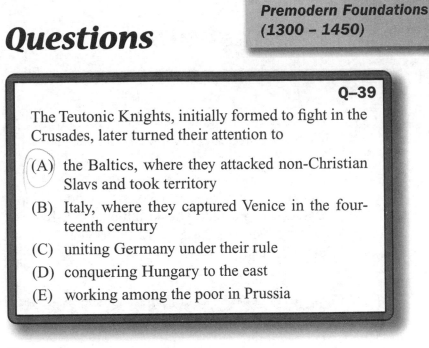

Q–39

The Teutonic Knights, initially formed to fight in the Crusades, later turned their attention to

(A) the Baltics, where they attacked non-Christian Slavs and took territory

(B) Italy, where they captured Venice in the fourteenth century

(C) uniting Germany under their rule

(D) conquering Hungary to the east

(E) working among the poor in Prussia

Your Answer _____

_____

Q–40

In Kievan Russia, the noble class of landowners was known as the

(A) intelligentsia

(B) serfs

(C) boyars

(D) laity

(E) clerics

Your Answer _____

_____

Correct Answers

A–39

(A) The Teutonic Knights were formed when the northern Europeans organized themselves to fight the Muslims in the Holy Land. Later, some of these knights found opportunities to expand into the northern coastal regions in present-day Poland. The knights established a strong German presence in the Baltics that lasted for centuries.

A–40

(C) Medieval Russia was a disunited mix of domains where princes fought to gain power and territory. The original center of Russian power was in the city of Kiev, where the boyars dominated society. The majority of people were landless peasants who struggled to survive while working the land for the elites.

Q–41

The heart of the medieval administration of the Roman Catholic Church was controlled by the pope and the

(A) Medici family in northern Italy

(B) German princes

(C) Swiss Guard in the Vatican

(D) mendicant orders like the Franciscans

(E) papal curia

Your Answer _____

_____

Q–42

The term *excommunication* means the

(A) control of a bishopric by the local nobles

(B) act of penance by an errant king

(C) disallowing a divorce sought by a believer

(D) extreme censure by the church of an individual that disallows that individual from receiving the sacraments

(E) denial of all communication between the pope and an offending prince

Your Answer _____

_____

Correct Answers

A–41

(E)   Over many centuries, the Roman Catholic Church administration grew larger and more complex. By the Middle Ages, cardinals comprised the administrative elite of the church, which made up part of the papal curia. Archbishops and other appointed church administrators filled in other levels of the curia, which managed large holdings throughout the world.

A–42

(D)   Excommunication was one of the most powerful weapons used by the church against those who opposed it. Kings were often cowed when the pope would excommunicate a monarch. It meant that the individual was cast out of the church and disallowed from receiving the sacraments. Not receiving the sacraments meant eternal damnation because one had to partake of the sacraments to be saved in the afterlife.

Q–43

During the Middle Ages, most European women who dedicated their lives to the church were from the

(A) peasant class

(B) landed aristocracy

(C) urban areas

(D) Mediterranean regions

(E) merchant class

Your Answer _____

_____

Q–44

While monks and nuns could live in religious isolation, they could also provide

(A) counsel to the College of Cardinals

(B) conscripts for the local lords

(C) social services for the poor

(D) schools for local peasant children

(E) translations of the Bible to the populace

Your Answer _____

_____

Correct Answers

A–43

(B)   Giving one's life to the church and becoming a nun was a respectable option for women from the landed classes. It released them from marriage and allowed some to pursue intellectual goals. Some became abbesses who ran convents, while others wrote of their lives and faith.

A–44

(C)   Monastic life took on many forms when religious orders were founded during the Middle Ages. Monks and nuns performed many functions, such as maintaining libraries, copying texts by hand, and serving the poor. Some orders took oaths of poverty for life and lived simple lifestyles.

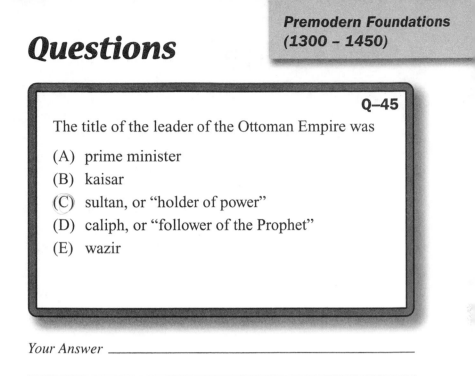

Q–45

The title of the leader of the Ottoman Empire was

(A) prime minister

(B) kaisar

(C) sultan, or "holder of power"

(D) caliph, or "follower of the Prophet"

(E) wazir

Your Answer _____

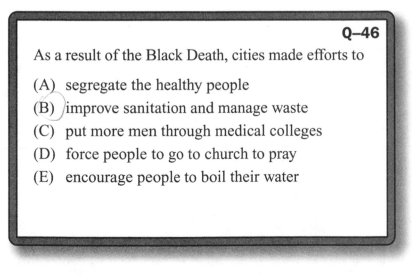

Q–46

As a result of the Black Death, cities made efforts to

(A) segregate the healthy people

(B) improve sanitation and manage waste

(C) put more men through medical colleges

(D) force people to go to church to pray

(E) encourage people to boil their water

Your Answer _____

Correct Answers

A–45

(C) After Mohammed died, leadership of the Islamic territories was given to the caliphs who had known the Prophet. After the first generation of Muslim leadership died, the Islamic world began to fragment and leadership became regional. As the Turks grew in power, they adopted the Abbasid title of sultan for their leader.

A–46

(B) The Black Death created incredible tension in medieval society. Medical science had little knowledge about the cause of the rampant disease. The church also seemed powerless to do anything against the deaths that resulted. After trial and experimentation, cities began to manage the basic cleanliness of their streets. Garbage and human waste, which was commonly deposited in the streets, was disposed of in an effort to improve sanitation.

Q–47

Some Europeans saw the fourteenth century as the apocalypse because of

(A) a comet that showed up in the heavens

(B) a rise in the practice of witchcraft

(C) a papal proclamation

(D) widespread death owing to pandemic and war

(E) a decline in the birthrate in rural areas

Your Answer _____

_____

Q–48

The term *dowry* means

(A) a legal fee paid to lawyers

(B) an amount of money paid by the bride's family to the groom's family

(C) a percentage of income given to the church

(D) a tax paid to the landowner by peasants

(E) laws against graft in medieval towns

Your Answer _____

_____

Correct Answers

A–47

(D) The combination of the horrors of the Black Death and wars that raged in Europe made the fourteenth century a calamitous one for those living in the era. Some Christians saw it as fulfilling a prophecy in the Bible about the "apocalypse," or end of the world. Some lost their faith, while others sought further signs that the world was ending. Strange religious cults sprang up and tried to find a way to appeal to God.

A–48

(B) The traditional dowry was a variable fee paid by the bride's family to the groom's family at the wedding. This custom evolved over many years in Europe and was an incentive for the male to marry a specific woman because of the wealth of her family.

Questions

The sketches above, drawn by Masaccio, reveal that in the era in which he lived,

(A) drawing was a fad in France

(B) people were infatuated with Napoli soldiers

(C) people were deeply and religiously pious

(D) artists were giving different meaning to the human form

(E) courtly manners were typical in Sicily

Your Answer _____

_____

Correct Answers

A–49

(D) Masaccio was one of the early artists who paved the way for new techniques in drawing and painting. He used perspective to create depth and greater dimension in his works. In the sketches shown, he strives for greater realism, showing a person in relaxed and casual settings. This differs from the posed and stiffer portraiture that was common during the time. Note the detail of the legs of his subjects, which portray the human body more realistically.

Q–50

He (the friar) knew the taverns well in every town
The barmaids and innkeepers pleased his mind
Better than beggars and lepers and their kind.

Based on the quote above, what commentary is being made by Chaucer about the Christian clergy of his day?

(A) The church was generous in giving friars a living allowance.

(B) Beggars were well cared for by the clergy.

(C) Innkeepers gave priests special rates at their establishments.

(D) Taverns did not welcome clergymen.

(E) Some priests were more concerned with living well than helping the needy.

Your Answer _____

_____

Correct Answers

A–50

(E)   Chaucer used satire to lampoon people in his own day. In his description of the local friar or priest, he suggests that some clergy were more often seen drinking than helping the poor. He gives the impression of a worldly church less interested in the welfare of the common people.

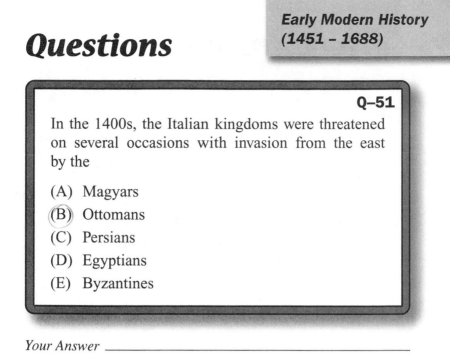

Q–51

In the 1400s, the Italian kingdoms were threatened on several occasions with invasion from the east by the

(A) Magyars

(B) Ottomans

(C) Persians

(D) Egyptians

(E) Byzantines

Your Answer _____

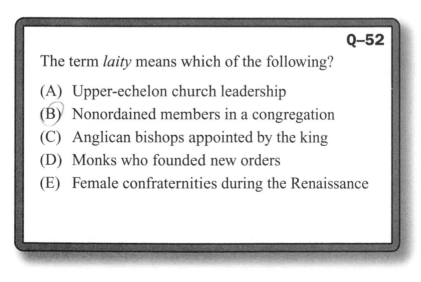

Q–52

The term *laity* means which of the following?

(A) Upper-echelon church leadership

(B) Nonordained members in a congregation

(C) Anglican bishops appointed by the king

(D) Monks who founded new orders

(E) Female confraternities during the Renaissance

Your Answer _____

Correct Answers

A–51

(B) As the Ottoman Turks grew stronger, their influence spread westward into Europe. The Ottomans developed a navy that dominated the Black Sea and then threatened southern Europe. Military campaigns kept the Italian peninsula in Christian hands. The Ottomans remained in control of the Balkans for centuries, leaving a strong Muslim presence there.

A–52

(B) The vast majority of Christian believers were members of congregations across Europe. The term *laity* refers to the common believers of the church. This term is still used to differentiate them from the ordained priests and pastors who lead the church services.

Questions

Q–53

The unification of Spain in the 1400s was accomplished by

(A) peaceful negotiations with Muslim Grenada

(B) allowing Muslim minorities to continue to practice their religion

(C) Italian mercenaries fighting for the pope

(D) the French monarchy invading Iberia

(E) the northern kingdoms of Aragon and Castile

Your Answer _____

Q–54

An early Christian humanist who translated the Greek New Testament into Latin was

(A) Martin Luther

(B) Zwingli

(C) John Calvin

(D) John Wyclyff

(E) Erasmus

Your Answer _____

Correct Answers

A–53

(E) Northern Spanish kingdoms began to push for a unified Christian Spain after 1420. During the fifteenth century, the kingdoms of Aragon and Castile were united through a royal wedding, which strengthened the military forces available to the Christians. Finally, in 1492, the last piece of Spain was retaken and the Moors were expelled or forced to convert.

A–54

(E) Humanism was a literary movement that began in Italy as early as the fourteenth century. Scholars wrote about theology and also about nonspiritual topics such as politics and the economy. Erasmus was one of the pioneering Christians, or northern, humanistic writers who brought new scholarship to the study of the Bible. Typical of humanist study was a rediscovery of the ancient texts written in Greek. The work of Erasmus was later used to translate the Bible into other European languages.

Q–55

Which of the following are examples of Italian city-states in the early modern period?

(A) Naples and Palermo

(B) Venice and Genoa

(C) Marseilles and Florence

(D) Rome and Nice

(E) Provence and Trieste

Your Answer _____

_____

Correct Answers

A–55

(B)   In the late medieval period, trade flourished in the Mediterranean. This produced the growth of powerful city-states in Italy. These city-states were some of the largest urban areas of the era, and some had populations exceeding 50,000. Large merchant fleets traveled in and out of these cities, where modern banks existed to help businesses invest in new ventures. Venice and Genoa had their own governments and military forces.

Questions

The art style of the painting shown above was typical of which period in Europe?

(A) The Rococo

(B) The postmodern

(C) The Pre-Raphaelite

(D) The Baroque

(E) The Renaissance

Your Answer _____

_____

Correct Answers

A–56

(E) The painting is a famous section of the ceiling of the Sistine Chapel painted by Michelangelo during the Renaissance. Commissioned by the pope, the ceiling portrays biblical themes while using the new artistic styles of the sixteenth century. The form of Adam being given life by God is typical of the Greco-Roman vision of the human body. The nude form and attention to musculature are classical in origin.

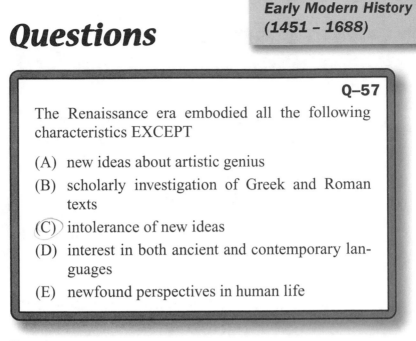

Q–57

The Renaissance era embodied all the following characteristics EXCEPT

(A) new ideas about artistic genius

(B) scholarly investigation of Greek and Roman texts

(C) intolerance of new ideas

(D) interest in both ancient and contemporary languages

(E) newfound perspectives in human life

Your Answer _____

_____

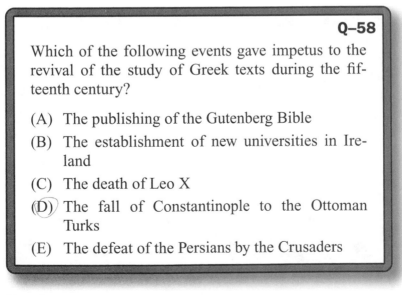

Q–58

Which of the following events gave impetus to the revival of the study of Greek texts during the fifteenth century?

(A) The publishing of the Gutenberg Bible

(B) The establishment of new universities in Ireland

(C) The death of Leo X

(D) The fall of Constantinople to the Ottoman Turks

(E) The defeat of the Persians by the Crusaders

Your Answer _____

_____

Correct Answers

A–57

(C) The Renaissance was an era when the medieval approaches to knowledge and life were challenged. A new intellectual energy emanated from fifteenth-century Italy, where new approaches to art and learning were evolving. New wealth produced from the successful trade in Italian cities sponsored study and the production of new works of art.

A–58

(D) The encroachment into southeastern Europe by the Ottoman Turks was constant during the 1400s. Byzantium, in present-day Turkey, had been a repository of ancient scholarship since the fall of the western Roman Empire. When the eastern empire fell to the Turks, many Greek scholars fled to Italy. They brought their knowledge and some Greek texts with them, which stimulated an interest in ancient works.

Q–59

What did the study of the humanities during the Renaissance help change within European society?

(A) The view that specialization was important

(B) A narrower view of the definition of education

(C) A rejection of the arts as a field of study

(D) The belief that only literature need be studied

(E) A new vision of education

Your Answer _____

_____

Q–60

Renaissance art departed from previous medieval styles by

(A) dealing only with biblical subjects

(B) devising unusual backdrops for paintings

(C) portraying the individual as an important subject

(D) presenting a two-dimensional view of the world

(E) learning from Muslim techniques

Your Answer _____

_____

Correct Answers

A–59

(E) The Renaissance created many new fields of scholarly study after the 1400s. Education was reorganized, and a new value was placed on broader learning. School curricula throughout Europe were revised, and the idea of the liberal arts was conceived.

A–60

(C) Renaissance artists were often paid by wealthy patrons to paint group or individual portraits. While medieval painting had dealt almost exclusively with biblical personalities and stories, the Renaissance highlighted the uniqueness of people in their own right. Indeed, individualism, as we know it today, is a Renaissance idea.

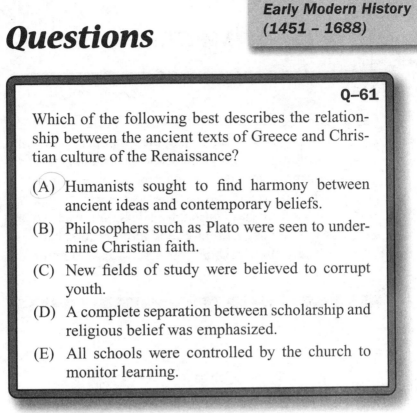

Q–61

Which of the following best describes the relationship between the ancient texts of Greece and Christian culture of the Renaissance?

(A) Humanists sought to find harmony between ancient ideas and contemporary beliefs.

(B) Philosophers such as Plato were seen to undermine Christian faith.

(C) New fields of study were believed to corrupt youth.

(D) A complete separation between scholarship and religious belief was emphasized.

(E) All schools were controlled by the church to monitor learning.

Your Answer _____

Q–62

After the Renaissance, the humanist curriculum began to include which of the following subjects?

(A) Theology and medicine

(B) Rhetoric and literature

(C) Cosmology and scholastic philosophy

(D) Abstract language and mechanics

(E) Sculpture and canonical commentary

Your Answer _____

Correct Answers

A–61

(A) For the most part, humanists were devout Christians who felt that their understanding of the world and God would be enhanced by returning to ancient learning. Some priest-scholars found similarities between Athenian philosophy and Christian beliefs, and went so far as to suggest that Greek thought foreshadowed some Christian ideas before the time of Jesus.

A–62

(B) Humanists looked to ancient approaches to knowledge to help them rethink education in the early modern period. Just as Socrates and Plato taught men how to speak and debate, so rhetoric became a feature of modern studies. Poetry and other literature became an important approach to language, and the study of both remains central in education today.

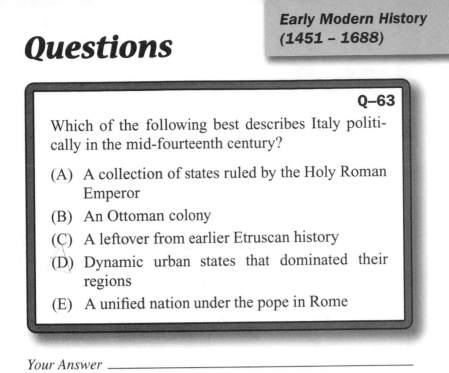

Q–63

Which of the following best describes Italy politically in the mid-fourteenth century?

(A) A collection of states ruled by the Holy Roman Emperor

(B) An Ottoman colony

(C) A leftover from earlier Etruscan history

(D) Dynamic urban states that dominated their regions

(E) A unified nation under the pope in Rome

Your Answer _____

_____

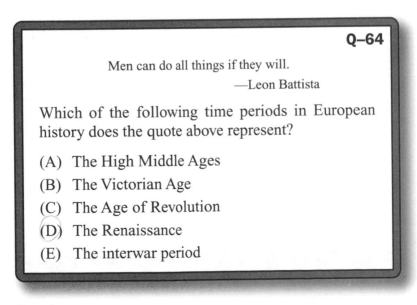

Q–64

Men can do all things if they will.

—Leon Battista

Which of the following time periods in European history does the quote above represent?

(A) The High Middle Ages

(B) The Victorian Age

(C) The Age of Revolution

(D) The Renaissance

(E) The interwar period

Your Answer _____

_____

Correct Answers

A–63

(D) Fourteenth-century Italy was a collection of domains, some of which were under direct church control. In the middle and northern regions, various city-states flourished because of the lucrative trade between Asia and the rest of Europe. The cities of Venice and Genoa were port cities that became European trading centers. Goods flowed from Asia through Italy to the north. The Italian countryside provided material for the manufacturing of textile goods that were later shipped to other parts of Europe.

A–64

(D) The Renaissance departed from the medieval view of humanity and found ways to celebrate the individual. The potential of the artist or political leader became a keynote of the era. Education and art were reconsidered and elevated the status of artist and scholar. This new intellectual direction in culture formed a new sense of the potential of human endeavor.

Questions

Q–65

In fourteenth-century Europe, the term *Hanseatic league* meant a

(A) treaty organization to prevent war in central Europe

(B) commercial association of northern cities to control trade and commerce

(C) sports league to promote competition between kingdoms

(D) confederation of nations that promoted diplomacy

(E) military treaty organization to defend Europe from the Mongols

Your Answer _____

Q–66

Which of the following goods were exported from Venice to northern Europe during the fourteenth century?

(A) Wool and silk

(B) Wine and corn

(C) Cotton and flax

(D) Porcelain and wood pulp

(E) Iron and salt

Your Answer _____

Correct Answers

A–65

(B) The Hansa incorporated more than eighty cities that dominated northern European trade in the early modern era. Led by port cities such as Hamburg and Bremen, this commercial league had a monopoly on goods being traded in northern Europe. This league was comprised of large parts of present-day northern Holland, Germany, and Scandinavia.

A–66

(A) Textiles were a major trade item moving from southern to northern Europe in the early modern era. Fleets left Venice and traveled to Holland, where goods could be sold to other traders in northern Europe. From there, the Hansa League sold the goods to other cities in the north. Wool was the main fabric worn by Europeans at this time; silk came from Asia and was much more expensive.

Questions

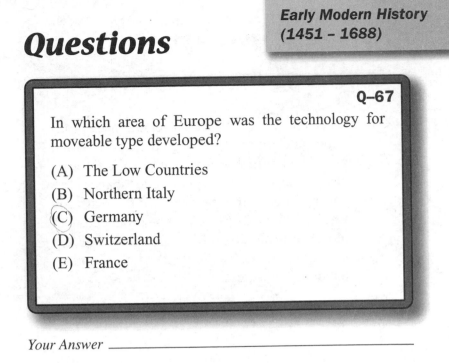

Q–67

In which area of Europe was the technology for moveable type developed?

(A) The Low Countries

(B) Northern Italy

(C) Germany

(D) Switzerland

(E) France

Your Answer _____

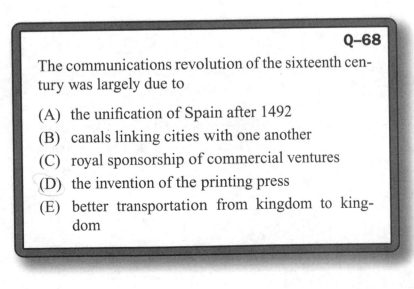

Q–68

The communications revolution of the sixteenth century was largely due to

(A) the unification of Spain after 1492

(B) canals linking cities with one another

(C) royal sponsorship of commercial ventures

(D) the invention of the printing press

(E) better transportation from kingdom to kingdom

Your Answer _____

Correct Answers

A–67

(C)   Mechanical printing was invented in the mid-1400s in Germany. Although the Chinese used woodblock printing earlier, it was the Europeans who used metal to press letter shapes onto paper. Letters could be arranged to create any text, and many copies could be produced with modest human effort. Mass-production of text became possible, which led to the modern publishing business.

A–68

(D)   Historians still debate the impact of the printing industry on Western history. Although most Europeans could not read in the 1500s, those who could were exposed to new ideas that helped shape the West. New philosophies and theologies spread in print and created movements that changed the course of history.

Q–69

Which of the following artists represented the peak of achievement during the Italian Renaissance?

(A) Michelangelo and Rubens

(B) Rembrandt and Holbein

(C) Donatello and da Vinci

(D) Holst and de Medici

(E) Mantegna and Vasari

Your Answer _____

Q–70

In European history, the term *artisan* refers to

(A) skilled producers of manually crafted goods

(B) factory laborers who are part of a team

(C) shopkeepers who sell specialized goods

(D) small farm employees

(E) helpers in a livery stable

Your Answer _____

Correct Answers

A–69

(C) In Renaissance Italy, artists like Donatello and Leonardo da Vinci were viewed as leading celebrities. Courted by leading nobility for their skill, some artists commanded high fees, and their works were great media productions of their day. They worked in many different media, such as paint or stone, and their imaginations were celebrated and given free rein.

A–70

(A) Artisans are people who learn a special skill and produce something with their own hands. They could be woodworkers or jewelers, but their operation tends to be small scale. Artisans learn a craft from a master over many years before setting up a shop of their own. Traditionally, European artisans practiced their craft for their entire adult lives or until they were unable to work.

Q–71

When I get a little money, I buy books;
and if any is left, I buy food and clothes.

—Erasmus

Which of the following Renaissance values does the statement above reflect?

(A) Nutrition is vital to the educated man.

(B) Scholarship and learning are vital parts of life.

(C) Clothes make the man.

(D) Commerce is to be celebrated in human affairs.

(E) Buying books is as important as one's relationships.

Your Answer _____

Q–72

To artists of the sixteenth century, beauty was often portrayed by depicting

(A) human invention and technology

(B) two-dimensional biblical characters

(C) church authority

(D) realistic human movement and emotion

(E) nature in epic settings

Your Answer _____

Correct Answers

A–71

(B)   Scholars like Erasmus committed their lives to learning and writing. His quote reveals the utmost value he and other Renaissance scholars placed on knowledge. Knowledge was gained through reading, so books were the key to learning. Books were so expensive in his time one had to budget carefully to be able to afford them.

A–72

(D)   Renaissance artists focused on human forms as a way to reveal beauty and truth. They painted realistic contemporary and biblical people in ways that expressed the painters' interest in the human form. Some artists would mix ancient and modern scenes to create connections across time. For example, portraits of patrons or scenes from the Bible were depicted as taking place in fourteenth-century Italy.

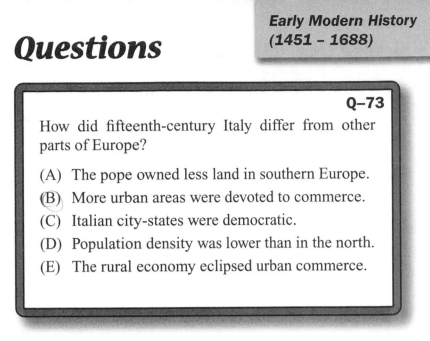

Q–73

How did fifteenth-century Italy differ from other parts of Europe?

(A) The pope owned less land in southern Europe.

(B) More urban areas were devoted to commerce.

(C) Italian city-states were democratic.

(D) Population density was lower than in the north.

(E) The rural economy eclipsed urban commerce.

Your Answer _____

_____

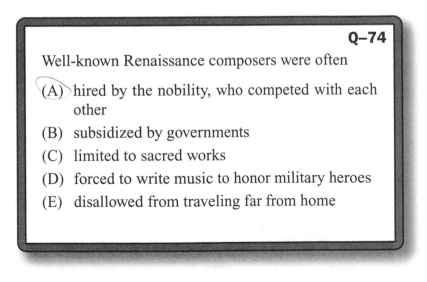

Q–74

Well-known Renaissance composers were often

(A) hired by the nobility, who competed with each other

(B) subsidized by governments

(C) limited to sacred works

(D) forced to write music to honor military heroes

(E) disallowed from traveling far from home

Your Answer _____

_____

Correct Answers

A–73

(B) Italy had some of the largest cities in the fifteenth century. Venice, Milan, Genoa, and Florence were thriving commercial centers that profited from their locations and the development of modern capitalistic practices. Other parts of Europe, such as France, were much more rural and had agriculture-based economies.

A–74

(A) Music developed into more complex forms during the Renaissance, and composers, like visual artists, became well known for their work. Both the church and royalty commissioned musical works. Some musicians traveled widely, and a composer might work in France, Italy, and Holland for different princes or kings. Royalty would offer high salaries for musicians to live at courts and compose special music for events and celebrations.

Questions

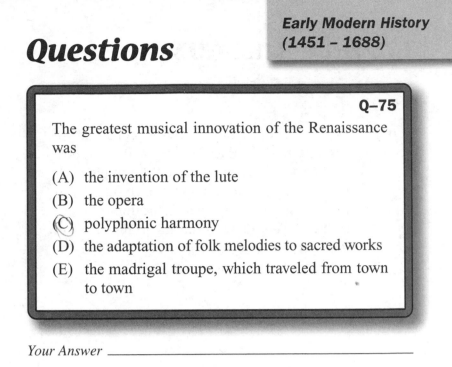

Q–75

The greatest musical innovation of the Renaissance was

(A) the invention of the lute
(B) the opera
(C) polyphonic harmony
(D) the adaptation of folk melodies to sacred works
(E) the madrigal troupe, which traveled from town to town

Your Answer _____

_____

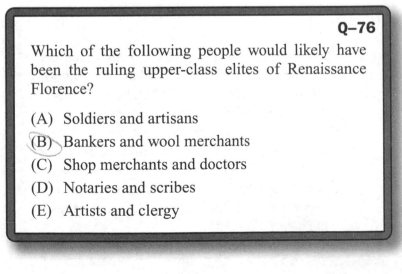

Q–76

Which of the following people would likely have been the ruling upper-class elites of Renaissance Florence?

(A) Soldiers and artisans
(B) Bankers and wool merchants
(C) Shop merchants and doctors
(D) Notaries and scribes
(E) Artists and clergy

Your Answer _____

_____

Correct Answers

A–75

(C) Most pre-Renaissance music consisted of a single melody line. In the 1400s, composers began to create works with multiple parts that existed in harmony with each other. This is known as *polyphonic*, meaning "many sounds." This more complex arrangement of tones created the modern sounds that frame musical composition today.

A–76

(B) Renaissance Florence was a commercial center where merchants and bankers traded goods and money on the open market. Florentine society was patriarchal, with leading businessmen at the top of society. Bankers and successful wool merchants controlled up to one-quarter of the wealth of this city. The excess wealth was used to build beautiful homes, which were decorated with the work of leading artists of the day.

Q–77

Artists of the northern Renaissance differed from their Italian counterparts by emphasizing

(A) the naked human figure

(B) biblical heroes from the Old Testament

(C) precise detail in their paintings

(D) a distorted view of reality

(E) secular subjects in their works

Your Answer _____

_____

Q–78

The large eastern European kingdom that buffered Russia from Poland in the late 1400s was

(A) Hungary

(B) Serbia

(C) Moldavia

(D) Lithuania

(E) Bohemia

Your Answer _____

_____

Correct Answers

A–77

(C) Artists from the Low Countries created brilliant paintings using new oil pigments and paid astonishing attention to detail. Artists in Flanders and Holland used their powers of observation to re-create people and nature with great realism. Many of their works also had religious themes that reflected the piety of the artists and their society. Their altarpieces are some of the masterworks of the period.

A–78

(D) Lithuania was a kingdom in northeastern Europe that rose in power by the end of the 1400s. Lithuanians and Poles defeated the Teutonic Knights and also stopped the spread of the last of the Mongols into Europe. Lithuania eventually created a dual state with Poland and lost more and more of its autonomy. In the end, both kingdoms were absorbed into neighboring domains.

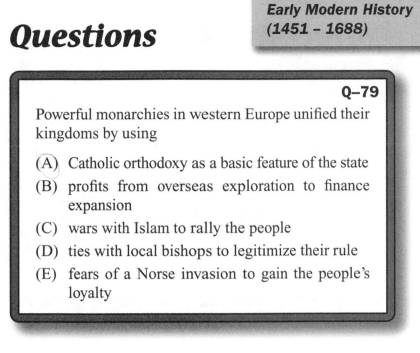

Q–79

Powerful monarchies in western Europe unified their kingdoms by using

(A) Catholic orthodoxy as a basic feature of the state

(B) profits from overseas exploration to finance expansion

(C) wars with Islam to rally the people

(D) ties with local bishops to legitimize their rule

(E) fears of a Norse invasion to gain the people's loyalty

Your Answer _____

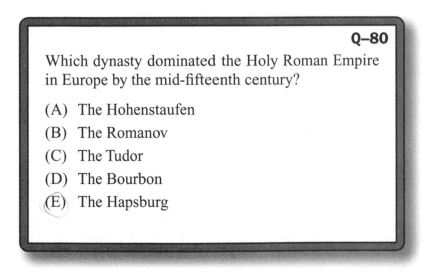

Q–80

Which dynasty dominated the Holy Roman Empire in Europe by the mid-fifteenth century?

(A) The Hohenstaufen

(B) The Romanov

(C) The Tudor

(D) The Bourbon

(E) The Hapsburg

Your Answer _____

Correct Answers

A–79

(A) Both Spain and France were united by using the Catholic Church to forge their national identities. The monarchy of Spain campaigned to rid the kingdom of religious minorities like Jews and Muslims. Non-Christians were sometimes compelled to convert to Catholicism or face expulsion. Both France and England went through periods in which uniform Catholicism was promoted.

A–80

(E) The Hapsburg family began its rise as they took territories along the Danube River in central Europe. This river was an important commercial route in Europe. Over time, controlling it brought wealth and power to the Hapsburgs. The Hapsburgs often used strategic marriages to consolidate their power and holdings in central Europe. The symbolic role of Holy Roman Emperor became a Hapsburg possession as the modern era dawned. In the end, the Hapsburgs controlled territory in France and Spain, which led to later wars with other monarchies.

Questions

Q–81

Only men of noble birth can obtain perfection. The poor, who work with their hands and have no time to cultivate their minds, are incapable of it.

—Lorenzo the Magnificent, 1488

What does the fifteenth-century commentary shown above reveal about the era?

(A) The poor should work less with their hands.

(B) The intellectual impact of the Renaissance was largely reserved for the elites of the day.

(C) Nobles wanted education to be available to all classes.

(D) People can reach perfection through the study of philosophy.

(E) The cultivation of the mind is important for all.

Your Answer _____

_____

Correct Answers

A–81

(B)   Lorenzo the Magnificent ruled Florence during the height of the Renaissance. Like other nobles of his day, he believed that the upper class deserved its privilege and that the poor were destined to a life of drudgery. The intellectual energy of the Renaissance did not affect the lower classes of that time period. The beneficiaries of the period were the wealthy merchants and the aristocracy, who had the leisure to enjoy art and music.

Q–82

The most stable and lasting democratic government in early modern European history was in the city of

(A) Venice

(B) Palermo

(C) Paris

(D) Florence

(E) Mantua

Your Answer _____

_____

Q–83

The custom of dueling between men in Europe required

(A) that the fight be to the death

(B) any cause that one might only imagine

(C) that only the combatants be in attendance

(D) that elaborate preconditions define any potential fight

(E) the king's approval

Your Answer _____

_____

Correct Answers

A–82

(A)   Both Venice and Florence had governments with some democratic mechanisms, but Florentine politics were much more corrupt and tempestuous. Venice created a democratic constitution that lasted for many years into the eighteenth century. It was still a limited democracy, however, with only landed noble males being allowed to vote or hold office.

A–83

(D)   Among men, private honor could be avenged or satisfied by challenging another man to a duel. Very specific rules had to be followed or the fighters could be arrested and punished by the local authorities. Witnesses had to be present, and all the rules had to be followed. This extralegal method of settling differences between people persisted into the modern era, but was eventually declared illegal throughout the continent.

Questions

Q–84

In addition to a period of great artistic productivity, the Renaissance was also a time of

(A) slave uprisings across Europe

(B) rampant disease in many parts of Europe

(C) diplomacy between growing kingdoms

(D) religious tranquility

(E) war and violence in many parts of Europe

Your Answer _____

_____

Q–85

In the second half of the fifteenth century, the dynasty that emerged victorious after civil war in England was the

(A) Lancaster dynasty

(B) Wessex dynasty

(C) Tudor dynasty

(D) Stuart dynasty

(E) Westminster dynasty

Your Answer _____

_____

Correct Answers

A–84

(E) The Renaissance was also a time of intense conflict. Civil war broke out in England, and Italy was wracked by fighting between various city-states and kingdoms. The Spanish succeeded in a bloody military expulsion of Jews and Muslims by 1500. Martial law became a common feature of life for some war-torn parts of Europe.

A–85

(C) The royal family of England divided into two factions in the late 1400s, and this lead to a long and brutal civil war. Called the War of the Roses, the houses of Lancaster and York fought for the throne for decades, until 1485. Henry Tudor, a relative of the Lancaster clan, was the eventual winner and became Henry VII. This new dynasty ruled England for over a century and created a more stable monarchy and powerful kingdom.

Q–86

Of mankind we can say in general that they are fickle, hypocritical and greedy of gain.

—Machiavelli, ca. 1511

What political view of humanity is revealed by the quote above?

(A) A generous view of people's motives and intentions

(B) A cynical observation of the selfishness of others

(C) People's unwillingness to share when convinced of the benefits

(D) The ability of leaders to count on the populace to be high-minded and fair

(E) People coming to each other's aid when needed

Your Answer _____

Q–87

The chronological order in which European kingdoms sailed to the Americas was

(A) Spanish, French, and Dutch

(B) Scandinavians, Spanish, and Portuguese

(C) English, Spanish, and Portuguese

(D) Scandinavians, Hebrews, and Spanish

(E) Spanish, Portuguese, and Irish

Your Answer _____

Correct Answers

A–86

(B) Machiavelli was a writer and political scientist during the Italian Renaissance. His book *The Prince*, became a classic in early modern Europe as he commented on the politics of the period. He wrote at length about the kind of rulers that were needed. Because of the conflict and violence of the time, Machiavelli described a leader who could rule with a strong hand. Machiavelli saw humankind as easily swayed by powerful personalities. He believed an effective ruler would need to use violence himself to stay in power and to be useful to his subjects.

A–87

(B) Evidence has proved that Scandinavians or Vikings were the first Europeans who sailed from their North Sea base and explored Greenland and present-day Canada. They did not stay long, however, and it was not until the late 1400s that western Europeans came to the Caribbean. The Portuguese had already pioneered the African route to Asia. They landed in South America in 1500.

Questions

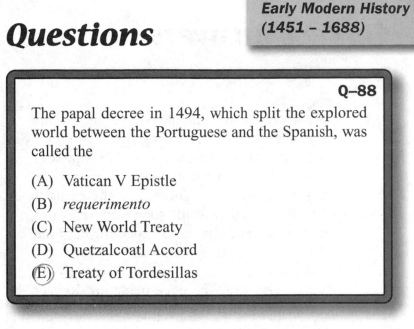

Q–88

The papal decree in 1494, which split the explored world between the Portuguese and the Spanish, was called the

(A) Vatican V Epistle

(B) *requerimento*

(C) New World Treaty

(D) Quetzalcoatl Accord

(E) Treaty of Tordesillas

Your Answer _____

_____

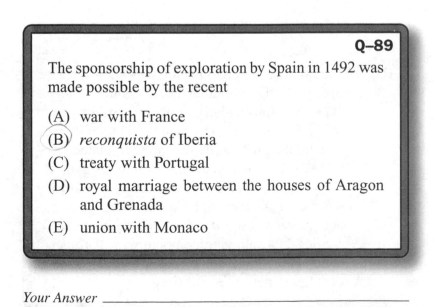

Q–89

The sponsorship of exploration by Spain in 1492 was made possible by the recent

(A) war with France

(B) *reconquista* of Iberia

(C) treaty with Portugal

(D) royal marriage between the houses of Aragon and Grenada

(E) union with Monaco

Your Answer _____

_____

Correct Answers

A–88

(E) Shortly after the initial voyage of Columbus, the pope was asked by Spain to give it a monopoly on exploration in the Americas. The Portuguese protested, and a line was redrawn that gave the Portuguese the rights to Brazil, which they would soon explore, as well as Africa and India. It was a confusing time. The Spanish initially believed they had found a shortcut to Asia as opposed to an entirely different continent. The pope made his decision arbitrarily, with little real geographical knowledge of the world.

A–89

(B) Christian leaders had been trying to win back Spain for the Christian church since before 1000. Muslims had occupied parts of the peninsula for centuries. The final retaking of Iberia by Christian monarchs was not completed until 1492, the same year that Columbus gained sponsorship to sail west to find Asia. The royal houses of Aragon and Castile were gaining new revenue from the captured southern territories and wanted to compete with Portugal, their neighbor, for trade routes that would access the riches of the Far East.

Q–90

By 1550, Portugal established colonies in which of the following distant places?

(A) Mexico, South Africa, and Australia

(B) Brazil, Arabia, and Ceylon

(C) Burma, Malaya, and China

(D) Brazil, Madagascar, and New Zealand

(E) East Africa, India, and South China

Your Answer _____

Q–91

The term *conquistador* means

(A) "savior of the people"

(B) "royal diplomat"

(C) "tiller of the soil"

(D) "pathfinder of the gods"

(E) "military adventurers exploring for the crown"

Your Answer _____

Correct Answers

A–90

(E)   Portugal was the first European kingdom to venture to Asia by sea. Sailing south around Africa, the Portuguese established their routes to India and later China and Japan. Access to the spices there made them wealthy for a time, but other European kingdoms with more money and power soon eclipsed them.

A–91

(E)   After the initial explorers sent by Spain, another group of military men gained sponsorship from the crown to look for riches and also convert the Americas to Christianity. These mostly young men were armed and aggressive emissaries of Spain who made contact with new peoples in the Americas. The result was the pacification of most native groups. The Spanish often used traditional tribal rivalries and allied themselves with one group to fight the other.

Questions

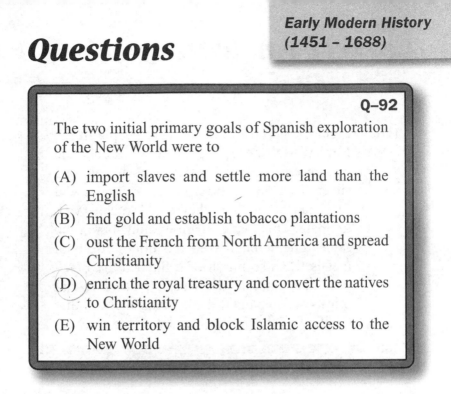

Q–92

The two initial primary goals of Spanish exploration of the New World were to

(A) import slaves and settle more land than the English

(B) find gold and establish tobacco plantations

(C) oust the French from North America and spread Christianity

(D) enrich the royal treasury and convert the natives to Christianity

(E) win territory and block Islamic access to the New World

Your Answer _____

_____

Correct Answers

(D) From the earliest contacts with people in the New World, the Spanish inquired about the existence of precious metals such as gold and silver. They found both in the Americas and extracted as much as they could to ship back to Spain. This made Spain wealthy, but at the same time it depressed the prices for both metals when so much of it flooded the European markets. The church also made sure that priests accompanied the conquistadors so that God's word would be shared with the natives.

Questions

Q–93

In what way did the Spanish exploration in the New World affect European economics?

(A) Silver and gold brought back from the New World created inflationary pressures.

(B) Wars with France enriched the royal treasury in Madrid.

(C) The pope blessed the marriage of Isabel and Ferdinand.

(D) Trade flourished with Italy.

(E) New treaties were written with the Holy Roman Empire.

Your Answer _____

_____

Correct Answers

A–93

(A) For two hundred years, Spain dominated the extraction of gold and silver from the New World. It made Spain very wealthy in the short term. But Spain used the money to finance some wars with other nations. These wars were often unsuccessful. The longer-term impact was a depreciation of both gold and silver because there was more of it being coined and traded in Europe. Spanish ships traveled to Asia and beyond, and thus Spanish silver also affected the economies of other parts of the world.

Q–94

The country is not very hot. The men are armed with bows and large arrows, strong shields of palm leaves bound with cotton, and pikes better than those of Guinea. Few swords were seen. They have four catapults for hurling stones but do not yet know the use of gunpowder.

—Dom Francisco, ca. 1505

The quote above, taken from a Portuguese document, reveals what about the Age of Exploration?

(A) Natives were largely friendly with Europeans.

(B) Military tactics were similar in the New World.

(C) Native cultures did not possess modern weaponry.

(D) Spears and pikes were effective defensive tools.

(E) Natives adapted quickly to European practices.

Your Answer _____

_____

Correct Answers

A–94

(C)   Spanish and Portuguese expeditions were routinely outnumbered by the natives they encountered. One advantage they enjoyed was the armor and guns that they used against the peoples of Asia, Africa, and the Americas. Many Europeans did die in battle against the natives, but gunpowder and cannons were very effective in creating awe and surprise in battle.

Questions

Q–95

A major impetus for the colonization of Brazil by Portugal was the European demand for

(A) cinnamon

(B) bananas

(C) sugar

(D) hemp

(E) pepper

Your Answer _____

_____

Q–96

A reason for the success of European joint-stock companies in Asia after 1650 was

(A) their ability to arm themselves and fight for their trading rights

(B) the failed alliance with Muslim sultans

(C) the acceptance of Christianity

(D) the booming cocoa trade in Malacca

(E) successful establishment of European-style trade guilds

Your Answer _____

_____

Correct Answers

A–95

(C)   Portugal largely ignored Brazil for decades after they had claimed it in 1500. It became a haven for pirates until the Portuguese discovered the money to be earned from sugar plantations. The climate was suited to the growing of sugarcane, which was brought from Africa and transplanted in the New World. For a time, Brazil produced most of the world's sugar, and many colonists came from Europe to work in the agricultural businesses that sprang up. Intermarrying with the natives, they created a multiracial society that is evident in Brazil today.

A–96

(A)   Joint-stock companies that originated in England, Holland, and France made aggressive inroads into Asia after 1650. These companies enjoyed the support of their monarchies back in Europe but also organized their own military capabilities. When necessary, they fought with local forces that opposed them and also with each other. In the 1600s, a series of wars took place in India, the Americas, Africa, and beyond as these companies competed for territory and market shares. In the end, England was the most successful of the commercial traders.

Questions

Q–97

Which of the following European kingdoms claimed territory in North America after 1500?

(A) Italy, England, and France

(B) England, Spain, and Holland

(C) France, Holland, and Turkey

(D) Ireland, England, and France

(E) France, Germany, and Spain

Your Answer _____

Q–98

The sale of indulgences by the Roman Catholic Church was needed to

(A) impress Italian kings

(B) fund expensive building projects such as Saint Peter's in Rome

(C) counter taxes gathered by Dutch princes

(D) pay for new monasteries in northern Europe

(E) raise money for more crusades to the Holy Land

Your Answer _____

Correct Answers

A–97

(B) Spain was the first European kingdom to claim land in North America. Britain, Holland, and France soon followed. The Spanish maintained their hegemony in Central America, while the French, British, and Dutch fought for control of eastern North America. A series of wars were fought over these territories, with the British claiming final victory after 1763.

A–98

(B) In Italy, the Roman Catholic Church had grown more powerful and wealthy throughout the Middle Ages. This wealth led to some corruption and exalted lifestyles by the church leadership. It also led to lavish expenditures and grandiose building projects, such as Saint Peter's in Rome, which would be the largest basilica ever built. The pope needed considerable income to pay for the huge construction projects, so sales of indulgences or church dispensations for the afterlife were sanctioned.

Questions

Q–99

About 1550, the globalization of the world economy under the Spanish began with

(A) the international silver trade
(B) the import of potatoes
(C) copper mining in California
(D) Chinese demand for European textiles
(E) English pirates stealing gold

Your Answer _____

Q–100

First ignored by the Europeans, North America (except for Mexico) finally drew settlers because of the

(A) gold found in Virginia
(B) legends of the Fountain of Youth
(C) friendly natives who helped the newcomers
(D) abundant fish and fur
(E) indigo that could be grown there

Your Answer _____

Correct Answers

A–99

(A) With the large output of silver from Mexican and Peruvian mines, the Spanish began to exchange their precious metal for goods worldwide. They created the first global currency with the coins they made. The Chinese especially wished to trade their silks and other wares for Spanish silver. From Europe to Asia, this silver became a globally traded commodity that affected economies in many different regions.

A–100

(D) The first attempts to colonize North America north of Mexico failed routinely. No real wealth could be found north of the Rio Grande, and native peoples were often hostile to Spanish and English settlements or missions. The North Atlantic Ocean was very difficult to sail, and many ships and passengers were lost, including some famous explorers. Sailors did find huge schools of fish, however, and this encouraged more exploration. Eventually the fur trade in Europe also stimulated more settlement by the French and English in the northern country.

Q–101

The term *bourgeoisie* can best be described as

(A) the rural aristocracy

(B) the urban wealthy class

(C) the landed peasantry

(D) the clerical elite

(E) royalty

Your Answer _____

Q–102

In the sixteenth century, the beginning of global European imperialism started with

(A) large colonial governments

(B) isolated trading posts in Africa and Asia

(C) English protectorates in Africa

(D) the slave trade in the Middle East

(E) manufacturing sites throughout India

Your Answer _____

Correct Answers

A–101

(B) The growing urban merchant class in Europe became known as the bourgeoisie. An earlier French term for medieval inhabitants of towns, the bourgeoisie were neither peasants nor nobility. This class of townspeople was called the merchant/artisan class. But in the end, *bourgeoisie* became a term to describe the nonaristocratic wealthy businesspeople who became more influential as the modern era dawned.

A–102

(B) Although the Portuguese and Spanish had sailed to Asia by 1520, they were not able to colonize such faraway locations. Instead they claimed and set up small trading ports and stations in India, the Spice Islands, and southern China. Goa and Macao were two such outposts, which were thousands of kilometers from Europe. Competition among these faraway trading centers was the start of the modern global business world we know today.

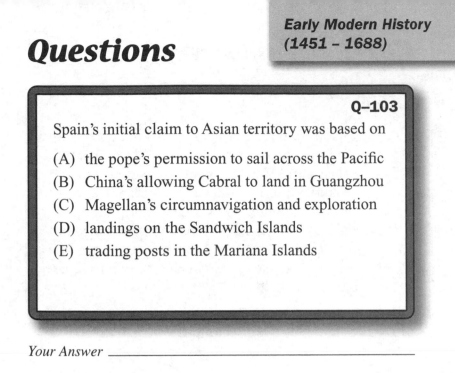

Q–103

Spain's initial claim to Asian territory was based on

(A) the pope's permission to sail across the Pacific

(B) China's allowing Cabral to land in Guangzhou

(C) Magellan's circumnavigation and exploration

(D) landings on the Sandwich Islands

(E) trading posts in the Mariana Islands

Your Answer _____

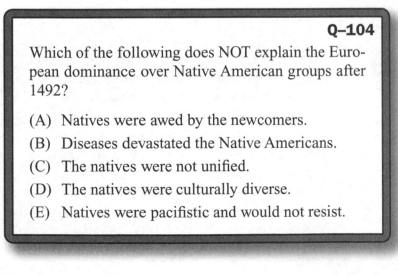

Q–104

Which of the following does NOT explain the European dominance over Native American groups after 1492?

(A) Natives were awed by the newcomers.

(B) Diseases devastated the Native Americans.

(C) The natives were not unified.

(D) The natives were culturally diverse.

(E) Natives were pacifistic and would not resist.

Your Answer _____

Correct Answers

A–103

(C) Spain followed Portugal in seeking a route to Asia, but Spanish explorers sailed west instead of east. In 1519, Magellan sailed around South America and into the Pacific Ocean. He landed in the Solomon, Mariana, and Philippine islands, which he claimed for the kingdom of Spain, his sponsor. This was the basis for Spain's Asian empire, which added to its large American holdings.

A–104

(E) Most native groups were experienced fighters when the Spanish arrived in 1492. Indeed, they had fought one another for centuries. The Europeans took advantage of this and would play different native groups against one another. Some Native American tribes and civilizations had sophisticated forms of government. The diseases brought by Europeans, however, decreased native populations by more than half within a century of Columbus's landing.

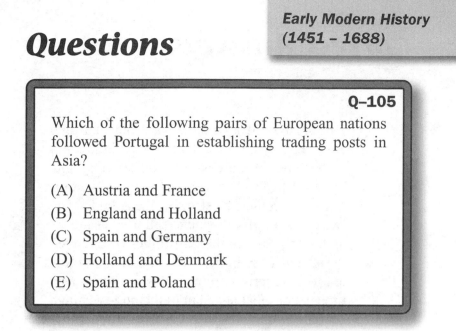

Q–105

Which of the following pairs of European nations followed Portugal in establishing trading posts in Asia?

(A) Austria and France

(B) England and Holland

(C) Spain and Germany

(D) Holland and Denmark

(E) Spain and Poland

Your Answer _____

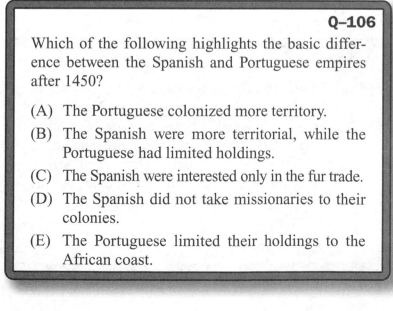

Q–106

Which of the following highlights the basic difference between the Spanish and Portuguese empires after 1450?

(A) The Portuguese colonized more territory.

(B) The Spanish were more territorial, while the Portuguese had limited holdings.

(C) The Spanish were interested only in the fur trade.

(D) The Spanish did not take missionaries to their colonies.

(E) The Portuguese limited their holdings to the African coast.

Your Answer _____

Correct Answers

A–105

(B)   Portugal could not maintain a strong maritime empire partly because it was a small kingdom with limited resources. Holland and England, however, had well-developed financial institutions that could invest in overseas trade. The Dutch and English began to sail to Asia and set up trading posts in the East Indies (later called the Dutch East Indies) and India. This trade led to long-term commitments by both maritime nations that lasted until the mid-twentieth century.

A–106

(B)   While the Portuguese ventured to Asia before the Spanish, the discovery of the New World gave Spain a much larger amount of claimed land after 1492. The Portuguese claimed a modest amount of land in Brazil and Africa, while the Spanish established colonies in Asia and Africa, as well as in North and South America.

Q–107

The first kingdom to sponsor the successful circum-navigation of the globe was

(A) Portugal

(B) England

(C) Hungary

(D) Holland

(E) Spain

Your Answer _____

_____

Q–108

Which of the following commodities was France most interested in finding in the New World?

(A) Rum

(B) Tobacco

(C) Fur

(D) Corn

(E) Sugarcane

Your Answer _____

_____

Correct Answers

A–107

(E)   In 1519, Magellan, sponsored by Spain, sailed west with five ships. This three-year voyage resulted in the first circling of the globe by an exploring nation. Only one ship made it around the world, and Magellan did not survive the trip. It established the Spanish as a Pacific power with a global empire. Spanish goods were traded from Asia to the Americas and then to Europe.

A–108

(C)   The French were most interested in finding and harvesting fur from the New World. Unlike Spain, the French made little effort to colonize the New World but were skilled in learning and adapting to local customs and the environment. In their search for skins and pelts for the European market, French hunters and trappers explored the rivers and woods of North America and learned the languages of Native American tribes they encountered.

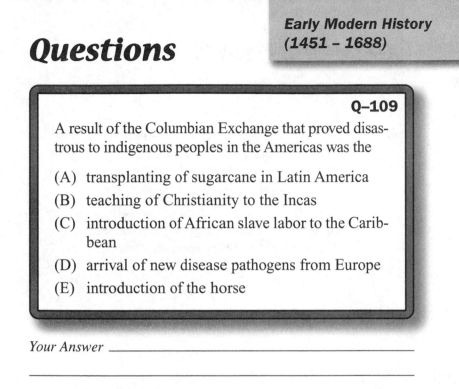

Q–109

A result of the Columbian Exchange that proved disastrous to indigenous peoples in the Americas was the

(A) transplanting of sugarcane in Latin America

(B) teaching of Christianity to the Incas

(C) introduction of African slave labor to the Caribbean

(D) arrival of new disease pathogens from Europe

(E) introduction of the horse

Your Answer _____

_____

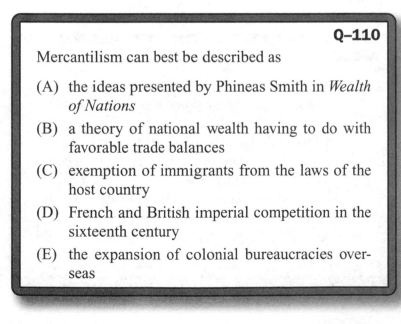

Q–110

Mercantilism can best be described as

(A) the ideas presented by Phineas Smith in *Wealth of Nations*

(B) a theory of national wealth having to do with favorable trade balances

(C) exemption of immigrants from the laws of the host country

(D) French and British imperial competition in the sixteenth century

(E) the expansion of colonial bureaucracies overseas

Your Answer _____

_____

Correct Answers

A–109

(D) Large demographic declines took place across North and South America when European diseases were passed on to the natives. Illnesses such as smallpox and influenza killed entire communities, with many of the victims being young children. Some tribal groups and civilizations lost up to 90 percent of their people.

A–110

(B) After 1500, leading European nations adopted an economic theory that national wealth could be gained through controlled trade, leading to a favorable balance between imports and exports. This meant that overseas empires could benefit a nation by supplying raw materials for manufacture. These goods could then be sold overseas, and money would flow into the host nation. More exports and fewer imports would be the end result.

Q–111

Which of the following was an impact of the Columbian Exchange in Europe?

(A) Severe famine was common in southern Europe.

(B) Tobacco use became common in the lower classes.

(C) Population rates rose steadily.

(D) Animal birthrates dropped.

(E) Epidemics ravaged the slave trade.

Your Answer _____

_____

Q–112

Which of the following enhanced Spanish access to Asian goods after 1500?

(A) The establishment of a trading center in Manila by 1565

(B) Access to goods through the Spanish colony at Capetown

(C) An alliance with the French in 1570

(D) Overland trade with China

(E) Ming ships landing in Europe in 1521

Your Answer _____

_____

Correct Answers

A–111

(C) The introduction of New World crops, such as the potato, made cheaper foods available to many people. Peasant families could cultivate new sources of carbohydrates and vitamins that nourished their children. In 1450, Europe was still recovering from the medieval bubonic plague, but by 1600, it saw a 25 percent increase in population. Europe then doubled its population in the next century.

A–112

(A) After Magellan claimed the Philippines for Spain in 1521, other Spanish expeditions followed to take control of the archipelago. Missionary priests set about converting the Filipinos to Catholicism, and commercial operations began. After 1565, a trade connection with Asia and the Americas was formed. Spanish ships sailed from Manila to Acapulco, where goods were then trans-shipped to Europe.

Questions

Q–113

The modern global economy was initiated with the

(A) use of coined bullion as money

(B) defeat of Spain by the English in 1588

(C) use of bank drafts to pay for trade goods

(D) European discovery of the Americas after 1492

(E) abolition of slavery in the 1800s

Your Answer _____

_____

Q–114

Which of the following was NOT a cause of the fragmentation of the Roman Catholic Church after 1517?

(A) The increased wealth of the church

(B) A decline in morality within the priesthood

(C) The sale of indulgences

(D) Challenges to papal authority by regional princes

(E) A growing belief in witches in western Europe

Your Answer _____

_____

Correct Answers

A–113

(D) After the creation of the Spanish and Portuguese overseas empires, the entire world was linked for the first time by ships. Maritime trade connected Europe to Africa, Asia, Australia, and the Americas. Money and goods flowed back and forth as capitalism grew more sophisticated. China became a key market for the Europeans because silk was in great demand. The Dutch followed the Spanish and Portuguese into the Asian market and set up trading posts in the East Indies.

A–114

(E) By 1500, many perceived that the Roman Catholic Church had become corrupt and overly concerned with worldly affairs. Because the Catholic Church had accumulated great wealth and power, corruption at the highest levels of church leadership was evident. Some bishops openly kept mistresses and fathered children. Martin Luther began a public discussion on the need of the church to reform itself from within. German princes used Luther's criticism of the Catholic Church to challenge papal authority and gain some independence for their domains.

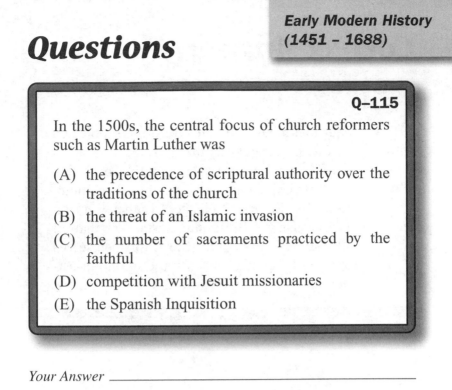

Q–115

In the 1500s, the central focus of church reformers such as Martin Luther was

(A) the precedence of scriptural authority over the traditions of the church

(B) the threat of an Islamic invasion

(C) the number of sacraments practiced by the faithful

(D) competition with Jesuit missionaries

(E) the Spanish Inquisition

Your Answer _____

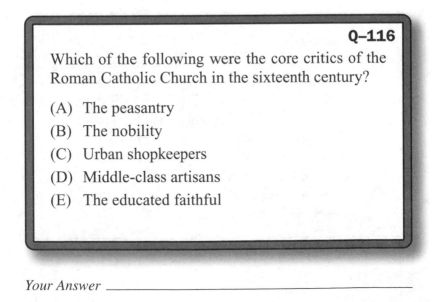

Q–116

Which of the following were the core critics of the Roman Catholic Church in the sixteenth century?

(A) The peasantry

(B) The nobility

(C) Urban shopkeepers

(D) Middle-class artisans

(E) The educated faithful

Your Answer _____

Correct Answers

A–115

(A)   Martin Luther and other reformers objected to Catholic traditions that did not have a basis in scripture. The sale of indulgences was the most objectionable of many Catholic practices that Luther challenged. Luther went on to translate the Bible into German so that all literate believers could read it for themselves and not be dependent on the Catholic priesthood to interpret God's word.

A–116

(E)   While many Christians observed behavior by clerics that was scandalous, it was mostly the well educated who voiced their disapproval. Writers like Chaucer and parish priests such as Zwingli noted the unchaste lifestyles of some priests and wrote about them. Other scholar-priests, such as Luther, looked to the scriptures to form a response to the scandals that were observed in the church.

Questions

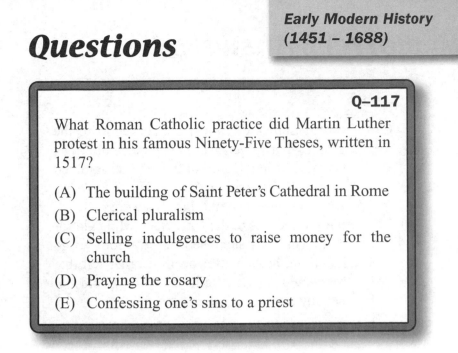

Q–117

What Roman Catholic practice did Martin Luther protest in his famous Ninety-Five Theses, written in 1517?

(A) The building of Saint Peter's Cathedral in Rome

(B) Clerical pluralism

(C) Selling indulgences to raise money for the church

(D) Praying the rosary

(E) Confessing one's sins to a priest

Your Answer _____

_____

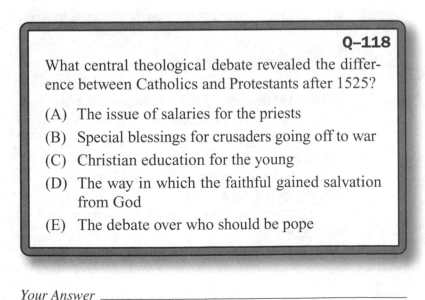

Q–118

What central theological debate revealed the difference between Catholics and Protestants after 1525?

(A) The issue of salaries for the priests

(B) Special blessings for crusaders going off to war

(C) Christian education for the young

(D) The way in which the faithful gained salvation from God

(E) The debate over who should be pope

Your Answer _____

_____

Correct Answers

A–117

(C)   Martin Luther was most concerned with the selling of indulgences. The pope authorized the sales of indulgences after he had initiated various building projects, such as the large basilica in Rome. The indulgences were believed to remit the sins of the Christians who paid for them. This was supposed to allow one to go directly to heaven after death. Luther felt that this would mislead believers who would not feel any remorse for their sins.

A–118

(D)   As Luther protested the sale of indulgences he was also questioning the merit of any human act in working toward the salvation of the individual sinner. He believed that one was saved through faith alone, while the Catholic Church maintained that a combination of faith and good works helped a person gain salvation. This essential debate was the core controversy that led to the split in western Christianity after 1525.

Questions

Q–119

What was the Protestant alternative to papal authority as the Reformation unfolded?

(A) Canonical records from the early church

(B) The Bible as the revealed Word of God

(C) Church councils in Germany after 1517

(D) Newly discovered letters from Saint Paul to Greek congregations

(E) The Book of Mormon

Your Answer _____

_____

Correct Answers

A–119

(B) Christian reformers, such as Luther, Calvin, and Zwingli, believed that the best way to reform the church was to return to early Christian values found in the Bible. They worked to translate the Bible for the common people and make it more accessible to Christians everywhere. The new printing technology helped make this happen. A larger and better-educated middle class also responded to this call for scriptural piety in northern Europe.

Questions

Q–120

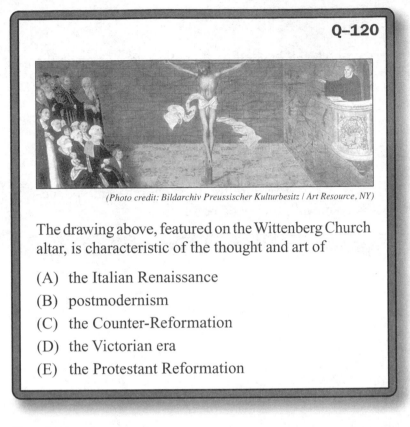

(Photo credit: Bildarchiv Preussischer Kulturbesitz / Art Resource, NY)

The drawing above, featured on the Wittenberg Church altar, is characteristic of the thought and art of

(A) the Italian Renaissance

(B) postmodernism

(C) the Counter-Reformation

(D) the Victorian era

(E) the Protestant Reformation

Your Answer _____

_____

Correct Answers

A–120

(E)   The altar painting, done by Lucas Cranach the Elder, shows a preacher (Martin Luther) pointing to the central figure of Jesus on the cross. This simple depiction shows the emphasis that Protestant reformers placed on the biblical story of the life of Christ as opposed to the traditions of the church. Their focus on Jesus was a departure from the church-centered medieval experience before 1450.

Questions

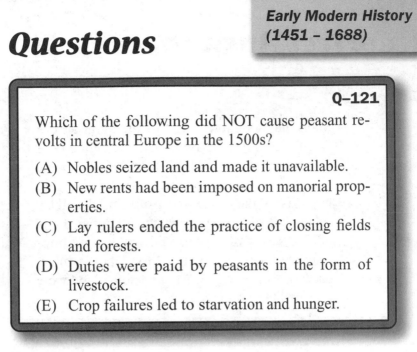

Q–121

Which of the following did NOT cause peasant revolts in central Europe in the 1500s?

(A) Nobles seized land and made it unavailable.

(B) New rents had been imposed on manorial properties.

(C) Lay rulers ended the practice of closing fields and forests.

(D) Duties were paid by peasants in the form of livestock.

(E) Crop failures led to starvation and hunger.

Your Answer _____

_____

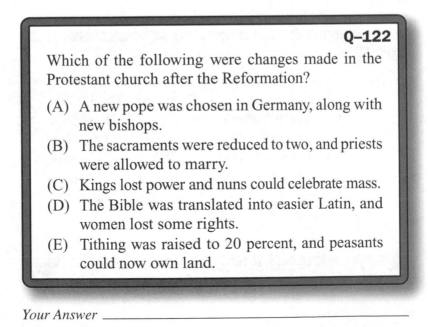

Q–122

Which of the following were changes made in the Protestant church after the Reformation?

(A) A new pope was chosen in Germany, along with new bishops.

(B) The sacraments were reduced to two, and priests were allowed to marry.

(C) Kings lost power and nuns could celebrate mass.

(D) The Bible was translated into easier Latin, and women lost some rights.

(E) Tithing was raised to 20 percent, and peasants could now own land.

Your Answer _____

_____

Correct Answers

A–121

(C)   Many factors contributed to the agrarian crisis of the 1500s. Bad harvests meant the poor went hungry. Nobles took land out of use and reserved it for themselves, causing smaller harvests for the peasantry. Both church and lay rulers collected various rents and duties. Only after a series of revolts did some conditions improve for the workers of the land. In many parts of Germany, forests and some land were returned to public use.

A–122

(B)   After 1525, Protestants looked to the Bible as their basis for church reform. The Lutheran and other Protestant churches allowed the clergy to marry because celibacy did not have a firm biblical tradition. While the Catholic Church had seven sacraments, the Protestants retained the two practiced in the scriptures: baptism and communion.

Questions

Q–123

Be it enacted by authority of this present Parliament that the King our sovereign lord, his heirs and successors kings of this realm, shall be taken, accepted and reputed the only supreme head in earth of the Church of England called Anglicana Ecclesia . . . .

The proclamation of 1534 shown above has to do with the

(A) king's trial in Parliament

(B) king's obedience to the pope

(C) Reformation in England

(D) war in Ireland

(E) Magna Carta

Your Answer _____

Correct Answers

A–123

(C)   The Act of Supremacy in 1534 was a dramatic break between the English crown and the Catholic Church in Rome. After being denied a divorce from his Spanish queen, Henry VIII created his own church and placed himself at its head. This power struggle between church and state revealed the growing power of monarchs in Europe, who were able to defy church authority.

Q–124

What was the central compromise included in the Peace of Augsburg in 1555?

(A) Catholic priests would be allowed to marry.

(B) Denmark apologized for its attack on the pope.

(C) The Netherlands would remain Catholic.

(D) Lutheranism was officially recognized by European rulers.

(E) Calvin was released from prison.

Your Answer _____

_____

Q–125

The motives of King Henry VIII of England in separating from the Roman Catholic Church in 1534 were both

(A) economic and personal

(B) personal and political

(C) carnal and traditional

(D) commercial and theological

(E) psychological and vengeful

Your Answer _____

_____

Correct Answers

A–124

(D)   In the 1540s, a war was fought in central Europe over imperial control of the many small domains in present-day Germany. The Peace of Augsburg allowed each territory to choose between Catholicism and Lutheranism. Most of the northern territories chose the new Lutheran faith, while the south remained Roman Catholic. Either way, state churches were established, and each person had to convert to the new official faith or be forced to leave. This legitimized some of the gains of the Protestant Reformation, gave more power to local rulers, and continued the fragmented rule in central Europe. Centralized and dynastic power was further weakened.

A–125

(B)   The perceived need for a male heir had much to do with the Protestant Reformation in England. Henry VIII married the wife of his dead brother and when she did not bear a son for him, he broke with Rome and created his own national church in England. This allowed him to marry again, but it was not until his third wife that he had a legitimate male heir, who became Edward VI. Henry was excommunicated from the Catholic Church but went his own way for personal and political reasons so that his dynasty would continue after his death.

STOP Take Test-Readiness Quiz 1 on CD
(to review questions 1–125)

Questions

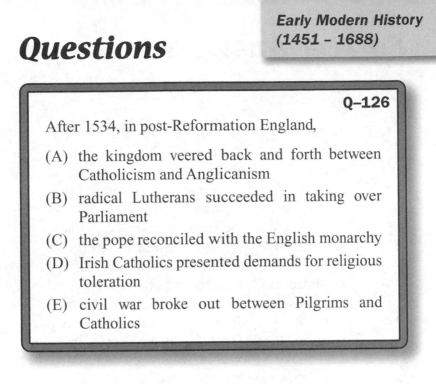

Q–126

After 1534, in post-Reformation England,

(A) the kingdom veered back and forth between Catholicism and Anglicanism

(B) radical Lutherans succeeded in taking over Parliament

(C) the pope reconciled with the English monarchy

(D) Irish Catholics presented demands for religious toleration

(E) civil war broke out between Pilgrims and Catholics

Your Answer _____

_____

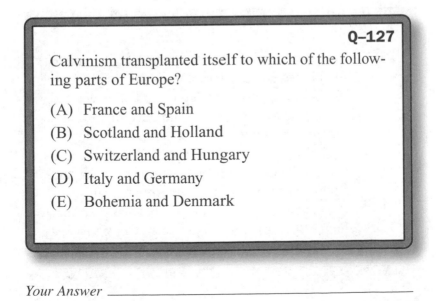

Q–127

Calvinism transplanted itself to which of the following parts of Europe?

(A) France and Spain

(B) Scotland and Holland

(C) Switzerland and Hungary

(D) Italy and Germany

(E) Bohemia and Denmark

Your Answer _____

_____

Correct Answers

A–126

(A) King Henry VIII broke with the Catholic Church, but his heirs were divided on how to maintain religious independence from Rome. Edward VI was pro-Protestant. However, Mary, his half-sister, who was devoutly Catholic, succeeded him. She persecuted those who followed the Protestant religion and had a number of them killed. In the end, Edward's other half-sister, Elizabeth I, steered a middle path by keeping the Church of England and dealing more leniently with dissident Catholics. Her long reign and the fact that she did not marry either a Catholic or a Protestant made for a more stable kingdom and religious atmosphere.

A–127

(B) The doctrines and discipline of Calvinism found converts in various parts of Europe. Calvin believed in a sovereign God who wanted his people to live simply and devoutly. French in origin, his doctrines became well established in Holland, Scotland, and parts of Switzerland and England. His emphasis on hard work and simple faith became an important feature of Protestantism as it spread beyond Europe. Italy, Bohemia, and southern Germany remained Catholic.

Questions

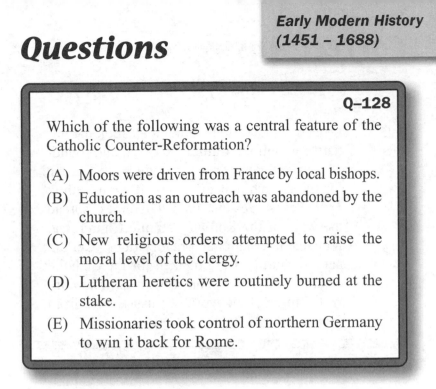

Q–128

Which of the following was a central feature of the Catholic Counter-Reformation?

(A) Moors were driven from France by local bishops.

(B) Education as an outreach was abandoned by the church.

(C) New religious orders attempted to raise the moral level of the clergy.

(D) Lutheran heretics were routinely burned at the stake.

(E) Missionaries took control of northern Germany to win it back for Rome.

Your Answer _____

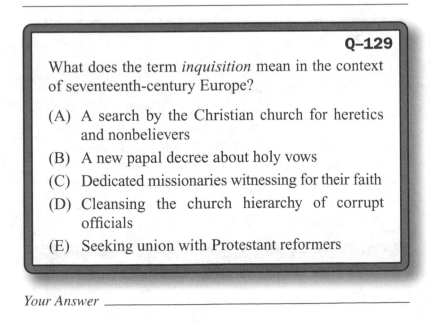

Q–129

What does the term *inquisition* mean in the context of seventeenth-century Europe?

(A) A search by the Christian church for heretics and nonbelievers

(B) A new papal decree about holy vows

(C) Dedicated missionaries witnessing for their faith

(D) Cleansing the church hierarchy of corrupt officials

(E) Seeking union with Protestant reformers

Your Answer _____

Correct Answers

A–128

(C) Dynamic and zealous individuals took the initiative within the Catholic Church and founded new religious orders to win back Europe for the church and to reform it from within. Franciscans, Jesuits, and Ursulines spread the work of the Roman Catholic Church and founded international organizations. Certain parts of Europe were retaken for the Catholic Church, and many people overseas were converted through the work of missionaries from these new orders.

A–129

(A) Some of the religious tension of the *reconquista* in Spain and the Reformation led to persecution in different parts of Europe. In Spain, tribunals were formed to find out heretical ideas and purge the kingdom of Jewish influence. This was partly due to older medieval anti-Semitism, but it was also a ploy to consolidate authority in a newly unified Christian kingdom.

Questions

Q–130

Which of the following policies had to be adopted by kingdoms in modern Europe because of large-scale warfare?

(A) Conscription was tried and abandoned as a failure.

(B) State-church authority diminished in northern Europe.

(C) Governments greatly increased taxes.

(D) Kings became more accessible to the people.

(E) Trade was deemphasized as a national priority.

Your Answer _____

Q–131

Which classes were the first to suffer from bad harvests and economic depression?

(A) Peasants and the urban poor

(B) Townspeople and shopkeepers

(C) Farmers and clergy

(D) Soldiers and merchants

(E) Nobility and manufacturers

Your Answer _____

Correct Answers

A–130

(C)　Warfare between powerful European king-doms grew in scope through the sixteenth and seventeenth centuries. As the size of armies increased, so did the expense of maintaining them. Food, weapons, and salaries now became large budget items for royal governments. Money had to be raised to sustain long campaigns, and new systems of taxation were devised to extract money from the population. Some of these taxes were on commerce and trade. The power to decide on these taxes became a key issue in some kingdoms.

A–131

(A)　Most of the population in seventeenth-century Europe lived in the countryside and made their living from the land. Poor harvests meant that peasants might suffer from malnutrition and the diseases that preyed on weakened bodies. Economic downturns hit the urban poor hard as they tried to survive on very little. This led to food riots in which the poor would steal bread or grain to survive.

Questions

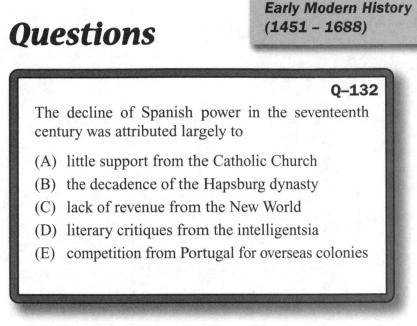

Q–132

The decline of Spanish power in the seventeenth century was attributed largely to

(A) little support from the Catholic Church

(B) the decadence of the Hapsburg dynasty

(C) lack of revenue from the New World

(D) literary critiques from the intelligentsia

(E) competition from Portugal for overseas colonies

Your Answer _____

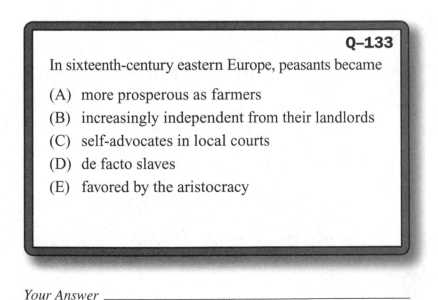

Q–133

In sixteenth-century eastern Europe, peasants became

(A) more prosperous as farmers

(B) increasingly independent from their landlords

(C) self-advocates in local courts

(D) de facto slaves

(E) favored by the aristocracy

Your Answer _____

Correct Answers

A–132

(B) The decadence of the Hapsburg royalty and the aristocracy in general helped Spain lose ground to other kingdoms in Europe after 1550. The incredible wealth of the Americas was squandered by the monarchy because expensive wars were initiated, which impoverished the government. The resulting malaise prevented Spain from keeping pace with France and England. France and England emerged as the great powers of modern Europe.

A–133

(D) Unlike the peasants of western Europe, the rural poor in the east had more and more rights taken from them. Over time, free peasants became serfs whose lives resembled that of slaves in several ways. Eastern European landlords used their political power to limit basic freedoms of the peasantry. Heavier labor obligations were imposed, and peasants could not move freely within their domains. Local lords had great power and would act as judge and jailer if a peasant or serf resisted the lords' power.

Q–134

In the seventeenth century, monarchs in eastern Europe were able to increase their power because

(A) frequent wars were fought with nearby kingdoms

(B) they suppressed their parliaments

(C) disease caused population declines

(D) relative peace reigned during the era

(E) the pope supported their policies

Your Answer _____

Q–135

What long-term impact did seventeenth-century absolutism in Prussia and Austria have on Europe?

(A) German militarism created a powerful legacy of expansionism.

(B) The Hapsburg dynasty was short-lived.

(C) England sought to emulate the German monarchy.

(D) Catholicism was mandated throughout central Europe.

(E) Bohemia revolted and wrote its own constitution in 1620.

Your Answer _____

Correct Answers

A–134

(A) The Thirty Years' War and other conflicts in the seventeenth century made for a tumultuous period. Kings and princes in eastern Europe used this to their advantage because the emergency of conflict allowed them to rule more decisively and cruelly. They raised revenue for their fighting and allowed the oppression of the peasant serfs who worked the land.

A–135

(A) Both Prussia and Austria evolved into powerful and absolutist states in the seventeenth century. Though Prussia would become more powerful and successful over time, the warfare involving both states would leave a strong militaristic stamp on the people of central northern Europe. Martial skill was celebrated, and loyalty to the monarchy took precedence over individual rights or ambitions. An army career was prestigious, and military science was an important field for young men to study.

Q–136

Hungary maintained a limited independence within the Hapsburg kingdom of Austria because

(A) all revolts were ruthlessly executed

(B) the Hungarian nobility had a national consciousness

(C) the Ottomans granted fewer freedoms during their occupation

(D) Charles VI was a liberal monarch

(E) the Catholic Church was sympathetic to Hungarian aims

Your Answer _____

Q–137

In the seventeenth century, Frederick of Brandenburg built his absolutist power base in Prussia by

(A) gaining support from the townspeople

(B) working with the peasants and giving them more rights

(C) writing a liberal constitution that shared power

(D) going to war with Sweden

(E) collaborating with the landed elites in northern Germany

Your Answer _____

Correct Answers

A–136

(B) The Austrian domain in central Europe was a patchwork of ethnic peoples dominated by the Hapsburg dynasty. The heavy hand of the ruling Hapsburgs had crushed most of these minorities, but the Hungarians fought back and won some concessions from the monarchy. The Hungarian nobility and even the peasantry had a better-developed sense of national identity and pride. This inspired them to fight back and negotiate some rights, which were granted as long as they remained loyal to the hereditary rule of the Hapsburgs.

A–137

(E) Powerful rulers, such as Frederick of Prussia and Louis of France, knew how to control the nobles under them. Some concessions were given as long as tax revenues continued to flow into the royal treasury. These tax revenues paid for larger standing armies and the lavish lifestyle of the monarch. The landed elites promised loyalty to the reigning monarch and raised monies from the lands they controlled. This resulted in few rights for the common people, who were taught to obey authority without question.

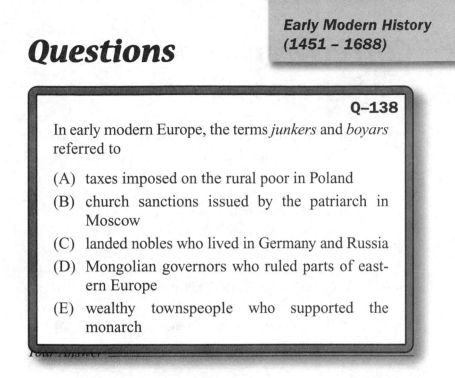

Q–138

In early modern Europe, the terms *junkers* and *boyars* referred to

(A) taxes imposed on the rural poor in Poland

(B) church sanctions issued by the patriarch in Moscow

(C) landed nobles who lived in Germany and Russia

(D) Mongolian governors who ruled parts of eastern Europe

(E) wealthy townspeople who supported the monarch

Your Answer _____

Q–139

The infamous Ivan the Terrible of Russia got his name by

(A) executing many boyars and peasants who resisted his rule

(B) slaughtering the priests who revolted in Muscovy

(C) killing Polish officers captured in the battle of Warsaw

(D) murdering his own family

(E) crushing the Polish-Lithuanian state

Your Answer _____

Correct Answers

A–138

(C)   Junkers were the landed nobles of northern Germany who helped support the Hohenzollern dynasty, which created the Prussian state in the seventeenth and eighteenth centuries. These landed elites owned large estates and had peasants work the land. Likewise, in Russia, the boyars were the landed elites who ruled their estates with great power over the enslaved serfs. Both the Hohenzollern and Romanov dynasties managed the nobles so that revenues could be raised and power could be maintained.

A–139

(A)   Ivan the Terrible was a cruel and paranoid ruler of Russia in the 1600s. He was the first ruler of Russia to take the title of tsar (equivalent to caesar) and was ruthless in his elimination of any perceived threat to his power. He imprisoned thousands and executed many from the nobility. He created a state in which all Russians were his servants and none were allowed to leave their localities.

Q–140

After 1500, the term *triangular trade* referred to

(A) Chinese goods flowing to Manila and then to the Americas

(B) spices from India being traded for slaves in Africa

(C) an economic network of goods and slaves between North America and Africa

(D) Portuguese trade between Brazil and South Africa

(E) goods being bought and sold in Mexico and New Spain

Your Answer _____

_____

Q–141

Which European nation dominated the East Asia spice trade in the seventeenth century?

(A) England

(B) Spain

(C) Portugal

(D) Holland

(E) France

Your Answer _____

_____

Correct Answers

A–140

(C) After the settlement of the Americas, trade routes evolved over which goods were shipped from the Caribbean to British America and then to Africa. Typically traded goods included molasses, tobacco, rum, and African slaves. The Spanish, British, and Portuguese colonies in the Americas demanded cheap labor, which slavery provided. Africans and Europeans both profited from the trading of goods and people through the nineteenth century.

A–141

(D) Although Portugal pioneered the spice trade out of Southeast Asia, the Dutch followed and quickly took charge of the lucrative trade. With a combination of large fleets and raw aggression, Holland took over various Portuguese and English trading posts. Ceylon, south of India, became one of a number of Dutch outposts. The important post of Malacca, situated on the Malay Peninsula, was taken in 1641, and the Dutch East India Company flourished for most of the seventeenth century.

Q–142

Key to the commercial success of the Dutch in the seventeenth century was their

(A) allegiance to the Roman Catholic Church

(B) authoritarian monarchy

(C) cotton industry

(D) banking system and stock exchange

(E) alliance with Spain

Your Answer _____

_____

Q–143

A primary goal of Elizabeth I of England was to

(A) placate radical Puritans

(B) strengthen the European economy

(C) marry another powerful continental monarch

(D) stabilize the Tudor dynasty and defend England against foreign threats

(E) maintain control of British America

Your Answer _____

_____

Correct Answers

A–142

(D) The 1600s have sometimes been called the Dutch century. This small republic became a major economic power in Europe and in the world because it developed a sophisticated financial system, as well as a robust maritime outreach. The Dutch later fought with the British over control of Africa and parts of North America. They also established the Dutch East Indies as an important Asian trading headquarters.

A–143

(D) Elizabeth I was the first long-term female monarch to reign over England. She dealt with various religious factions in post-Reformation England, including those who wished her dead. Her biggest challenge, however, came from overseas when Spain tried to invade England in 1588. Catholic Spain declared Elizabeth a servant of the devil and called on all Catholics in England to overthrow her. A determined English naval defense and fortuitous weather helped England turn back the Spanish fleet.

Questions

Q–144

Early Russia grew out of a principality centered in the city of

(A) Minsk

(B) Kiev

(C) Saint Petersburg

(D) Novgorod

(E) Cracow

Your Answer _____

Q–145

The Thirty Years' War was largely fought against which royal dynasty in Europe?

(A) The House of Hapsburg in Austria

(B) The Brandenburgers of Saxony

(C) The House of Tudor in England

(D) The Medicis of Florence

(E) The Fuggars of Amsterdam

Your Answer _____

Correct Answers

A–144

(B) Russia was established by Vladimir I when he and an army of Varangians retook Kiev and Vladimir I became the grand prince. In converting to Orthodox Christianity, Kiev became the center of the eastern faith. The center of power eventually shifted to Moscow when later Russian monarchs consolidated their power.

A–145

(A) The Thirty Years' War was an on-again, off-again conflict that took place in the 1600s in central Europe. Largely an outcome of the Protestant Reformation, it was fought over territory in present-day Germany. Mercenaries, nobles, and freemen fought in the conflict, which was part civil war and part religious war. The Hapsburgs represented the zealous Catholic impulse to reclaim parts of Europe for the Roman Catholic Church, while the Danish, Dutch, and Swedish armies were fighting for their new Protestant beliefs. Some historians explain the prolonged disunity of Germany as stemming from this conflict.

Q–146

During the Thirty Years' War, Sweden pursued a policy of

(A) helping the Hapsburgs against Prussia

(B) supporting the oppressed Protestants in central Europe

(C) allowing Huguenots to settle in Scandinavia

(D) siding with England in the recapture of the Low Countries

(E) remaining neutral

Your Answer _____

Q–147

Which of the following most accurately describes the political system of Brandenburg-Prussia in the seventeenth century?

(A) Parliamentary republic

(B) Confederation of cantons

(C) Limited democracy

(D) Absolutist monarchy

(E) Commercial oligarchy

Your Answer _____

Correct Answers

A–146

(B) During the third and Swedish phase of the long war, Gustavus Adolphus led an army to fight against the Catholic Hapsburgs. Germany was a patchwork of Protestant and Catholic domains, and the Protestant Scandinavians sought to protect the rights of their fellow believers. Swedish military success meant that Protestant gains in northern Germany would later be made permanent in the postwar settlements.

A–147

(D) Prussian absolutism was consolidated under King Frederick William. The landed junkers were not able to resist the Hohenzollern dynasty, which built an absolute monarchy in Prussia. The nobility accepted demands for military funding and gave into royal demands for obedience. This allowed the nobility to retain their local power while serving the king.

Q–148

In 1571, the Ottoman expansion into Europe was halted by

(A) the Hapsburg army at Vienna

(B) Hungarian troops at Bucharest

(C) the Byzantine forces at Constantinople

(D) the Bulgarians at the gates of Sofia

(E) the Mameluke Empire in the Aegean Sea

Your Answer _____

Q–149

Ottoman political and military power waned in the seventeenth century because of

(A) defeats by the French

(B) tensions between Sunni and Shiite factions

(C) a Turkish civil war

(D) reformers who undercut the sultan in Istanbul

(E) ethnic strife and bureaucratic in-fighting

Your Answer _____

Correct Answers

A–148

(A) The Ottoman victory at Constantinople meant that Islam was at the frontier of Europe. Suleiman the Magnificent captured large parts of southeastern Europe, including Bosnia, Romania, and the Ukraine. Christians finally banded together and created the Christian Holy League to oppose Islamic expansion into central Europe. Decisive battles at Vienna and Lepanto in the 1500s gave the Holy League important victories that stopped further Ottoman incursions.

A–149

(E) The Ottoman imperial expansion began to dissipate after two centuries of growth. One reason was that the ruling elites in Istanbul became increasingly corrupt. Another reason was that the many ethnic groups they had conquered created numerous administrative issues, and the government became increasingly rigid. The Christian Europeans successfully denied the Ottomans any further territory after the late seventeenth century and, in fact, began to win back sections of eastern Europe for Christian kings.

Q–150

Which of the following explains why Russia lagged behind western Europe in its development?

(A) The eradication of Islam from Central Asia

(B) The influence of the Ottomans in their affairs

(C) Massive immigration after the Mongol invasion

(D) Poor economic management

(E) Authoritarian rulers and cultural isolation

Your Answer _____

Q–151

Suleiman the Magnificent won the title of "the Law-giver" by

(A) prosecuting Jews in Islamic courts

(B) codifying local laws and granting autonomy to religious minorities

(C) forcing conversion of Christians to Islam

(D) creating legal councils in the provinces

(E) forming a legalistic theocracy

Your Answer _____

Correct Answers

A–150

(E) Russia took longer to develop into a nation-state for a number of reasons. Russian monarchs and rulers tended to be heavy-handed and despotic, giving the Russian people little control over their lives and no practice in governing themselves. Russia also suffered a period of rule by the Mongols, which isolated them culturally from the rest of Europe in the late medieval period. Even Peter the Great, who wanted Russia to emulate other, more modern kingdoms, was an old-fashioned autocrat who limited the freedoms of his people.

A–151

(B) The Ottoman Empire ruled many different peoples in eastern Europe from the 1600s to the 1900s. Ottoman rule was relatively tolerant, and different religions were allowed to practice their own faiths and administer their own legal traditions. Suleiman had his government codify regional legal traditions, which helped centralize the far-reaching Ottoman authority across the empire.

Questions

Which of the following was NOT an implication of the Copernican hypothesis of 1543?

(A) Earth was just another planet.

(B) The universe was vast in scope.

(C) The stars were at rest in the heavens.

(D) The cosmos was created by an intelligent deity.

(E) Aristotelian physics were disproved.

Your Answer _____

_____

Correct Answers

A–152

(D) Influenced by the Renaissance thinking of his day, Copernicus preferred the earlier Greek view of the solar system, which had the sun at its center. Copernicus theorized that the planets revolved around a stationary sun. This was a considerable departure from the writings of Aristotle and Ptolemy, which proposed an earth-centered system. Knowing the controversy that he was about to create, Copernicus wrote a book about his views, but it was not published until after his death.

Q–153

By the aid of the telescope anyone may behold the Milky Way which so distinctly appeals to the senses that all disputes which have tormented philosophers through so many ages are exploded by the irrefutable evidence of our eyes.

—Galileo Galilei, 1630

What intellectual changes in the seventeenth century does the quote above reveal?

(A) Established authority was challenged by new methods.

(B) The telescope was used to prove church doctrine.

(C) Orthodox views of the heavens were being proved.

(D) The observations of Copernicus were discredited.

(E) The church supported traditional astronomy.

Your Answer _____

_____

Correct Answers

A-153

(A)   Many observers of the heavens began to question older explanations of the relationships among heavenly bodies. Copernicus and Brahe were two scientists who questioned the earlier propositions of Aristotle and Ptolemy. Galileo was a mathematician who incorporated the ideas of inertia and motion to speculate about the heavens. His use of controlled experiments to prove natural phenomena was a new tool for the questioning scientist. It challenged the authority of older academics and the church, which sanctioned ancient ideas that fit its view of creation.

Q–154

The mercantilist theory of economics in the seventeenth century held that

(A) the rule of kings was divinely sanctioned by God

(B) some local autonomy was useful when setting up colonial rule

(C) slavery was unjust and must be abolished

(D) colonies existed for the financial benefit of the mother country

(E) free trade was vital to the economic survival of the kingdom.

Your Answer ———————————————————

Q–155

The Peace of Westphalia was part of the settlement of the

(A) Irish uprising after 1630

(B) war between Prussia and Denmark

(C) War of Spanish Succession

(D) Thirty Years' War

(E) Swiss invasion of Italy

Your Answer ———————————————————

Correct Answers

A–154

(D)   The Age of Exploration created many overseas colonies for European nations. Historians have debated the benefits of these colonies, but the belief in mercantilism was part of the thinking of the time period. Modern manufacturing was just beginning, and the need for raw materials was growing. The mercantilist theory maintained that cheap raw materials would allow factories in the mother or home country to make goods that they could sell to other nations. This resulted in an advantageous trade scenario where national wealth increased.

A–155

(D)   The post-Reformation order in northern Europe was chaotic and violent. For a generation, northern Protestant armies fought with Catholic forces over German territory. The Peace of Westphalia settled the end of the Thirty Years' War and granted certain German states their independence. Central Europe remained politically and culturally fragmented after the fighting.

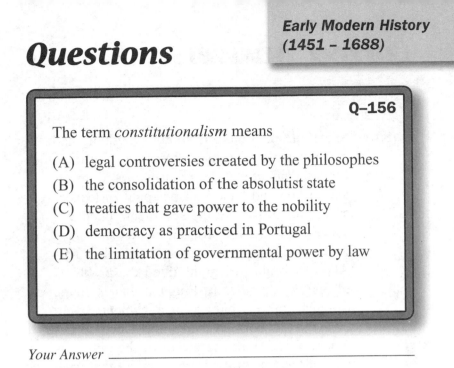

Q–156

The term *constitutionalism* means

(A) legal controversies created by the philosophes

(B) the consolidation of the absolutist state

(C) treaties that gave power to the nobility

(D) democracy as practiced in Portugal

(E) the limitation of governmental power by law

Your Answer _____

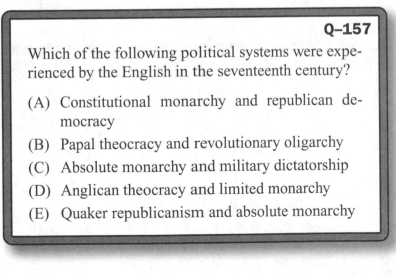

Q–157

Which of the following political systems were experienced by the English in the seventeenth century?

(A) Constitutional monarchy and republican democracy

(B) Papal theocracy and revolutionary oligarchy

(C) Absolute monarchy and military dictatorship

(D) Anglican theocracy and limited monarchy

(E) Quaker republicanism and absolute monarchy

Your Answer _____

Correct Answers

A–156

(E) Since ancient times, different kingdoms had experienced monarchy, dictatorship, and some limited democracy. Power structures were often ad hoc and based on personal instead of shared authority. By the seventeenth century, some kingdoms like Russia and Austria gave most of the power to their monarchs. This Age of Absolutism highlighted the problems of one-person rule. In England and Holland, different power-sharing arrangements were evolving that borrowed on ancient ideas of democracy. Limiting the power of the king was part of the constitutional movement that gave nobles and later common people more say in their government.

A–157

(C) England went through considerable political turmoil in the seventeenth century. It replaced one dynasty with another, and civil war broke out. The war pitted the forces of old-fashioned monarchy against militant Protestant ideas that sought to replace the king with a representative body (Parliament). After the Parliamentarians won, they briefly adopted a dictatorship. When this became unpopular, the monarchy was restored, but it had to share power with the Parliament.

Q–158

The European concept of balance of power found its origin in the period after the

(A) Glorious Revolution

(B) Peace of Westphalia, which ended the Thirty Years' War

(C) death of Suleiman the Magnificent

(D) rise of the Papal States

(E) discovery of the Americas by Portugal

Your Answer _____

_____

Q–159

The art and literature during the reign of Louis XIV has been called

(A) Baroque

(B) French postmodern

(C) Gothic

(D) French classicist

(E) neo-Roman

Your Answer _____

_____

Correct Answers

A–158

(B) After the settlement of the Thirty Years' War with the Peace of Westphalia, agreements between kingdoms attempted to create a balance of power so that no kingdom could become too powerful. Adjustments were made to territories so that some would gain and others would lose influence. A kind of balance was also created between the Catholic south and the Protestant north so that neither branch of Christianity would be dominant.

A–159

(D) The excesses of the Baroque style inspired a reaction that became known as French classicism. Artists and writers created a more spare style inspired by classical Greece and Rome. The virtues of balance and restraint were celebrated. The court of Louis XIV served as a showcase of this style. The royal court sponsored ballets and compositions that expressed a simple grandeur. This art also revealed the great confidence of a nation at the peak of its cultural and political influence.

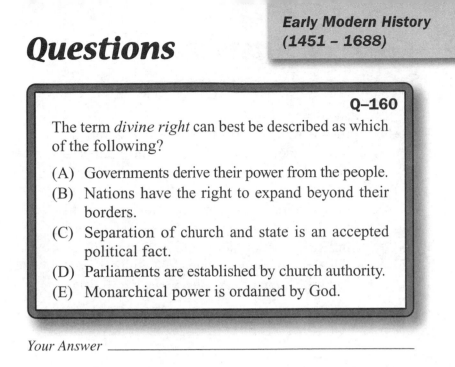

Q–160

The term *divine right* can best be described as which of the following?

(A) Governments derive their power from the people.

(B) Nations have the right to expand beyond their borders.

(C) Separation of church and state is an accepted political fact.

(D) Parliaments are established by church authority.

(E) Monarchical power is ordained by God.

Your Answer _____

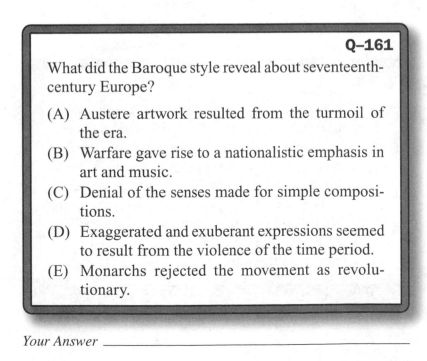

Q–161

What did the Baroque style reveal about seventeenth-century Europe?

(A) Austere artwork resulted from the turmoil of the era.

(B) Warfare gave rise to a nationalistic emphasis in art and music.

(C) Denial of the senses made for simple compositions.

(D) Exaggerated and exuberant expressions seemed to result from the violence of the time period.

(E) Monarchs rejected the movement as revolutionary.

Your Answer _____

Correct Answers

A–160

(E) In the Age of Absolutism, kings claimed to have authority from God to rule their kingdoms. This combining of religious and political dynamics rationalized the rule of the few over the many. Both church and royalty fostered this belief and preached that to oppose the king was to oppose God. In the 1600s, as the Enlightenment began, recognition of the rights of humans began to surface in Europe.

A–161

(D) Baroque art and music seemed a wild departure from the past. Colorful and energetic, baroque art seemed overexpressive. Scholars today see the style as a high-water mark in European culture, noting that it may have resulted because of the post-Reformation tensions that caused so much controversy and war. The sensuous, rich works may have provided an escape from the war and chaos of the era.

Q–162

Part of the reason women were often accused of being witches in the early modern era was

(A) new evidence of sorcery within society

(B) the Council of Trent

(C) religious fervor and tensions within the church during the Reformation

(D) the mass confessions of women who had sold their souls

(E) widespread plague in Poland

Your Answer _____

_____

Q–163

In seventeenth-century western Europe, cultural patterns showed a tendency toward

(A) emulating all things French

(B) simple and plain works of art

(C) relatively little creativity in art and music

(D) returning to medieval styles

(E) romanticizing rural life

Your Answer _____

_____

Correct Answers

A–162

(C)   Many common superstitions combined to lead people to fear some women as spiritual allies of the devil. People sought answers to explain misfortune, and individual women were used locally as scapegoats. The devil and witches were blamed for calamities such as crop failure or mental illness. The spirit world was a tangible part of religious beliefs at this time in history, and the heightened spiritual controversies of the Reformation also encouraged zealotry.

A–163

(A)   In the 1600s, France enjoyed its greatest political and cultural influence in Europe. The courts of Europe looked to France for fashion as well as a stylish approach to monarchy. The court of Louis XIV was seen as the most lavish and accomplished in the world. Kings would send their young people to study and learn from the French. French manners and humor were copied by royal families across the continent.

Questions

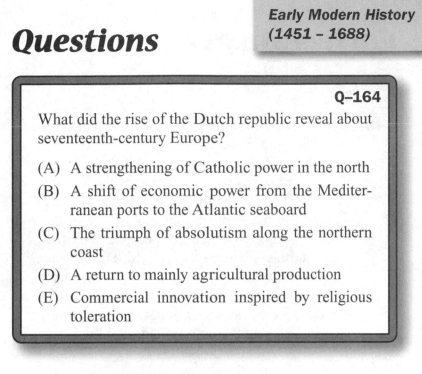

Q–164

What did the rise of the Dutch republic reveal about seventeenth-century Europe?

(A) A strengthening of Catholic power in the north

(B) A shift of economic power from the Mediterranean ports to the Atlantic seaboard

(C) The triumph of absolutism along the northern coast

(D) A return to mainly agricultural production

(E) Commercial innovation inspired by religious toleration

Your Answer _____

_____

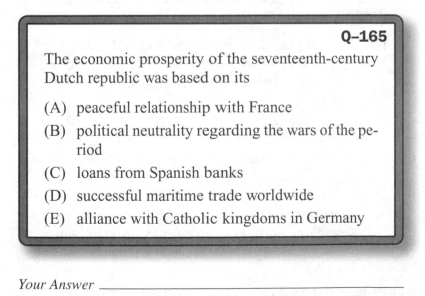

Q–165

The economic prosperity of the seventeenth-century Dutch republic was based on its

(A) peaceful relationship with France

(B) political neutrality regarding the wars of the period

(C) loans from Spanish banks

(D) successful maritime trade worldwide

(E) alliance with Catholic kingdoms in Germany

Your Answer _____

_____

Correct Answers

A–164

(B) The Dutch eventually eclipsed the Italians as traders and manufacturers in the seventeenth century. They were successful fishermen and also factory managers. Located on the northern coast of Europe, the Dutch could import and export to many nearby kingdoms. The quality of Dutch goods gained a respectable reputation, and business was well regulated. Dutch banks were also important sources for investment. Within 150 years of the start of the Renaissance, economic power was shifting northward from Italy and Spain to Holland and England.

A–165

(D) For a period of about one hundred years, the Dutch Republic was very successful in dominating European trade and shipping. Amsterdam became the center of much of the buying and selling in northern Europe. Investment allowed the building of large merchant fleets that sailed between Asia and Europe. Profits were high, and the spice trade made fortunes for many Dutch investors. Finally, wars and competition with other kingdoms, such as France and England, led to an overextension of Dutch resources. By 1700, the Dutch republic began to decline in importance as a trading power.

Q–166

In the seventeenth century, Russia was traumatized by

(A) Teutonic invasion

(B) the assassination of the tsar

(C) mass deportations of the peasantry

(D) religious schism and peasant revolts

(E) poor harvests and severe inflation

Your Answer _____

_____

Q–167

Which of the following resulted from the Edict of Fontainebleau in 1685?

(A) Protestantism was effectively outlawed in France.

(B) Religious tolerance became the law of the land.

(C) Catholic schools had to welcome Huguenot students.

(D) The Portuguese were expelled from France.

(E) France became less culturally diverse.

Your Answer _____

_____

Correct Answers

A–166

(D) In the seventeenth century, Russian peasants lived in abject conditions, and revolts were a natural consequence of desperate poverty. The Eastern Orthodox Church had long been a stabilizing force in the kingdom, but when religious controversy over traditional beliefs broke out in the mid-seventeenth century, many left the church in protest. Western ideas were also making some inroads into Russia, which caused additional tensions between the classes.

A–167

(E) Believing in the idea of "one country, one faith," Louis XIV undid the earlier Edict of Nantes and made Protestantism difficult to practice in France. Huguenot churches were burned, and many Protestants left France for more friendly kingdoms such as England and Holland. Many of these emigrants were skilled professionals. This loss undermined the economy of France to some degree and heightened the religious tensions of the time period.

Questions

Q–168

The struggle between Parliament and the king of England in the seventeenth century revealed

(A) great religious turmoil in the aftermath of the Reformation

(B) social unrest between the Welsh and the Scottish

(C) the first movement toward the abolition of slavery

(D) a stronger monarchy in the kingdom

(E) resurgent influence of the cardinals

Your Answer _____

Q–169

What did the trial of Galileo reveal about seventeenth-century Europe?

(A) Constant conflicts between German princes and the pope

(B) The challenge of science to literal interpretations of the Bible

(C) Spanish and Portuguese competition over the colony of Brazil

(D) Attempts to add new books to the Bible

(E) The impact of the Moors on Christian culture

Your Answer _____

Correct Answers

A–168

(A) Religion was the most divisive issue in England after the break with Rome under Henry VIII. While Elizabeth I steered a middle course during her reign, the succeeding Stuarts were not so neutral with regard to the role of the church in England. Some were openly Catholic, which threatened the Protestant majority in London. Economic issues forced a showdown between the king and Parliament and, in the end, war broke out between the two factions. The royalists lost this fight, and the reconstituted monarchy that followed was much less powerful.

A–169

(B) Galileo followed in the footsteps of Brahe and suggested an alternative to the geocentric view of the solar system. By suggesting that the sun was the center of our solar system, he contradicted some orthodox interpretations of Old Testament scripture. Science was forced to conform to traditional church beliefs, which resulted in Galileo's trial and conviction. As punishment, he was put under house arrest for the remainder of his life.

Q–170

Which of the following events ended in regicide in the seventeenth century?

(A) The trial of Galileo

(B) The English civil war

(C) The Lisbon earthquakes

(D) The War of Spanish Succession

(E) The Ottoman invasion of the Balkans

Your Answer _____

_____

Q–171

Which of the following royal houses ruled England in the seventeenth century?

(A) Tudor and Saxe-Coburg

(B) Lancaster and Stuart

(C) Tudor and Stuart

(D) York and Tudor

(E) Stuart and Windsor

Your Answer _____

_____

Correct Answers

A–170

(B)   Between 1642 and 1648, tensions between the king and the Parliament led to civil war in England. Parliament was dominated by the expanding middle class, and many of its members were Puritans. They defeated the king and tried him in Parliament. Found guilty of treason and tyrannical rule, Charles I was executed in public in London. This regicide (killing the monarch) set a precedent in English history for the possible removal of an unjust or even unpopular king.

A–171

(C)   Elizabeth I carried on the Tudor rule of England but, having no heir, the dynasty died with her. Her cousin, James VI of Scotland, was chosen to succeed her and thus began the Stuart period in British history. This dynasty was quite troubled because religious and political tensions tore the kingdom apart. Civil war and the beheading of the king himself are the most dramatic examples of the turmoil during the Stuart period.

Questions

Q–172

The seventeenth-century struggle between the king of England and Parliament was complicated by

(A) the marriage of King William to a Catholic

(B) French interference in English politics

(C) the attempted assault by the Spanish armada

(D) economic crisis in the cities

(E) intense religious factionalism

Your Answer _____

Q–173

The Protestant Reformation successfully challenged the idea of

(A) the divine right of kings

(B) mercantilist economics

(C) Aristotelian physics

(D) male superiority over women

(E) hereditary rule

Your Answer _____

Correct Answers

A–172

(E) The political fallout of the Protestant reformation in England took more than a century to resolve. English churchgoers were split among Anglicans who followed the national church, Catholics who adhered to the old faith, and Calvinists who took a more radical stand in wanting change. King James was married to a Catholic from France and had many problems dealing with Parliament, which was dominated by the Calvinist Puritans. The Anglican Church was finally upheld, but the monarchy lost considerable power to the people in Parliament.

A–173

(A) Church reformers first challenged the pope in the sixteenth century, starting a precedent for resisting authority. In the seventeenth century, more nobles and the middle class began to resist the traditional monarchical rule in Europe. The most dramatic examples of this resistance occurred in Holland and England, where monarchies were retained but were given limited roles to play in national politics.

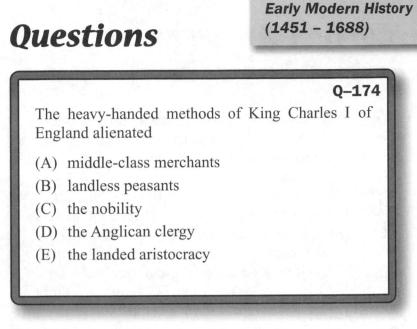

Q–174

The heavy-handed methods of King Charles I of England alienated

(A) middle-class merchants

(B) landless peasants

(C) the nobility

(D) the Anglican clergy

(E) the landed aristocracy

Your Answer _____

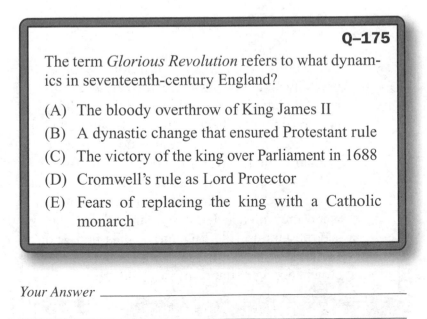

Q–175

The term *Glorious Revolution* refers to what dynamics in seventeenth-century England?

(A) The bloody overthrow of King James II

(B) A dynastic change that ensured Protestant rule

(C) The victory of the king over Parliament in 1688

(D) Cromwell's rule as Lord Protector

(E) Fears of replacing the king with a Catholic monarch

Your Answer _____

Correct Answers

A–174

(A)   By 1630, England had grown into a powerful economic nation, which stimulated the growth of the middle class. The English middle class were mostly merchants who bought and sold goods in the urban areas of the kingdom. When King Charles could not get Parliament to pass tax laws to fund his treasury, he devised his own taxes. He taxed shipping, which had a direct impact on merchants and their businesses. This and other tensions would cause the kingdom to fracture into civil war in 1642.

A–175

(E)   The English civil war left religious tensions unresolved as long as there was the possibility of a Catholic monarch on the throne. This became more real when James II appointed Catholics in his government and married a Roman Catholic. When the queen bore a son, a Catholic line of kings seemed a reality. Anti-Catholic nobles engineered a royal transition when they invited King William of Holland, a Protestant, to rule England. James fled, and Parliament made it illegal for a Catholic to be crowned king or queen of England.

Q–176

Which of the following is most closely associated with John Locke?

(A) The overthrow of the French church

(B) The creation of the modern Irish state

(C) The rejection of absolutist rule

(D) The rights of women to attend university

(E) The elimination of mannerism as an artistic style

Your Answer _____

Q–177

What does the term *scientific method* mean when used in modern history?

(A) Using traditional knowledge to gain information

(B) Creating random hypotheses about nature

(C) Honoring previous discoveries to explore the universe

(D) Making systematic observations of nature to prove a hypothesis

(E) A pre-Victorian sponsorship of geographical exploration

Your Answer _____

Correct Answers

A–176

(C)   John Locke was an influential political philosopher who was widely read during the Enlightenment. Like other thinkers of his day, he believed that humans lived in a state of nature before civilization created rules and traditions. In a purer state, humans have rights, such as freedom and the right to own property, that are natural. These ideas opposed the traditional monarchy, which often limited personal freedoms. Those who agreed with Locke began to resist royal authority and consider alternatives to single-person rule.

A–177

(D)   The Scientific Revolution of the seventeenth and eighteenth centuries saw a flurry of European scientific activity. Relying on reason and intelligence, scientists used inductive principles. Proceeding from the particular to the general, they believed humans could understand more of the natural world. One would make observations and then suggest an explanation. Controlled experiments would prove or disprove the explanation. One of the pioneers in this new approach was Francis Bacon, who believed the approach would benefit humankind with knowledge and power.

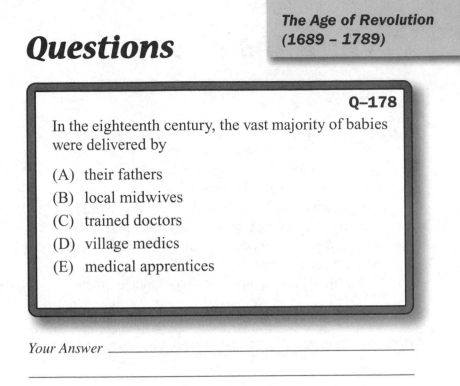

Q–178

In the eighteenth century, the vast majority of babies were delivered by

(A) their fathers

(B) local midwives

(C) trained doctors

(D) village medics

(E) medical apprentices

Your Answer _____

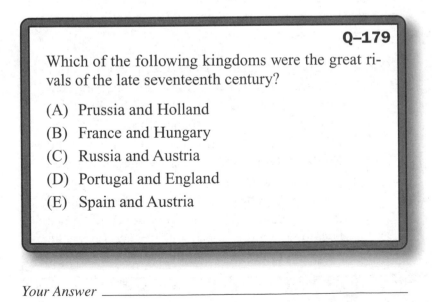

Q–179

Which of the following kingdoms were the great rivals of the late seventeenth century?

(A) Prussia and Holland

(B) France and Hungary

(C) Russia and Austria

(D) Portugal and England

(E) Spain and Austria

Your Answer _____

Correct Answers

A–178

(B) The knowledge of childbirth was often handed down from woman to woman in local areas. Sometimes regulated by a guild, midwives assisted in the labor process and sometimes treated small children. At the time, childbirth was considered to be a normal and spontaneous occurrence, so doctors rarely became involved. Friends and relatives were often in attendance because births took place in homes. If any drugs were used, they were organic and gathered from the surrounding countryside.

A–179

(E) Spain and Austria were the great Catholic monarchies of Europe in the seventeenth century. In 1701, a war was fought to determine the successor to the Spanish throne. This war pitted France and Spain against Austria and England. Other nations also joined to try and gain some advantage from the power struggle. A complex series of treaties eventually settled the conflict. Spain began its decline, and France became the more dominant western European kingdom in the next century.

Questions

Q–180

Which of the following languages replaced Latin as the language of culture and scholarship by 1700?

(A) English
(B) German
(C) Greek
(D) French
(E) Italian

Your Answer _____

Q–181

To keep quiet is the first civic duty.

—Prussian minister, 1738

What does the statement above reveal about German culture in the eighteenth century?

(A) Civic responsibility to the state was a German value.
(B) Obedience to the state was prized.
(C) Those who were outspoken were prized.
(D) Politicians were supposed to keep speeches short.
(E) Only the kaiser could speak on national matters.

Your Answer _____

Correct Answers

A–180

(D) Since the time of the Roman Empire, Latin had been the language of learning and scholarship. As the official language of the Roman Catholic Church, it was also figured in the worship of many people. With the Renaissance, and later the Enlightenment, there was a backlash against the church and its traditions. Although a Catholic kingdom, France became the vanguard of the new secular philosophies of modern Europe. As the court of Versailles flourished, French arts and letters became highly regarded, and the French language was the most popular across the European continent.

A–181

(B) German absolutism was strong in Prussia-Brandenburg because the monarch was able to dominate the landed nobility. The crown had police who kept an eye on those who spoke out against the monarchy. Duty to the state was emphasized above all else. Germans were impressed with the need to keep one's opinions to oneself. This trained people to be uncritical and passive toward the state and its government.

Questions

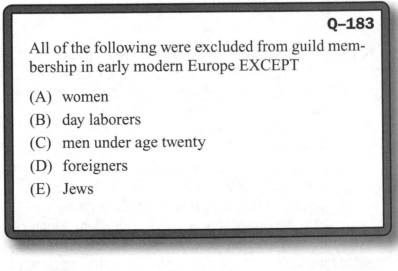

Q–182

Between 1700 and 1750, which of the following was the most profitable import to Europe from the Americas?

(A) Rum

(B) Sugar

(C) Cotton

(D) Corn

(E) Indigo

Your Answer _____

_____

Q–183

All of the following were excluded from guild membership in early modern Europe EXCEPT

(A) women

(B) day laborers

(C) men under age twenty

(D) foreigners

(E) Jews

Your Answer _____

_____

Correct Answers

A–182

(B) Colonies in South and Central America found that Europe's demand for sugar grew larger and larger. Hundreds of sugar plantations were started in Brazil, in Cuba, and on the island colonies in the West Indies. Sugar cultivation needed a lot of manual labor, which stimulated the slave trade from Africa. Large-scale production of sugar and molasses made many people rich because European tastes changed with the availability of the sweetener.

A–183

(C) In towns and cities, the guilds continued to regulate much of business and manufacturing in early modern Europe. Boys often became apprentices at a fairly early age and lived in the workshops where they learned a trade. Masters who trained the apprentices had great power over their young trainees. Those who mastered a craft could gain some social status and later open their own shop. Guild membership was often limited to males from established families.

Questions

Q–184

What does the term *cottage industry* mean in the context of early modern Europe?

(A) Factories that were built on the outskirts of a large city

(B) Peasants making saleable goods in their homes in the country

(C) The housing industry in the 1700s

(D) Luxury goods made in suburbs

(E) Industrial output of urban workers

Your Answer _____

_____

Q–185

The population rise in Europe after 1750 was caused mostly by

(A) the need for soldiers in frequent wars

(B) polygamy, which became more common

(C) increased immigration from North Africa

(D) lower mortality rates in all age groups

(E) great advances in medicine

Your Answer _____

_____

Correct Answers

A–184

(B) As the demand for manufactured goods rose along with the population numbers, rural peasants became involved in the small-scale manufacture of goods. They made goods in their homes or cottages and were paid by the piece. This was usually in addition to the farmwork they were engaged in. Goods made by the rural poor were usually textiles or housewares in the eighteenth century.

A–185

(D) The bubonic plague had come and gone in Europe for reasons still being debated by historians. Although local epidemics still broke out, they passed and people began to live longer throughout Europe. Birthrates also rose in the countryside, where more food was available. Advances in medicine in the eighteenth century were not of great importance in accounting for the higher birthrate.

Questions

Q–186

Eighteenth-century animal husbandry was greatly improved by the introduction of

(A) selective breeding

(B) genetic manipulation of animal DNA

(C) segregating livestock

(D) in vitro fertilization of cows

(E) more veterinarians being trained in royal colleges

Your Answer _____

_____

Q–187

The Dutch of the eighteenth century were skilled managers of their available land through the practice of

(A) mechanized plowing

(B) closing off fields to the peasantry

(C) drill planting

(D) water drainage and land reclamation

(E) using day laborers on farms

Your Answer _____

_____

Correct Answers

A–186

(A) English aristocrats were very keen to find better horses for fox hunting, so they experimented with breeding certain horses. The results encouraged the practice with other animal groups, such as pigs and dogs. Farmers became students of this new practice and noted how superior it was to the older, more haphazard practices. Larger and stronger animals for farmwork resulted.

A–187

(D) Holland had vast acreage that was marshy and flooded by the sea tides. The Dutch drained huge tracts of land and built dykes and barriers so they could farm the reclaimed land. Their engineers became some of the most skilled in the world, and other nations came to study their methods. Other nations that had long coastlines, such as Russia and England, learned from the Dutch how to better manage land along the sea.

Q–188

The most common deadly combination that led to local population declines were

(A) disease and pogroms

(B) religious strife and immigration

(C) epidemic and civil war

(D) war and plague

(E) famine and disease

Your Answer _____

_____

Q–189

Urban guilds grew with the population of eighteenth-century Europe and were sanctioned by the government because

(A) masters trained more apprentices

(B) wealthy patrons wanted quality merchandise

(C) the church supported the city workers

(D) warfare increased demand for guild-produced goods

(E) they were efficient collectors of taxes and fees

Your Answer _____

_____

Correct Answers

A–188

(E)   Although war was a factor in population declines in some areas, more common were the phenomena of famine and accompanying disease. If a harvest was bad, the local rural poor would begin to starve and opportunistic diseases would often cause death. These famines were often regional, depending on the crop being grown or the weather in a particular year.

A–189

(E)   The reputation of urban guilds was at its high-water mark in the eighteenth century. Cities were growing, and demand for products was also increasing. Governments saw the benefit of the guilds as collectors of fees and also producers of high-quality goods. These monopolies were sanctioned by the government but regulated from within.

Questions

Q–190

The trend toward wage work in eighteenth-century Europe was most often seen among the

(A) urban middle classes

(B) absentee landlords

(C) urban and rural poor

(D) unmarried women

(E) widows and gentry

Your Answer _____

Q–191

What political belief would John Locke and Jean-Jacques Rousseau have had in common?

(A) Might is right.

(B) Government can occur only with the consent of the governed.

(C) Monarchy is ordained by God.

(D) Theocratic rule is effective.

(E) Rule by a philosopher-king is necessary.

Your Answer _____

Correct Answers

A–190

(C)   Households of the lower classes had opportunities to become more industrious in the 1700s because a new economy was evolving. Women with families could do piecework and earn money for household necessities. Children were often enlisted to participate in earning more for the family. Although the work was often mindless and repetitive, it also gave some families upward mobility and empowered women as wage earners.

A–191

(B)   John Locke and Jean-Jacques Rousseau were leading political thinkers during the Enlightenment. They suggested that natural laws governed men and that social contracts were entered into to protect the rights of the people. If the government does not serve the people, then it can be changed or overthrown. Rousseau believed that political power lies with the people, so they should control government.

Q–192

Newton's great achievement was to present the modern world with

(A) the law of inverse relationships

(B) a complex view of how motion and mass were related in the universe

(C) the first heliocentric view of the solar system

(D) a reconciliation between science and religion

(E) philosophical views of the heavens

Your Answer _____

_____

Q–193

The establishment of the medieval university was crucial in allowing

(A) nobles to send their sons away for an education

(B) an open discourse between the laity and the church hierarchy

(C) the children of the middle classes to become court officials

(D) priests to be trained for the work of the church

(E) a sense of open and free inquiry in the early modern era

Your Answer _____

_____

Correct Answers

A–192

(B) Newton was able to bring together previously unconnected ideas involving mathematics, physics, and astronomy. He cited Kepler, Copernicus, and Galileo as he explained the law of universal gravitation. This explained the relationships between mass and attraction in the universe. His work gave the movement of the planets a mathematical explanation and proved more directly the place of the sun in the solar system.

A–193

(E) Universities were formed in large towns during the Middle Ages to train doctors, lawyers, and other professionals. Although a small segment of society, these educated men made up the intelligentsia of the western world. Philosophers and thinkers were allowed some independence from the theology of the church. After the Renaissance, universities broadened their fields of study and incorporated the study of astronomy and physics. New approaches in critical thinking made for new discoveries in the natural sciences.

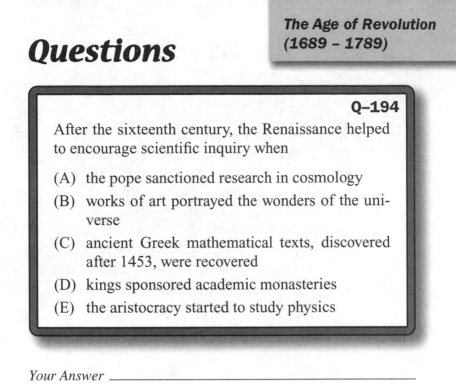

Q–194

After the sixteenth century, the Renaissance helped to encourage scientific inquiry when

(A) the pope sanctioned research in cosmology

(B) works of art portrayed the wonders of the universe

(C) ancient Greek mathematical texts, discovered after 1453, were recovered

(D) kings sponsored academic monasteries

(E) the aristocracy started to study physics

Your Answer _____

_____

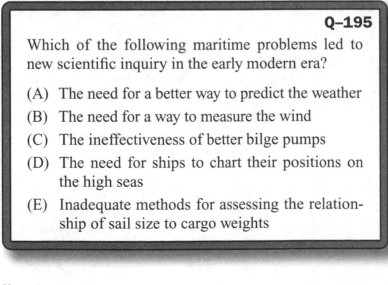

Q–195

Which of the following maritime problems led to new scientific inquiry in the early modern era?

(A) The need for a better way to predict the weather

(B) The need for a way to measure the wind

(C) The ineffectiveness of better bilge pumps

(D) The need for ships to chart their positions on the high seas

(E) Inadequate methods for assessing the relationship of sail size to cargo weights

Your Answer _____

_____

Correct Answers

A–194

(C) After the fall of Constantinople to the Ottoman Turks, some Greek scholars and their libraries were relocated to Italy. These texts revealed lost knowledge of the natural world and also the scholastic controversies of ancient Athens. An interest in science also led wealthy families, such as the Medicis of Florence, to sponsor experimentation. This yielded new knowledge and also some criticism from conservative theologians and academics.

A–195

(D) The need for ships to know where they were geographically led to new mathematical breakthroughs in Europe. King John of Portugal had sponsored mathematical research to find better ways for sailors to chart where they were. This research allowed maps to be drawn and exploration to be documented. Charts of the African coast and South America were well-kept secrets at this time in history, when nations competed with one another to build empires.

Q–196

What does the term *empiricism* mean in the context of the Scientific Revolution?

(A) Economic ideas from Adam Smith's writings

(B) Inductive reasoning based on observation and experience

(C) A new view of quantum physics

(D) An intellectual vision of the modern era

(E) Science and philosophy joined in theory

Your Answer _____

_____

Q–197

Which of the following is most closely associated with René Descartes?

(A) Creation of the field of spatial physics

(B) New laws based on tolerance and reason

(C) The rights of the people to elect their leaders

(D) The French Revolutionary credo

(E) A fresh and skeptical approach to philosophy

Your Answer _____

_____

Correct Answers

A–196

(B) The scientific method is based on what one can observe in nature. Once observed, phenomena can be explained through reasoning. Empiricism is crucial to the process because it depends on information that is seen and experienced. Francis Bacon promoted this new approach to gaining knowledge because he saw the Aristotelian approach as too speculative and haphazard.

A–197

(B) René Descartes was one of the most original and important thinkers of the eighteenth century. He demanded proof of the reality of ideas and would reject traditional approaches if they did not stand up to his high standards of evidence. He separated knowledge into two spheres, the physical and the spiritual. He placed ultimate importance on the ability to think and discern the truth. Like many Enlightenment thinkers, he believed in reason and preached religious tolerance.

Questions

Q–198

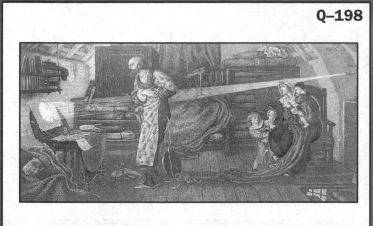

The etching above illustrates the interests and values of the

(A) Scientific Revolution

(B) Victorian era

(C) belle époque

(D) interwar period

(E) Renaissance

Your Answer _____

_____

Correct Answers

A–198

(A)   In the etching, a man shows a woman and children the movement of the planet Venus across the sun. The clothing and artwork places it in the eighteenth century during the Scientific Revolution. At the time, viewing the heavens was fashionable, and scientific demonstrations were well attended. Kingdoms recruited scientists and mathematicians to live at court and teach the nobles about new ideas.

Questions

Q–199

After 1550, Africans who were forced into slavery by Europeans were most often

(A) religious minorities

(B) kidnapped traders

(C) jailed prisoners

(D) prisoners of war

(E) Bantu tribespeople

Your Answer _____

Q–200

The Scientific Revolution of the seventeenth and eighteenth century was mainly an

(A) economic interlude

(B) educational movement

(C) agricultural phenomenon

(D) intellectual transition

(E) interim development

Your Answer _____

Correct Answers

A–199

(D) African tribes often warred with one another, and a common outcome of fighting was the capture of the members of other tribes. When Europeans started offering money for slaves, the capture of other Africans became a feature of the international slave trade. Lucrative relationships were developed between certain coastal African tribes and the European slave traders.

A–200

(D) The Scientific Revolution did not affect the people of Europe directly until later. Most people still could not read or write. In the eighteenth century, scientists were engaged in many different endeavors that amounted to an intellectual revolution within elite society. New approaches to gathering knowledge and information set the tone for academic research in the modern era.

Q–201

Religious wars are not caused by the fact that there is more than one religion, but by the spirit of intolerance . . . the spread of which can only be regarded as the total eclipse of human reason.

—Baron De Montesquieu, 1748

The quote above is typical of what opinion in the eighteenth century?

(A) Human reason is a fallible thing.

(B) There have been many religious wars in history.

(C) Many religions are the bane of society.

(D) Reason is the only antidote for intolerance.

(E) Aristocrats need to demonstrate reason in their daily lives.

Your Answer _____

_____

Correct Answers

A–201

(D) The thinkers who defined the Enlightenment believed that human reason was the most important of all faculties. Many of the philosophers were critical of the church, which they saw as old-fashioned and given to superstition. France experienced barbarism in the fighting between Catholics and the Protestants. The philosophers pointed to the history of religious wars as proof of the muddled thinking of people of faith. In the quote above, Montesquieu suggests that religions can coexist if reason prevails. Thus, tolerance was a value that was preached in Enlightenment writings.

Q–202

All of the following were hallmarks of the reign of Frederick the Great EXCEPT

(A) building up the Prussian military

(B) granting religious toleration

(C) making Prussia more aristocratic than before

(D) abolishing torture in most legal cases

(E) granting Polish autonomy in the east

Your Answer _____

_____

Q–203

The freeing of the serfs in eighteenth-century Austria led to

(A) brutal discrimination against the peasants

(B) alienation between the nobility and the monarch

(C) intense debate among the clergy

(D) a condemning decree from the Vatican

(E) civil war

Your Answer _____

_____

Correct Answers

A–202

(E) Frederick the Great was famous for being a tolerant and conscientious monarch. He admired the French philosophes of the eighteenth century, who urged that legal rights be recognized and that the accused not be mistreated. He remained an autocrat, however, and was a social conservative. As monarch, he was militarily aggressive and led Prussia into two wars during his reign. Prussia gained territory to the east at the expense of Poland.

A–203

(B) Joseph II of Austria was an ambitious reformer who issued thousands of decrees in an effort to change many traditions in his kingdom. He proclaimed the equality of all before the law as well as many other liberal ideas. Unfortunately, his kingdom was not ready for so many changes so quickly. The nobility was angered over his freeing of the serfs, who were the source of much revenue for the landed elites. In the end, many of Joseph's reforms did not last after his death.

Q–204

What was the method used to choose the monarch of Poland in the eighteenth century?

(A) The hereditary monarchy was handed down to the oldest male.

(B) The king was elected by the nobles.

(C) The monarch was appointed to the throne by the bishop of Warsaw.

(D) The tsar of Russia chose the Polish ruler.

(E) A council of princes met to cast lots.

Your Answer _____

Q–205

Which of the following explains the partition of Poland in 1795?

(A) Rival neighbors overwhelmed the state and divided it up.

(B) Civil war led to its disintegration.

(C) The Reformation helped create a disunited people.

(D) The absolutist monarch went too far and the people rebelled.

(E) Russia absorbed all Polish territory after winning a war.

Your Answer _____

Correct Answers

A–204

(B) The Polish monarch was elected by the nobles, which greatly limited the power of the king. The power struggles between the Roman Catholic nobility and the monarch had been a longstanding feature of Polish history. It is one reason that Poland grew weaker as other nearby kingdoms, such as Prussia and Austria, became stronger, with powerful dynasties in control. This would lead to Poland's demise at the end of the 1700s.

A–205

(A) Poland was unfortunate in both its geography and its political leadership in the eighteenth century. Surrounded by powerful neighbors, it was not able to resist Russia, Austria, and Prussia all at the same time. Over time, its territory was lost to these neighbors. In 1795, the final partition of all Polish territory was accomplished. The Polish people became minorities in large domains ruled by foreigners.

Questions

Q–206

What did the term *philosophes* mean in the eighteenth century?

(A) Soldiers fighting for the monarchy

(B) French aristocrats who sided with the church

(C) Italian merchants in support of the nobility

(D) Cardinals who challenged the pope

(E) French thinkers who challenged authority

Your Answer _____

Q–207

All of the following were famous eighteenth-century French philosophes EXCEPT

(A) Rousseau

(B) d'Alembert

(C) Montesquieu

(D) Voltaire

(E) Richelieu

Your Answer _____

Correct Answers

A–206

(E) The intellectual history of Europe was greatly altered in the eighteenth century by the philosophical writings of different French thinkers. Called philosophes, they wrote on the power of reason and criticized the ignorance of their time period. In particular they criticized the church, which they saw as medieval and backward. Their influence also reinforced the cultural dominance of France during this time.

A–207

(E) France produced many of the great thinkers and social critics of the eighteenth century. These men wrote about the ills they perceived in European culture and were widely read in their day. All of the above men were philosophers and writers except Richelieu, who was a famous cardinal and minister during the reign of Louis XIII.

Q–208

The salons of the Enlightenment were famous for

(A) hosting discussions of literature and philosophy
(B) creating tensions between Catholics and Protestants
(C) urging the abolition of the monarchy in France
(D) a decrease in the literacy rate
(E) influencing monarchs to reform their kingdoms

Your Answer _____

Q–209

Which of the following territories were taken from Spain in the Treaty of Utrecht?

(A) Naples and the Netherlands
(B) Savoy and Switzerland
(C) Poland and Sicily
(D) Alsace and the Netherlands
(E) Brittany and Naples

Your Answer _____

Correct Answers

A–208

(A) The emphasis on critical thinking during the Enlightenment encouraged intellectual discourse. In upper-class France, wealthy women would host salons where people could come and discuss famous books or the new philosophies that were emerging. These salons were fashionable and even prestigious. It was another way for ideas to gain popularity and to promote the many new books being published.

A–209

(A) The War of Spanish Succession did not go well for Spain. The Treaty of Utrecht took considerable foreign territory from the Spanish kingdom and parceled it out to other kingdoms. Spain lost Italian territories in Naples, Sardinia, and Sicily. It was also forced to cede the Netherlands to Austria. Poland was divided up by Austria and Russia, while Switzerland remained independent.

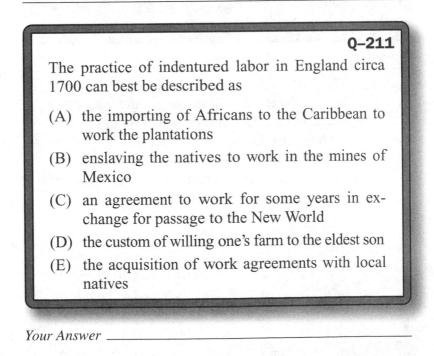

Q–210

When d'Alembert made a distinction between the "truly enlightened public" and the "blind and noisy multitude," he revealed the

(A) need for education for the middle classes

(B) tensions between the nobility and the church

(C) elitism of the eighteenth-century philosophes

(D) new attitudes toward the merchant classes

(E) open discourse among all classes during the Enlightenment

Your Answer _____

Q–211

The practice of indentured labor in England circa 1700 can best be described as

(A) the importing of Africans to the Caribbean to work the plantations

(B) enslaving the natives to work in the mines of Mexico

(C) an agreement to work for some years in exchange for passage to the New World

(D) the custom of willing one's farm to the eldest son

(E) the acquisition of work agreements with local natives

Your Answer _____

Correct Answers

A–210

(C) Historians have debated the impact of the Enlightenment on the common people. Educated and literate people were the minority in society in the eighteenth century. Well-read people such as the philosophes could champion the lower classes, but they actually did not come into much contact with them. Among the educated elite, there was a common mistrust of the lower classes, who they saw suffering in superstition and ignorance. The distinction by d'Alembert reveals this because the common people are characterized as "blind and noisy." This elitism reveals some of the class tensions of the era.

A–211

(C) The demand for cheap labor in British America helped create work-for-passage agreements between landowners and poor immigrants. Many farms were growing cash crops, such as tobacco and cotton. These farms needed additional laborers in the fields. The arrangement appealed to many poor Europeans who wanted to make a new life in the Americas but did not have the money to get started. In exchange for a period of work (i.e., seven years), they could aspire to become farmers themselves over time. Some laborers were also petty criminals who were given the option of going to the New World instead of remaining in an English prison.

Questions

Q–212

From about 1680 to 1725, the balance of power shifted radically in eastern Europe. Russia, Brandenburg-Prussia, and Austria rose at the expense of which three powers in decline?

(A) Poland, the Papal States, and the Holy Roman Empire

(B) France, Poland, and Sweden

(C) Venice, Denmark, and Saxony

(D) Poland, Sweden, and the Ottoman Empire

(E) Finland, Sweden, and Poland

Your Answer _____

_____

Correct Answers

A–212

(D) Venice, the Holy Roman Empire, and the Papal States were no longer factors in the European balance of power in that period. Although France suffered in major wars from 1686 to 1715, it did not cease to be a great power. Because Finland was not independent until 1918, that leaves the only possible combination of Poland, Sweden, and the Ottoman Empire. Sweden to the north, Poland to the west, and the Ottoman Turks to the south were adversely affected by wars with Prussia, Russia, and Austria.

Q–213

Gravity, the falling of accelerated bodies on the earth, the revolution of the planets in their orbits, their rotations round their axis, all this is mere motion. Now motion cannot perhaps be conceived any otherwise than by impulsion; therefore all those bodies must be impelled. But by what are they impelled? All space is full, it therefore is filled with a very subtle matter, since this is imperceptible to us; this matter goes from west to east, since all the planets are carried from west to east.

—Voltaire, 1778

The primary message of the quote above is to show Voltaire's

(A) agreement with the theories of Copernicus

(B) determination to oppose the theology of the church

(C) interest in the work of Newton

(D) desire for scientific accord with Einstein

(E) support for the work of alchemists in France

Your Answer _____

_____

Correct Answers

A–213

(C) The quote focuses on the scientific speculation about gravity and motion, two ideas much written about by Isaac Newton. Voltaire was a great admirer of Newton, and this quote shows that Voltaire was also speculating on what causes things to move and the wind to blow. The thinkers of the Enlightenment read one another's works and were inspired by new scientific discoveries.

Questions

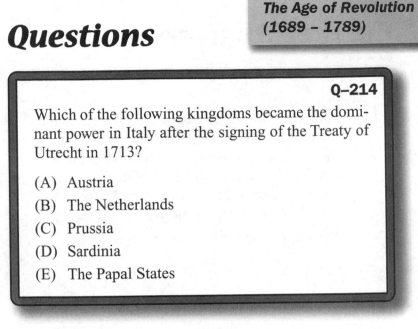

Q–214

Which of the following kingdoms became the dominant power in Italy after the signing of the Treaty of Utrecht in 1713?

(A) Austria

(B) The Netherlands

(C) Prussia

(D) Sardinia

(E) The Papal States

Your Answer _____

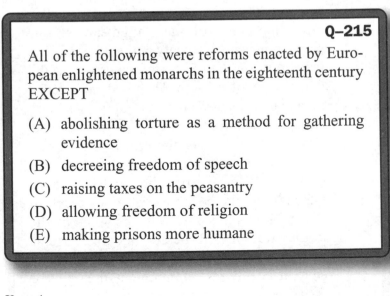

Q–215

All of the following were reforms enacted by European enlightened monarchs in the eighteenth century EXCEPT

(A) abolishing torture as a method for gathering evidence

(B) decreeing freedom of speech

(C) raising taxes on the peasantry

(D) allowing freedom of religion

(E) making prisons more humane

Your Answer _____

Correct Answers

A–214

(A) Although the Papal States still existed in Italy in the eighteenth century, Austria was the dominant power in southern Europe after the War of Spanish Succession. Spain had been forced to surrender territory in Italy to Austria. This left the Hapsburg throne with more power in the Mediterranean.

A–215

(C) The philosophes of the Enlightenment saw many injustices in society and commented on them. A major theme was tolerance, especially in the realm of religion. The most enlightened monarchs issued decrees to allow their subjects to worship the religion of their choice. Basic rights such as the freedom to speak out and criticize the government were radical ideas of the time period. The cruelty of police methods and the horrible conditions found in prisons at this time were also deplored by the leading reformers. Liberal kingdoms, such as Sweden and Austria under Joseph II, attempted to make progress in improving the rights of the accused and the imprisoned.

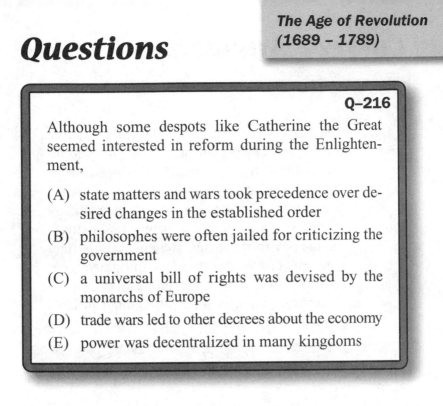

Q–216

Although some despots like Catherine the Great seemed interested in reform during the Enlightenment,

(A) state matters and wars took precedence over desired changes in the established order

(B) philosophes were often jailed for criticizing the government

(C) a universal bill of rights was devised by the monarchs of Europe

(D) trade wars led to other decrees about the economy

(E) power was decentralized in many kingdoms

Your Answer _____

_____

Correct Answers

A–216

(A)   Some rulers such as Frederick II and Catherine the Great seemed interested in enlightened reforms during their reigns in the eighteenth century. The writings of the philosophes of France had an impact on some elites. However, raising money for large standing armies and extending the power of the state were more important concerns during the so-called Enlightenment. Some reforms were made into legal codes, but in general, changes were not enough to have great impact on the common person.

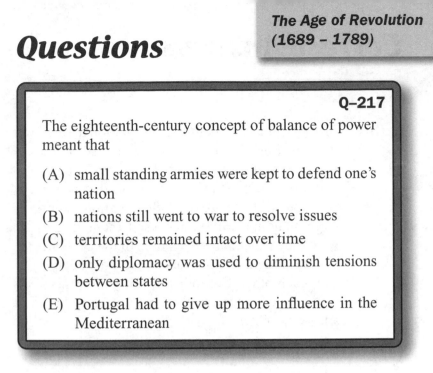

Q–217

The eighteenth-century concept of balance of power meant that

(A) small standing armies were kept to defend one's nation

(B) nations still went to war to resolve issues

(C) territories remained intact over time

(D) only diplomacy was used to diminish tensions between states

(E) Portugal had to give up more influence in the Mediterranean

Your Answer _____

Q–218

Which of the following is most closely associated with Immanuel Kant?

(A) Defining the field of metaphysics and examining moral philosophy

(B) Creating a workable diplomatic model for nation-states

(C) Mapping out the motives for imperialism

(D) Advocating full suffrage for women

(E) The denial of a universal morality

Your Answer _____

Correct Answers

A–217

(B) In the eighteenth century, international relations in Europe tried to maintain a sense of balance, where no single nation could dominate the others. This did not mean that peace was the ultimate goal. Rather, nations kept large standing armies and used them to get what they wanted. In the middle of the century, nations fought major wars to gain advantage over each other. Combinations of nations also fought one another so that some military balance was achieved.

A–218

(A) Immanuel Kant was one of the best-known thinkers of the late Enlightenment in northern Europe. He was concerned with the ways humans know what they know. He compromised between the empiricists and the rationalists, and believed in the "laws of the mind." He wrote extensively on three unknowable realms: God, freedom, and immortality. Because these realms are outside the human experience, they could not be scientifically proven. Still, they were believed to be vital to moral philosophy.

Q–219

The idea for emancipation of Russian serfs came to an end during the reign of Catherine the Great when

(A) priests declared themselves against it

(B) the nobles refused to cooperate with the monarch

(C) war with Austria intervened

(D) a bloody uprising led by a cossack threatened the regime

(E) Poland tried it and failed

Your Answer _____

_____

Q–220

In rural areas, the traditional solution to the problem of soil exhaustion was

(A) heavy use of chemical fertilizers

(B) letting a field lie fallow for a time

(C) selling the land to someone else

(D) surveying the land

(E) religious rituals and blessings by a priest

Your Answer _____

_____

Correct Answers

A-219

(D)   Although sympathetic to the plight of the landless peasantry because of the writings of Voltaire, Catherine the Great experienced a large serf revolt early in her reign. The uprising almost toppled the monarchy, but the revolt collapsed from within. After its collapse, Catherine permitted the nobility to oppress the peasants and did not attempt to alter the feudal status quo. Thus, Russia remained mired in the past, and economic order was built at the expense of the poor workers of the land.

A-220

(B)   The patterns of planting and harvesting gave farmers valuable knowledge about the soil they were working. If they planted wheat, they knew that the soil would be depleted and the field would not yield a good crop the following year. If there was enough organic fertilizer, they could use that to replenish the lost nutrients in the soil. Usually, however, the farmers would leave the ground fallow or unplanted for a year, so that the natural chemicals could be replenished. This put limits on the productivity of available land and had to be carefully managed.

Questions

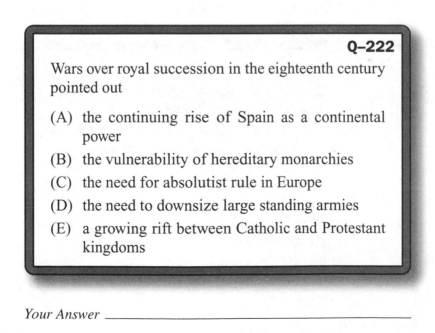

Q–221

In which of the following areas of Europe did Protestantism become dominant?

(A) Italy and Ireland

(B) Southern Germany and Austria

(C) France and Spain

(D) Scandinavia and England

(E) Holland and Portugal

Your Answer _____

_____

Q–222

Wars over royal succession in the eighteenth century pointed out

(A) the continuing rise of Spain as a continental power

(B) the vulnerability of hereditary monarchies

(C) the need for absolutist rule in Europe

(D) the need to downsize large standing armies

(E) a growing rift between Catholic and Protestant kingdoms

Your Answer _____

_____

Correct Answers

A–221

(D) Protestantism eventually established itself in northern Europe, which included Scandinavia, northern Germany, England, and Holland. The Roman Catholic Church remained established in France, Italy, Austria, Bavaria, Ireland, and Poland.

A–222

(B) Both Spain and Austria experienced crises involving the transition between a ruling monarch and his political heirs. In both cases, large wars were fought to determine who would take the throne in these kingdoms. When the wars were settled, the monarchies of Spain and Austria both lost territory. This underscored the problems arising from competing claims to a throne, or interference from outside the kingdom to settle the issue.

Questions

Q–223

The agricultural enclosure movement was often opposed by the nobles because

(A) it was thought to be heretical

(B) no one could see the benefit

(C) artisans were left out of the process

(D) it required an initial large investment

(E) there was no advantage in terms of harvest yields

Your Answer _____

_____

Q–224

The term *diaspora* can best be described as the

(A) festivals that were observed in Spanish colonies

(B) expansion of the sugar trade in Latin America

(C) acquisition of new colonies or areas

(D) scattering of a people to different parts of the world

(E) establishment of scientific principles

Your Answer _____

_____

Correct Answers

A–223

(D) The older system of open fields and common property came under criticism when the techniques of crop rotation began being used. Demarking the land with stone or wood fences was seen as beneficial in allowing better soil management. Nobles, who wanted maximum profits from their holdings, would resist the enclosure movement because of the investment needed in the short term.

A–224

(D) At different times in history, certain peoples have dispersed and scattered, usually as a result of conquest and/or captivity. In Europe, Germans, Gypsies, and Armenians found themselves transplanted to other parts of the continent or elsewhere in the world. This led to a cultural transference, in which pockets of ethnicity would exist within a larger culture. The movement of Europeans and Africans to the New World after 1500 led to a huge diaspora of many different peoples.

Q–225

The painting above

(A) introduces abstract images with everyday scenery

(B) condemns the gap between rich and poor in France

(C) documents the life of the eighteenth-century bourgeoisie

(D) favors the monarchy and single-person rule

(E) advertises the fashion of the upper classes

Your Answer _____

Correct Answers

A–225

(C) The artist of the painting was Jean-Baptiste-Simeon Chardin. He painted plain still-life and realistic scenes of the Paris bourgeoisie. Patronized by Louis XV, Chardin was well known in his lifetime. His paintings show a realistic view of the people in prerevolutionary France.

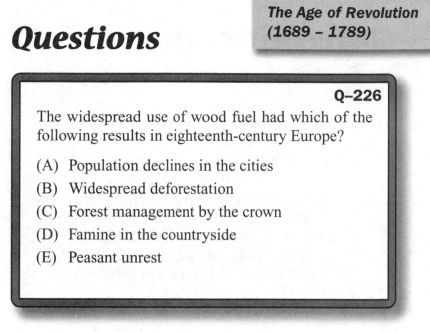

Q–226

The widespread use of wood fuel had which of the following results in eighteenth-century Europe?

(A) Population declines in the cities

(B) Widespread deforestation

(C) Forest management by the crown

(D) Famine in the countryside

(E) Peasant unrest

Your Answer _____

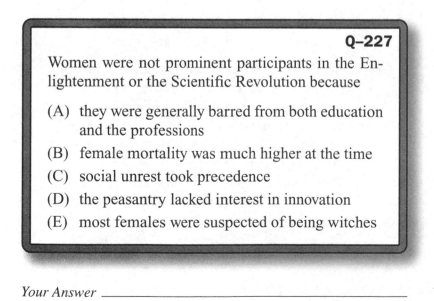

Q–227

Women were not prominent participants in the Enlightenment or the Scientific Revolution because

(A) they were generally barred from both education and the professions

(B) female mortality was much higher at the time

(C) social unrest took precedence

(D) the peasantry lacked interest in innovation

(E) most females were suspected of being witches

Your Answer _____

Correct Answers

A–226

(B) Both farming and new industries needed fuel in the 1700s, and wood was the most widely used. Today, England, Romania, and Hungary have less than 10 percent of the trees that existed in 1300. The fabled Sherwood Forest (of Robin Hood fame) once covered over 10,000 acres of land, but it now contains less than 700 acres. The lack of wood fuel forced people to use other fuels such as coal to keep warm.

A–227

(A) In the early modern era, daughters were not educated or groomed for professional life by their parents. The main goal of the family was to have daughters marry into a good family. Higher education was male dominated, and the number of literate women was small. While some upper-class families would see to the education of a daughter, fewer than 10 percent of women were literate.

Questions

Q–228

The Sovereign is absolute; for there is no other Authority but that which centers in his single Person, that can act with a Vigour proportionate to the Extent of such a vast Dominion.

—Catherine the Great, 1767

Which of the following is best supported by the quote above?

(A) Authority resides in the aristocracy.

(B) Democracy is the political ideal.

(C) Absolute monarchy is the only governing principle.

(D) A king must be vigorous.

(E) An empire has regional governors.

Your Answer _____

Q–229

The term *demographics* can best be described as

(A) the spreading of the Jesuit order

(B) the granting of freedom to individual slaves

(C) understanding the tax methods of nations

(D) anticolonial movements in Latin America

(E) the study of population patterns and growth

Your Answer _____

Correct Answers

A–228

(C) When Catherine said "the Sovereign is absolute," she was referring to herself as the empress of Russia. She believed in absolutism and here expressed that authority must be centered in one person (herself) so that she could act quickly when the need arose. Although considered an enlightened despot, she had no intention of giving power to the people she ruled. She was born a princess and schemed to take the throne from her husband. Once in power, she did all she could to consolidate the power of the Russian monarchy.

A–229

(E) Historians have always been interested in the concentrations of human settlement. The specific study of population trends is called demographics. Throughout history, populations have grown at varying rates depending on births and the movements of people. Death rates also affect growth patterns and can be tied to medical care and diseases that periodically ravage a local population. Plagues, whether widespread or isolated, have been a recurring phenomenon. The last wave of bubonic plague struck Marseilles in the early 1700s and killed almost 100,000 people before it dissipated.

Q–230

Great Britain joined Austria in the War of Austrian Succession of 1740 because

(A) it was attacked by Prussia

(B) France had become too powerful on the continent

(C) of agreements between the two kingdoms before the war

(D) the Hapsburgs had borrowed a lot of money from London banks

(E) of rival claims in the New World

Your Answer _____

_____

Q–231

All of the following are components that define a nation EXCEPT

(A) financial indexes

(B) history

(C) language

(D) religion

(E) traditional rivalries with other nations

Your Answer _____

_____

Correct Answers

A–230

(B) The War of Austrian Succession was fought because there was no male heir to the Hapsburg throne in Vienna. Charles VI wanted to give the throne to his daughter, Maria Theresa. Although many nations had agreed to recognize Maria's legitimacy as monarch, once Charles was dead, a war broke out over the succession. France thought the Austrian Empire was vulnerable and attacked. Great Britain came to Austria's aid because it was alarmed by the growing might of France and did not want one kingdom to dominate the continent.

A–231

(A) Many things define a nation or people. There is a shared experience over time and also key cultural components, such as a common language and a belief system shared by most citizens. Some dynamics such as competing religious beliefs or the existence of more than one language may cause tension, but there will be an overarching sense of what it is to be a German, for example, or a Canadian.

Q–232

General improvements to the water supply and sewage disposal in Europe led to

(A) the eradication of the plague

(B) poor harvests in the Low Countries

(C) massive immigration to the New World

(D) poor economic results

(E) better public health and higher birthrates

Your Answer _____

Q–233

What does the term *joint-stock company* mean?

(A) Trading firms that are privately owned

(B) A public business venture financed by stockholders who risk their money

(C) Christian companies that sponsored missionaries overseas

(D) A family business handed down to the sons

(E) A corporation sponsored by the monarch

Your Answer _____

Correct Answers

A–232

(E) Two of the most devastating diseases in urban Europe were typhoid and typhus. These water-borne diseases were especially deadly for children and young adults. As cities became better managed, they improved the available drinking water. The management of human sewage was also important because the pollution of rivers had been a major cause of spreading disease in the past. With cleaner water available, people were healthier and birthrates increased. Infant mortality also decreased, which boosted population growth.

A–233

(B) Joint-stock companies originated in England, Holland, and France and were a new investment vehicle after 1650. Private investors with capital would buy units called shares of stock and become partners in a venture. With the Age of Discovery, Europeans invested in overseas businesses, and stock exchanges sprang up in London, Amsterdam, and Paris, allowing people to buy shares in different companies. These companies often enjoyed the support of their monarchies back in Europe, but they also organized their own military capabilities. This aspect of capitalism is part of the founding of the modern economy in Europe.

Q–234

Which industry employed the most Europeans before the nineteenth century?

(A) Weapons

(B) Dairy

(C) Iron and steel

(D) Textiles

(E) Agricultural food processing

Your Answer _____

Q–235

The Treaty of Paris in 1763 was part of the settlement of the

(A) Seven Years' War

(B) war between Prussia and Denmark

(C) War of Spanish Succession

(D) Thirty Years' War

(E) Swiss invasion of Italy

Your Answer _____

Correct Answers

A–234

(D) The textile industry involved different phases of working with woolens and linen material. Before the 1900s, most textile work was done in cottages, where the rural poor had looms and dying vats for processing and making cloth. Handloom work was often done by the entire family. Men, with the help of the women, usually operated the loom; children helped by doing tasks that suited their smaller hands.

A–235

(A) The eighteenth century saw a number of wars break out in Europe, but the most far-flung was the Seven Years' War, also known as the French and Indian War in North America. In part, this war highlighted the rekindling of the past medieval rivalry between England and France. Other kingdoms also joined the war. For example, Russia sought to diminish the new power of Prussia in eastern Europe. Since the war spread to North America and Asia, where colonial claims were being contested, this war is considered to be the first global conflict in modern history.

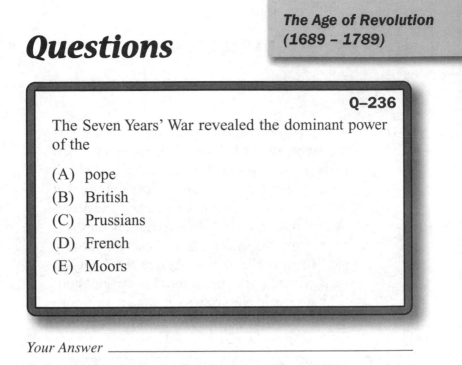

Q–236

The Seven Years' War revealed the dominant power of the

(A) pope

(B) British

(C) Prussians

(D) French

(E) Moors

Your Answer _____

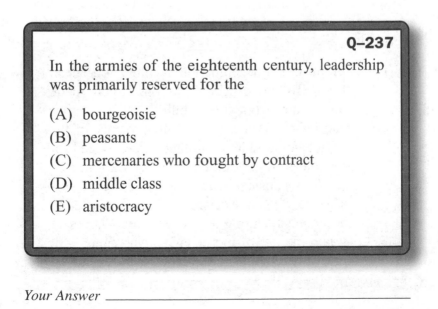

Q–237

In the armies of the eighteenth century, leadership was primarily reserved for the

(A) bourgeoisie

(B) peasants

(C) mercenaries who fought by contract

(D) middle class

(E) aristocracy

Your Answer _____

Correct Answers

A–236

(B) The Seven Years' War that ended in 1763 saw the emergence of the global power of Great Britain. Victories in Europe, India, and North America left Great Britain with an empire that now spanned the globe. France became a secondary power, having lost territories on three continents. Holland had also been eclipsed by the British in the century before the Treaty of Paris. The importance of naval power in establishing a world empire was proven in the Seven Years' War, and the navy of Great Britain was the best in the world.

A–237

(E) In most major eighteenth-century European kingdoms, the officer corps was largely made up of men from the nobility. Military honor and fame was regarded as the province of the aristocracy, and its young men were trained for fighting from a young age. Serving in time of war was considered an important rite of passage that all young aristocrats were supposed to accomplish. During the Seven Years' War, there was some use of mercenaries, who came with preorganized units and their own leadership.

Questions

Q–238

Which of the following nations supplied mercenary troops in the Seven Years' War?

(A) Switzerland and small German states

(B) Ottoman Turkey and Hungary

(C) Sicily and Sardinia

(D) Spain and Naples

(E) Portugal and Holland

Your Answer _____

Q–239

The philosophes of the eighteenth century supported which kind of government?

(A) Theocracy

(B) Enlightened despotism

(C) Limited self-rule

(D) Totalitarian dictatorship

(E) Democracy with universal suffrage

Your Answer _____

Correct Answers

A–238

(A)   The Swiss had long been famous for providing professional fighting men for European wars. In the eighteenth century, armies grew larger and larger, which meant the demand for soldiers grew accordingly. Nations such as Britain and Austria hired foreign soldiers to fight with them and for them. Smaller German principalities also had regiments for hire, which were used by the side that could pay them the most.

A–239

(B)   Philosophes, such as Voltaire, preferred an enlightened monarch who would use his or her power for the benefit of the people. Such rulers kept their absolute rights over the people but used their power to care for the kingdom and its people. In the ideal, somewhat similar to the idea of Plato's philosopher-king, this ruler would be wise and not behave selfishly or use oppression to control his subjects. Some eighteenth-century monarchs admired Voltaire and made some limited reforms in the name of tolerance and humanity.

Q–240

Which of the following eighteenth-century European empires were the most multiethnic in character?

(A) Ottoman and Austrian

(B) German and Austrian

(C) Russian and Swiss

(D) German and Ottoman

(E) French and Sardinian

Your Answer _____

Q–241

Which of the following were components of British mercantilist policy in the eighteenth century?

(A) Interagency Acts, which angered British Canadians

(B) Navigation Acts, which mandated use of British ships

(C) Anti-Swedish boycotts

(D) French trade agreements about fishing in Nova Scotia

(E) Naval Stores Acts, which imported pitch from Spain

Your Answer _____

Correct Answers

A–240

(A)   Both the Ottoman and Austrian empires were very diverse and multiethnic in composition. The Turks ruled over Arabs, Bosnians, and Romanians, while the Austrians had control over Serbs, Hungarians, Czechs, and others. The difficulty in ruling a large and diverse population would challenge both empires and lead to their eventual dissolution.

A–241

(B)   The Navigation Acts were enacted to manage trade and shipping between Britain and the rest of the world. If British ships handled imports, the money stayed inside the nation. If other nations were allowed to ship goods into the nation, they would share the profits. Mercantilism aimed to create an internal system of importation so that all goods were handled by persons and companies connected to the mother country. The policy was meant to take profits away from other nations in competition with England, such as Holland and France.

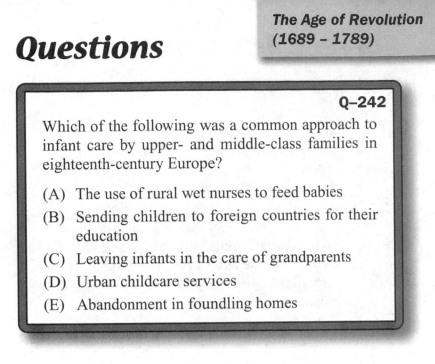

Q–242

Which of the following was a common approach to infant care by upper- and middle-class families in eighteenth-century Europe?

(A) The use of rural wet nurses to feed babies

(B) Sending children to foreign countries for their education

(C) Leaving infants in the care of grandparents

(D) Urban childcare services

(E) Abandonment in foundling homes

Your Answer _____

_____

Correct Answers

A–242

(A)   In middle- and upper-class society, breastfeeding was considered common, so mothers would give their newborns to other women to nurse in the first months of the baby's life. Wet nurses often lived in the country, so the baby would live temporarily away from home. Infant mortality was still quite high and many children died before the age of ten. The wealthy could also afford nannies, who basically raised and taught the children.

Man being born, as has been proved, with a title to perfect freedom and an uncontrolled enjoyment of all the rights and privileges of the law of Nature, equally with any other man, or number of men in the world, hath by nature a power not only to preserve his property—that is, his life, liberty, and estate, against the injuries and attempts of other men.

—John Locke, 1689

The quote above expresses the philosophy of the period in history known as the

(A) Renaissance

(B) Commercial Revolution

(C) Enlightenment

(D) Great Schism

(E) Industrial Revolution

Your Answer _____

_____

Correct Answers

A–243

(C)   The 1600s saw a flowering of new ideas about society and politics. French and British thinkers began to explore the relationship between the people and their government. They considered people to be in a state of nature, which suggested certain universal rights. Locke was one of the great political philosophers of this time period, now labeled the Enlightenment.

Questions

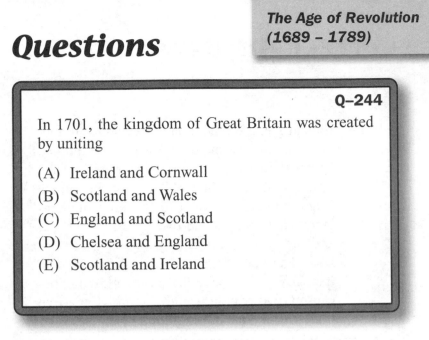

Q–244

In 1701, the kingdom of Great Britain was created by uniting

(A) Ireland and Cornwall

(B) Scotland and Wales

(C) England and Scotland

(D) Chelsea and England

(E) Scotland and Ireland

Your Answer _____

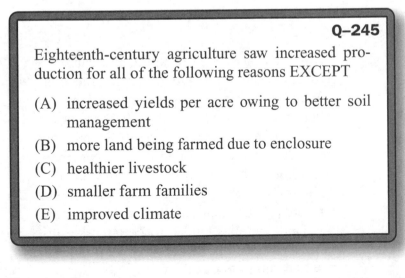

Q–245

Eighteenth-century agriculture saw increased production for all of the following reasons EXCEPT

(A) increased yields per acre owing to better soil management

(B) more land being farmed due to enclosure

(C) healthier livestock

(D) smaller farm families

(E) improved climate

Your Answer _____

Correct Answers

A–244

(C)   England and Scotland had been separate medieval kingdoms and often fought one another. When the succession problem arose in 1603 upon the death of the childless Elizabeth I, the English monarchy went to the king of Scotland. This brought the two kingdoms closer, and the two were formally united a century later. The poor financial state of Scotland in the early 1700s made the union attractive because Great Britain would encourage tax-free trade within the new kingdom.

A–245

(D)   Historians have been debating the causes of the agricultural revolution during the eighteenth century and looking for explanations about the increased output of farmers in Europe. The enclosure movement helped bring more land under direct farmer management. The cultivations of more hay allowed more feed for livestock, which increased the size of herds. Crop rotation allowed better use of the land. Families tended to be large because farmers wanted the children to help out with the unending work of the farm.

Questions

Q–246

Which of the following composers were most prominent during the high baroque period of modern music?

(A) Rachmaninoff and Lizst

(B) Handel and J. S. Bach

(C) Buxtahude and Mozart

(D) Chopin and Debussy

(E) Beethoven and Mendelssohn

Your Answer _____

Q–247

Medicine in the eighteenth century discovered new ways to prevent disease by

(A) building more hospitals

(B) burning the homes of the infected

(C) bleeding patients who were ill

(D) amputating infected limbs

(E) inoculation

Your Answer _____

Correct Answers

A–246

(B)   J. S. Bach and Handel were two of the most prolific composers of the eighteenth century. Both were German, but both were influenced by Italian compositions and genres. Handel and J. S. Bach composed works in most of the existing genres, from opera to fugues. At this time, it was common for well-known composers to work for a generous monarch, as Handel did for George II of England.

A–247

(E)   One of the scourges of the early modern era was smallpox, which killed many people. Lady Montague in England had heard of a technique from Turkey where people were purposely infected with smallpox so that they would have the fever but then develop antibodies to fight the disease. She introduced this practice to western Europe in 1721. Though risky, it became a standard method in the modern era of protecting people against some diseases.

Q–248

In 1753, a Scottish surgeon published his findings that scurvy was

(A) common among rural women

(B) connected to heart disease

(C) a blood disease

(D) a vitamin C deficiency

(E) a problem encountered during severe winters

Your Answer _____

_____

Q–249

Which of the following tactics did British diplomacy use to counter French power in the eighteenth century?

(A) Creating alliances with multiple kingdoms

(B) Enacting trade embargos

(C) Disputing the succession of the French monarchy

(D) Using the Roman Catholic Church to limit French power

(E) Attacking French outposts in the Caribbean

Your Answer _____

_____

Correct Answers

A–248

(D) The relationship between diet and health was just being discovered in the eighteenth century. A doctor in Scotland knew that men at sea suffered from a malady known as scurvy, which caused teeth to fall out and bleeding. Upon experimenting with fruit juices, he found that lemon juice would either halt the progress of the disease or cure it all together. This was a medical breakthrough, especially for the Royal Navy, which had barrels of lemons and limes put on every ship to maintain the health of its sailors.

A–249

(A) Great Britain was active in creating different alliances with nations that were also concerned with the rise of French power. Britain aligned itself with Austria, France's great rival during the eighteenth century, and also signed a treaty with Prussia, which tended to be anti-French. Britain's new king was from Germany, which further connected England with central Europe.

Questions

Q–250

Rococo art and music departed from the earlier Baroque by producing a

(A) heavy and dark impression

(B) light and airy feeling

(C) monochromatic style of expression

(D) series of neoclassical themes

(E) derivative genre that was briefly popular

Your Answer _____

_____

The Industrial Revolution (1790 – 1914)

Q–251

Liberté, egalité, fraternité is the motto associated with the

(A) Cuban Revolution

(B) Reign of Fear

(C) Russian Revolution

(D) French Revolution

(E) Commercial Revolution

Your Answer _____

_____

Correct Answers

A–250

(B)   Rococo paintings are often busy and use pastel colors to convey a sense of floating on a cloud. Palaces and churches from the period had ceilings painted with decorative themes, such as birds, cherubs, ribbons, and flowers. The art was busy and very colorful. While Baroque style seemed formal and heavy, the Rococo aimed to be charming and light.

A–251

(D)   Born out of the Enlightenment philosophies of the eighteenth century, French revolutionaries called for new political freedoms and more equality for the people. New ideas of government and politics developed the thought that rights should be guaranteed to the people. Abstract concepts of liberty and freedom became a part of the political discourse of the eighteenth century.

 Take Test-Readiness Quiz 2 on CD
(to review questions 126–251)

Q–252

After the French Revolution, the ideals of republican liberty in France were

(A) fully achieved by the Directory

(B) compromised by the dictatorship of Napoleon

(C) partially realized under Robespierre

(D) embraced by the Roman Catholic Church

(E) confused with democratic liberalism

Your Answer _____

Q–253

Which of the following nations formed an informal coalition against France after the execution of Louis XVI?

(A) Prussia, Italy, and Austria

(B) Britain, Spain, and Austria

(C) Russia, Denmark, and Britain

(D) Germany, Belgium, and Portugal

(E) Holland, Ireland, and Spain

Your Answer _____

Correct Answers

A–252

(B)   The era after the French Revolution was politically chaotic and was complicated by the threats of foreign invasion. After a period of oligarchic rule, Napoleon rose to power and took complete control of the national government. A strong leader, he paid lip service to the revolutionary motto of liberty, but he was more interested in maintaining his own power and achieving military goals.

A–253

(B)   The act of regicide, or killing the monarch, in revolutionary France was seen as barbaric and dangerous by other regimes in Europe. The Catholic monarchies of Austria and Spain were also particularly incensed with the anticlerical flavor of the French Revolution. France responded by building up the largest army ever assembled and trained. By 1794, the French army had over 1 million men and began to win battles against the antirevolutionary forces.

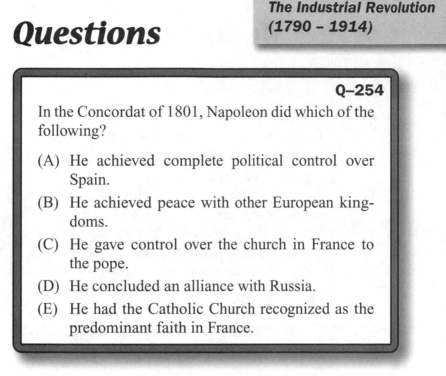

Q–254

In the Concordat of 1801, Napoleon did which of the following?

(A) He achieved complete political control over Spain.

(B) He achieved peace with other European kingdoms.

(C) He gave control over the church in France to the pope.

(D) He concluded an alliance with Russia.

(E) He had the Catholic Church recognized as the predominant faith in France.

Your Answer _____

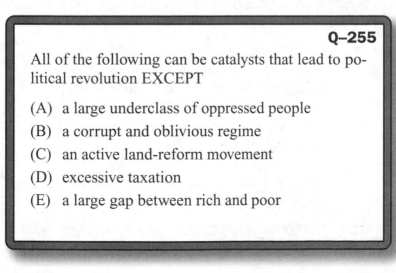

Q–255

All of the following can be catalysts that lead to political revolution EXCEPT

(A) a large underclass of oppressed people

(B) a corrupt and oblivious regime

(C) an active land-reform movement

(D) excessive taxation

(E) a large gap between rich and poor

Your Answer _____

Correct Answers

A–254

(E) After the coup of 1799, Napoleon made peace with the Roman Catholic Church. Although not a believer himself, Napoleon placated the pope by recognizing that most French people were still Catholic. In agreeing to this, the church did not get back the land taken by the revolutionary government. In the end, it meant the end of official enmity between Rome and Paris. This lessened the role of religion in the wars that would sweep across the continent in the next decade.

A–255

(C) Revolutions are often more likely with a conservative and uncaring leadership. Often land reform is desperately needed to give the peasantry a stake in their work. Aristocrats usually resist such reforms and seek to maintain their own power base. Whether one looks at the French or the Russian Revolution, corrupt leadership and a small wealthy elite often give the poor no option but to revolt.

Q–256

A major encouragement to industrialization in the nineteenth century was the development of

(A) labor unions

(B) steam power

(C) reform movements

(D) land grants

(E) transoceanic shipping lanes

Your Answer _____

Q–257

The survival of Great Britain during the Napoleonic period was primarily due to

(A) the collapse of Italian nationalism

(B) its alliance with Portugal

(C) its dominant naval power

(D) Prussian duplicity in switching sides during the war

(E) the leadership of Lord Baltimore

Your Answer _____

Correct Answers

A–256

(B) The ability to move people and goods is an important capability for industrialized nations. During the Industrial Revolution, steam power helped make ships and trains faster and more efficient. Steam-powered trains replaced canals as a much more effective way to move goods over long distances.

A–257

(C) Napoleon was the leader of one of the great continental armies in European history. He was thwarted on the high seas, however, by the power of the British Royal Navy. In the Mediterranean and in the Atlantic, the French navy could not defeat the British. This protected Britain from invasion and also disrupted French overseas trade. British naval power was able to play a pivotal role in the eventual defeat of Napoleon in 1814.

Q–258

The paintings of Goya played a role in

(A) encouraging Spanish nationalism during the Napoleonic era

(B) helping keep peace between Spain and France after the revolution

(C) romanticizing the life of the rural poor in Portugal

(D) eclipsing the work of the Dutch masters during the nineteenth century

(E) promoting Protestantism in France after 1800

Your Answer _____

_____

Q–259

The final defeat of Napoleonic France was mostly caused by

(A) the resistance of the United States to the practice of impressment at sea

(B) overextension of its military reach

(C) Prussian naval power

(D) the disintegration of its overseas empire

(E) the defeat at Trafalgar

Your Answer _____

_____

Correct Answers

A–258

(A) The Napoleonic wars spread beyond the borders of France and had a large impact on neighboring Spain. Napoleon put his own brother on the Spanish throne, which prompted protests from the Spanish. The occupying French used arbitrary arrests and executions to attempt to control the restless population. Goya painted dramatic scenes of Spanish defiance in the face of French oppression. This further catalyzed Spanish nationalism and eventually led to the defeat of the French in Iberia.

A–259

(B) Napoleon was successful in controlling different parts of Europe during the first decade of the nineteenth century. But his reach was exceeded when he invaded Russia in 1812. Formerly an ally of France, Russia decided to withdraw from the economic union that Napoleon thrust on his allies. The invasion of Russia was a disaster for France because its military power was weakened by a costly and remote campaign. Napoleon never regained his former power and was finally defeated in 1814 and forced into exile.

Questions

Q–260

The chief aim of the Napoleonic continental system was to

(A) forge an alliance with Great Britain

(B) bring most of the Mediterranean under French control

(C) intimidate the Irish into attacking Scotland

(D) exclude British trade from the rest of Europe

(E) partition Germany among the powers of Europe

Your Answer _____

_____

Q–261

Which of the following was NOT a result of Napoleon's Grand Empire?

(A) Feudal dues were abolished in some conquered territories.

(B) Belgium's nationhood was recognized.

(C) Serfdom was ended in many parts of Europe.

(D) Heavy taxes were levied in occupied territories.

(E) German nationalism was given a boost.

Your Answer _____

_____

Correct Answers

A–260

(D) By 1810, Napoleon was the great power in Europe because he had conquered and intimidated the powers around him. The one nation he could not control was Great Britain, which was militarily intact and protected by its powerful navy. Napoleon tried to deny British access to the economy of Europe, but this was unsuccessful in the end. Russia and other former French allies joined Britain in resisting Napoleon's hegemony.

A–261

(B) Napoleon saw himself as a conquering liberator who spread the ideals of the French Revolution. This meant recognizing the rights of the peasantry or serfs. Although some reforms resulted, many Germans and Spanish saw the French as foreign oppressors. This gave rise to new national sentiments and led to Napoleon's eventual downfall. The extended France was called the Grand Empire and reached its apex in 1810. After 1810, the empire began to fragment as more and more kingdoms opposed French domination.

Q–262

The Constitutional Charter of 1814 achieved which of the following in France?

(A) The Bourbon dynasty was reinstated as a limited monarchy.

(B) All rights were restored to the aristocracy.

(C) Protestantism was banned.

(D) Austrian occupation of Paris was formalized.

(E) Louis XVIII became an absolutist sovereign.

Your Answer _____

_____

Correct Answers

A–262

(A)   The Charter of 1814 allowed for the return of the Bourbons after a generation of exile. Louis XVIII accepted many of the reforms of the revolution, and his restored monarchy was essentially a constitutionally limited one. In the end, he reigned only ten years, and the monarchy did not prove popular in post-revolutionary France.

Q–263

The poster above is evocative of which era in modern European history?

(A) The belle époque

(B) The Victorian era

(C) The Gay Nineties

(D) The Napoleonic era

(E) The interwar period

Your Answer _____

_____

Correct Answers

A–263

(B) The reign of Queen Victoria coincided with the rapid industrialization of western Europe. Chief among the new technologies that appeared was the steam-powered railroad systems that began to connect Europe. The poster is British and shows that trains gave people access to once-remote regions, such as Scotland. Families were able to vacation in areas that had been inaccessible before modern transportation was available.

Q–264

In the preindustrial era, European goods were often moved via

(A) barges that connected different countries

(B) wagons on paved roads

(C) human-made canals that connected cities

(D) mule trains across the countryside

(E) crude steam-powered trucks

Your Answer _____

Q–265

Which of the following features of the British nation encouraged industrialization after 1780?

(A) A large population

(B) Technological know-how

(C) Available capital for investment

(D) A government friendly to business interests

(E) All of the above

Your Answer _____

Correct Answers

A–264

(C)   In the eighteenth century, canals were built in different parts of western Europe to help move goods to the marketplace. These were often human-made spurs that left existing rivers and went across the countryside regardless of elevation gain. Many locks were built to allow canal boats to follow the terrain. These canals enjoyed a half century of usefulness until they were replaced by the railroads, which were more efficient.

A–265

(E)   Great Britain was the first modern industrial nation. It possessed all the ingredients that a country needs to develop beyond the preindustrial stage. It had a thriving textile industry with wool and cotton as the most common products. Cotton mills were among the first factories to be built in the late eighteenth century. There were many agricultural laborers who adapted to factory work in nineteenth-century Britain. There was also a stable government that often voted in the interests of investors who were expanding their industries in Britain and around the world.

Q–266

Which two technological innovations greatly stimulated the textile industry in Great Britain by 1795?

(A) The cotton woofer and spinning jenny

(B) The astrolabe and shuttlecock

(C) The barometer and flying loom

(D) The spinning jenny and the water frame

(E) The wool splicer and lateral woof

Your Answer _____

_____

Q–267

In the early years of the Industrial Revolution, factory owners often sought to hire

(A) older married women

(B) children abandoned by their parents

(C) nobles down on their luck

(D) educated middle-class people

(E) retired clergy

Your Answer _____

_____

Correct Answers

A–266

(D) In the eighteenth century, cotton had to be imported into Great Britain from other parts of the world, such as India or the United States. Cotton was an easier fabric to manufacture, especially after the invention of the spinning jenny, which greatly increased the ability to produce yarn and thread. This and the water frame helped textile manufacturers expand their operations and create more cloth. These inventions catalyzed the growth of the cotton industry because clothes could be made faster and cheaper.

A–267

(B) Working conditions in factories were often poor, and some adults balked at working in them. There was a large population of orphaned and abandoned children who were available to factory managers. These children had often been left in the care of local parishes or churches. Sometimes opportunistic parish officers apprenticed these children out to factory recruiters, and they worked long hours in unsafe factory conditions. This was a type of de facto slavery, and conditions were brutal for the young workers.

Q–268

Nineteenth-century Great Britain was remarkable in the

(A) strictness of its mercantilistic policies

(B) oppressive nature of its monarchy

(C) devotion it showed to King George II

(D) freedom it allowed to private entrepreneurs

(E) liberal policies it implemented in India

Your Answer _____

Q–269

Early eighteenth-century factories were often located on

(A) the coast

(B) mountainsides

(C) canals built by steam shovels

(D) the sides of valleys

(E) rivers

Your Answer _____

Correct Answers

A–268

(D) England had evolved into a relatively liberal constitutional monarchy by 1800. It maintained a respected monarchy while giving more power to the people through the governing Parliament. It was much less regulatory of businesses than other European nations in the same time period. This encouraged people to invest their money in new enterprises, which helped create the great merchant class in Britain in the nineteenth century.

A–269

(E) Many of the early factories were water powered, making flowing rivers an ideal source of natural power to industrialists. The flowing water drove large water wheels, and the mechanical energy was used to power the water frames and power looms. New towns grew up rapidly around these factories, and many jobs were created.

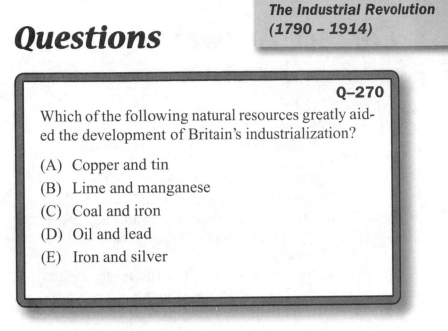

Q–270

Which of the following natural resources greatly aided the development of Britain's industrialization?

(A) Copper and tin

(B) Lime and manganese

(C) Coal and iron

(D) Oil and lead

(E) Iron and silver

Your Answer _____

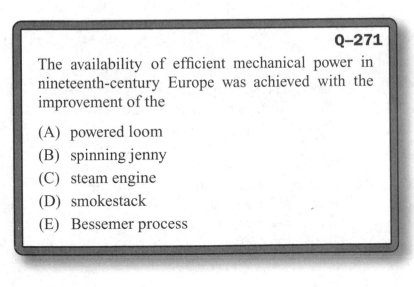

Q–271

The availability of efficient mechanical power in nineteenth-century Europe was achieved with the improvement of the

(A) powered loom

(B) spinning jenny

(C) steam engine

(D) smokestack

(E) Bessemer process

Your Answer _____

Correct Answers

A–270

(C)　The industrialization of Great Britain was furthered with the discovery of new methods for making iron and, later, steel. Coal was a vital material used in making higher-quality iron. Higher temperatures and new methods allowed for impurities to be removed from the raw iron. Iron became the favored material for new machines used in the manufacturing sector. When new transportation technology evolved in shipping and railroads, the demand for iron increased many times. This led to a boom in heavier industries in Britain.

A–271

(C)　The first steam engines used in Europe were inefficient but were used in mines and early factories. In the eighteenth century, specific improvements were made so that larger and larger machines generated more power. Soon, steam power was being used to move ships and operate looms in factories. Fuel in the form of coal was cheap and plentiful, so steam was an inexpensive solution to power needs in western Europe. Great Britain led the way in steam technology and helped it industrialize ahead of other nations.

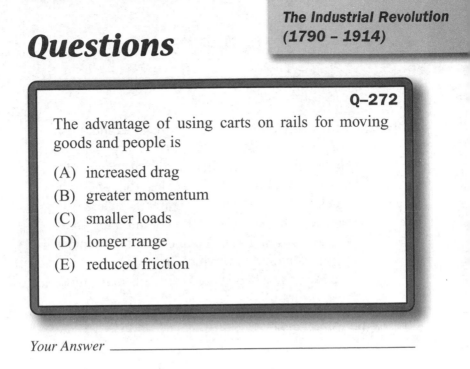

Q–272

The advantage of using carts on rails for moving goods and people is

(A) increased drag

(B) greater momentum

(C) smaller loads

(D) longer range

(E) reduced friction

Your Answer _____

_____

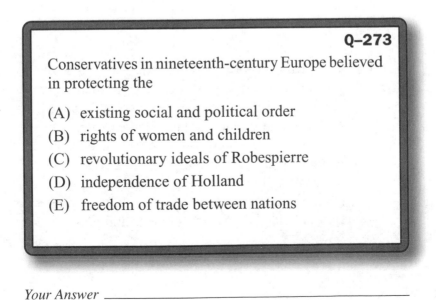

Q–273

Conservatives in nineteenth-century Europe believed in protecting the

(A) existing social and political order

(B) rights of women and children

(C) revolutionary ideals of Robespierre

(D) independence of Holland

(E) freedom of trade between nations

Your Answer _____

_____

Correct Answers

A–272

(E) Miners discovered that humans could push wagons on rails much more easily than on roads. Rails were first made of wood, but wooden rails were not durable. Iron, and later steel, replaced wood and created even less friction with the wheels of the container. As rails became stronger, larger, and heavier, vehicles could ride on them, which helped give rise to the use of steam-powered railroads in the nineteenth century.

A–273

(A) The basic posture of the conservative is opposition to change. Conservatives in the nineteenth century began to develop an alternative to the revolutionary ideals of the American and French Revolutions. They believed that while change was natural over time, it should not be revolutionary in nature. They worked to preserve the political and social status quo as they defended their own interests and power.

Q–274

The industrial term *division of labor* in manufacturing means the

(A) creation of specialized tasks on the factory floor

(B) establishment of union organizations

(C) worker makes the product entirely

(D) creation of more management layers in a company

(E) labor gets divided into different factory shifts

Your Answer _____

_____

Q–275

Traditional elites in nineteenth-century Europe consisted mostly of

(A) Catholic priests and middle-class merchants

(B) company officials and lower nobility

(C) professionals and businesspeople

(D) peasants and artisans

(E) aristocrats and high-level bureaucrats

Your Answer _____

_____

Correct Answers

A–274

(A)   As industrialization became more complex, labor needed to become more specialized. Workers would learn one task in the manufacturing process and do only that. The task could be attaching the wheels to a car or polishing a glass piece on a truck. This created more efficiency but also made work more rote and repetitive.

A–275

(E)   With the defeat of Napoleon, the traditional conservatives in Europe were able to reconsolidate their power. These landed aristocrats sought to reestablish the monarchy and the privileges of the old order. Governments were also dominated by entrenched bureaucracies. Leadership was often in the hands of the landowners and the officials who helped run the kingdoms.

Q–276

Mass manufacturing of machines became more efficient after 1830 with the use of

(A) plastic presses

(B) cast-iron parts

(C) handmade steel parts

(D) iron smelting

(E) interchangeable parts

Your Answer _____

Q–277

Which of the following were important forces of ideological change in nineteenth-century Europe?

(A) Fascism and neoconservatism

(B) Nationalism and liberalism

(C) Moralism and Leninism

(D) Victorian ideals and Marxism

(E) Globalism and monarchism

Your Answer _____

Correct Answers

A–276

(E) Interchangeable parts meant that many phases of making a device could be standardized. The fewer the parts, the more simple the machine and the easier it was to clean and maintain. Repair was also easier. This was true of everything from steam locomotives to cannons.

A–277

(B) The nineteenth century proved to be an important transition for conservatives and liberals. The economic and technological changes of the 1800s meant new challenges for all people. While liberals continued to promote the ideals of the eighteenth-century revolutions, conservatives used nationalism to appeal to their supporters. Nationalism gave rise to new countries and also helped support established leaders.

Questions

Q–278

The postwar order after the defeat of Napoleon was fashioned at the

(A) Treaty of Helsinki
(B) Geneva Convention
(C) Congress of Vienna
(D) Versailles Convention
(E) Berlin Congress

Your Answer _____

Q–279

A political stance that favored progressive change would be called

(A) anarchistic
(B) libertarian
(C) conservative
(D) radical
(E) liberal

Your Answer _____

Correct Answers

A–278

(C) The four nations that banded together to defeat France in 1814 met in Vienna to establish a lasting peace for Europe. Prussia, Great Britain, Russia, and Austria met to deal with a defeated France and redraw the map of Europe. The hope was to build a balance of power that would last. The agreements were generally lenient toward France and had strong defensive features should any power rise up and upset the balance.

A–279

(E) In the 1800s, liberal and conservative political thinking emerged to separate parties and candidates from one another. Some, like Marx, favored change and believed in revolution when the circumstances called for it. Others, like Burke in England, saw revolution as dangerous and sought to preserve the way things were. Progressive change is the goal of the liberal, who wants to work within the system to see the world improve.

Q–280

After 1815, the European congress system was used somewhat regularly to

(A) create alliances against Russia

(B) raise taxes from kingdoms

(C) settle international disputes and maintain the peace

(D) punish France for the Napoleonic wars

(E) isolate Great Britain politically

Your Answer _____

Q–281

Which of the following was the primary goal of the Holy Alliance in Europe after 1815?

(A) Suppressing the liberal legacy of eighteenth-century revolutions

(B) Supporting the Catholic Church

(C) Ensuring that Russia did not become too dominant in eastern Europe

(D) Mandating nonintervention in the affairs of other countries

(E) Creating a balance between Protestant and Catholic kingdoms

Your Answer _____

Correct Answers

A–280

(C) The Congress of Vienna established the longer-term Quadruple Alliance among Great Britain, Austria, Prussia, and Russia. These powers moved to isolate France without punishing her and maintain a workable peace in Europe. Throughout the nineteenth century, the four powers would meet when needed if there was a potential crisis to attend to. Their commitment to a rational balance of power meant that general war was avoided and the 1800s were relatively peaceful.

A–281

(A) After the Napoleonic era, the most conservative kingdoms were Austria and Russia. They sought the support of Prussia in a campaign to discourage liberal reform in Europe. The three monarchies formed the Holy Alliance after the Congress of Vienna in 1815. Their desire was to maintain the prerevolutionary status quo that kept monarchs in power. Whenever liberalism rose up, as in Spain or in Sicily, the Holy Alliance would do what it could to stamp out change to the old order.

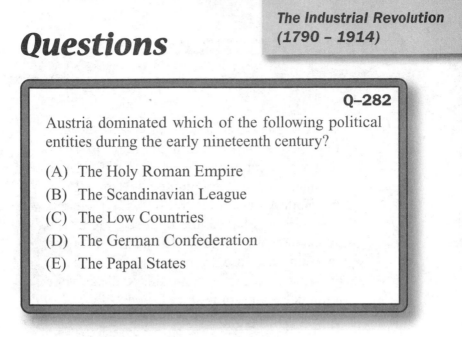

Q–282

Austria dominated which of the following political entities during the early nineteenth century?

(A) The Holy Roman Empire

(B) The Scandinavian League

(C) The Low Countries

(D) The German Confederation

(E) The Papal States

Your Answer _____

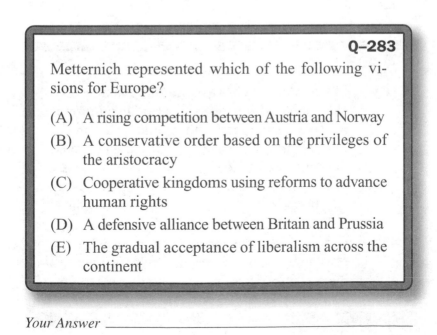

Q–283

Metternich represented which of the following visions for Europe?

(A) A rising competition between Austria and Norway

(B) A conservative order based on the privileges of the aristocracy

(C) Cooperative kingdoms using reforms to advance human rights

(D) A defensive alliance between Britain and Prussia

(E) The gradual acceptance of liberalism across the continent

Your Answer _____

Correct Answers

A-282

(D) The Congress of Vienna sponsored the creation of the German Confederation in 1815. This was a loose union of over thirty small German domains, including the larger Prussia. Both Austria and Prussia were members of the Holy Alliance and opposed any liberal trends in central Europe. They used spies and deception to observe progressive groups in universities and in the media. Radicals were intimidated and sometimes killed.

A-283

(B) Prince Metternich was a middle-ranking Austrian noble who rose to great political prominence in the nineteenth century. A foreign minister under the Hapsburgs, he engineered the conservative peace after the French defeat at Waterloo. He believed in a strong monarchy and bureaucracy based on traditional values. He blamed the bloodshed of the Napoleonic period on the dangerous liberal ideas of the revolutions and worked tirelessly to undo all the reforms of the French Revolution and preserve the peace.

Q–284

Which of the following philosophers glorified the nation-state in his writings?

(A) Giuseppe Mazzini

(B) Friedrich Nietzsche

(C) Arthur Schopenhauer

(D) Georg Hegel

(E) Charles Fournier

Your Answer _____

Q–285

The revolutions of 1848 yielded which of the following results?

(A) The deposing of the pope

(B) The establishment of the Second Republic in France

(C) Marxist states being created in eastern Europe

(D) New progress made by union workers

(E) Suffrage rights being expanded in Russia

Your Answer _____

Correct Answers

A–284

(D) Georg Hegel was a German philosopher who built on the ideas of Kant. Hegel saw history moving in a certain direction, toward the founding of national states. As a German, Hegel was anticipating the later political unification of his own culture. He believed history was a clashing of opposing ideas that would yield a new synthesis. This synthesis suggested the combining of peoples with a common culture into a new political entity. Nationalists used these ideas to further their campaigns, which led to the unification of Germany and Italy later in the nineteenth century.

A–285

(B) Liberals opposed to the rule of Louis Philippe rioted in Paris in early 1848. The king abdicated and a new assembly was created. This new government was made up of mostly moderate and some radical republicans. The two factions did not work well together and the assembly did not last. The nephew of Napoleon was elected during the upheaval and moved to undo the liberal advances of the republicans. He disbanded the assembly and reestablished authoritarian control.

Q–286

The Reform Act of 1832 had which of the following effects in Great Britain?

(A) The monarchy was strengthened.

(B) The number of males who could vote was doubled.

(C) The poor were given more employment by the government.

(D) The slave trade was allowed to continue.

(E) The workday was lengthened in mines.

Your Answer _____

_____

Q–287

Positivism was associated with which of the following nineteenth-century thinkers?

(A) Auguste Comte

(B) Prince Metternich

(C) Louis Napoleon

(D) Friedrich Engels

(E) Louis Kossuth

Your Answer _____

_____

Correct Answers

A–286

(B) One of the main goals of British liberals in the nineteenth century was expanding suffrage rights. Attempts to change voter requirements were met with strong opposition in the House of Lords. The Reform Act revised qualifications for males to vote so that one did not have to own so much property to qualify. The property qualification was ten pounds, which still disallowed many men from being able to vote. Even so, twice as many men were able to vote after 1832.

A–287

(A) Positivism was a nineteenth-century refutation of earlier theology and philosophy. Some people rejected traditional religious beliefs and turned to science as the sole source of truth. They believed that positive knowledge was based in natural phenomena and could be proved by scientific observation. Comte was a pioneer of the positivistic way of thinking and believed in focused investigations into reality. He rejected what could not be proved and believed that a new search for social truth would replace religion.

Questions

Q–288

Transatlantic voyages in the nineteenth century were shortened to weeks with the introduction of

(A) steam-powered boats

(B) new navigational equipment

(C) larger lateen sails

(D) larger prows

(E) steel hulls

Your Answer _____

_____

Q–289

By the mid-nineteenth century, which city had replaced Amsterdam as the financial capital of Europe?

(A) Paris

(B) Rome

(C) Glasgow

(D) London

(E) Berlin

Your Answer _____

_____

Correct Answers

A–288

(A) Early steamships combined engine power with sails to move faster on the water. One such steamship sailed from England to America in seventeen days in 1816. This was twice as fast as earlier schooners that used only wind power. Soon steamships were built for both ocean voyages and local river travel. Steam allowed ships to travel easily upriver, which stimulated the domestic cargo business.

A–289

(D) Holland dominated European banking in the eighteenth century, but Great Britain took the lead in financial activity in the next century. Dutch banks remained important, but the growth of British banking took the lead. The stock market in London grew as more and more investment was raised for ventures all over the world. The British banking industry grew along with the imperial interests that Great Britain now had on five continents.

Questions

Q–290

(Photograph © by Dave Cooper)

What new nineteenth-century technology is displayed in the picture above?

(A) Radio navigation

(B) Iron plows

(C) Subway systems

(D) Horse-drawn streetcars

(E) Steam-powered railroads

Your Answer _____

_____

Correct Answers

A–290

(E)   In 1830, railroads started in Great Britain as the first mass overland passenger systems. At first, rail companies were private, but later, many European nations nationalized their systems. The first trains were rather slow but could still travel more quickly than horse-drawn wagons. Soon the white and black smoke of steam locomotives became a common sight as more and more track was laid across the continent.

Questions

Q–291

What nineteenth-century ideologies are highlighted in the painting above?

(A) Idealism and conservatism

(B) Realism and jingoism

(C) Liberalism and nationalism

(D) Marxism and Leninism

(E) Fascism and liberalism

Your Answer _____

Correct Answers

A–291

(C)   The painting *Liberty Leading the People* by Delacroix is one of the most famous works of art representing the postrevolutionary era in France. It portrays the political turmoil of the nineteenth century that led to violence in France in 1830 and 1848. It shows the people rising up to change the government and, in the center, shows a woman who represents liberty and freedom. She holds the flag of France, which gives a strong nationalistic tone to the image.

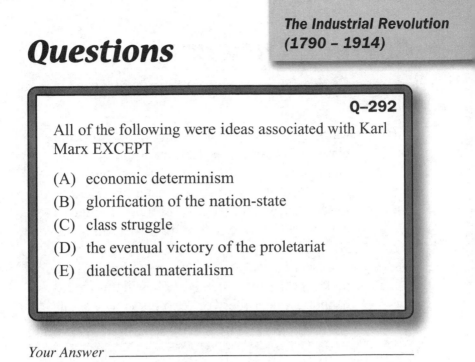

Q–292

All of the following were ideas associated with Karl Marx EXCEPT

(A) economic determinism

(B) glorification of the nation-state

(C) class struggle

(D) the eventual victory of the proletariat

(E) dialectical materialism

Your Answer _____

Q–293

The Crimean War helped inaugurate which of the following professions?

(A) Chemical engineering

(B) Corporate law

(C) Investment banking

(D) Modern nursing

(E) Political science

Your Answer _____

Correct Answers

A–292

(B) Marx believed in the power of the working class (proletariat) and wanted the working class to seize control of production in the modern industrial system. As a materialist, he believed that material forces produce change, a concept referred to as economic determinism. His view of history was one of class struggle that would lead to revolution as the workers took over the economy. He believed this would happen all over the world, so his view was internationalist, as opposed to nationalist.

A–293

(D) In the 1850s, the Crimean War was fought in the north Black Sea area and many died from wounds and disease. There was no organized system for treating the sick and wounded on the battlefield, so medical attention was ad hoc. Florence Nightingale saw the situation and organized field hospitals and care for the wounded. Her work marks the beginning of the modern nursing profession and demonstrated that women were capable of helping in public wartime roles.

Questions

Q–294

Which of the following explains the so-called Eastern Question of the nineteenth century?

(A) The Prussian takeover of Polish territory after 1820

(B) The decline of Ottoman Turkey in the Balkan region

(C) Russia's interest in Finland

(D) The ethnic tensions within the Austria-Hungarian Empire

(E) Wilhelm II's desire to unite with Bavaria

Your Answer _____

Q–295

All the following are features of Marxist theory EXCEPT

(A) class struggle

(B) capitalistic benefits

(C) proletarian overthrow of moneyed interests

(D) bourgeois exploitation of the workers

(E) international unity of all workers

Your Answer _____

Correct Answers

A–294

(B) Ottoman Turkey had been a powerful empire in the East for centuries, but by 1800, it was in decline. The Ottomans lost more and more territory to Austria, and Russia became interested in east European territory. This upset the balance of power in Europe because large nations sought to take advantage of Turkish weakness. The Crimean War was a result of English and French attempts to thwart Russian expansion.

A–295

(B) Marx wrote of the predicted overthrow of capitalism by the workers. He saw the bourgeoisie as the moneyed interests who used the workers and took the profits. For Marx, capitalism was the great evil. He saw all of history in terms of class struggle, in which the rich exploited the poor. His theories formed the basis for later socialist/communist movements in Russia and China.

Q–296

Early factory workers found it difficult to adjust to

(A) higher salaries

(B) regular hours under close supervision

(C) shorter work days

(D) cleaner facilities to work in

(E) being around so many other people

Your Answer _____

_____

Q–297

The European textile industry suffered in the early nineteenth century when

(A) Germany declared war on Denmark

(B) a revolution in Haiti disrupted business

(C) the United States boycotted goods from France

(D) a cotton blight struck

(E) cheap British goods flooded continental markets

Your Answer _____

_____

Correct Answers

A–296

(B) Before the industrial era, workers would get paid by the piece and could work at home, often at odd hours. With the building of factories, many workers had to be organized into shifts. A twelve-hour shift and management oversight meant a more disciplined work experience. This was a difficult transition for many who were used to working in their cottages without supervision. It took a generation for workers to adjust to the new, more regimented work experience.

A–297

(E) After 1820, the industrial capacity of Britain increased dramatically. It was able to outproduce the rest of Europe combined. This meant that cheap British goods were able to undersell textiles from other parts of the continent. The Low Countries were still recovering from the Napoleonic wars, which did not affect Great Britain directly. Soon Britain's economic power was dominant and the rest of Europe was trying to emulate its success.

Questions

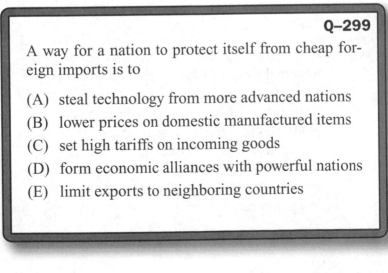

Q–298

The Industrial Revolution gave a boost to which of the following industries in nineteenth-century Europe?

(A) Fishing and transportation
(B) Metalworking and construction
(C) Silk weaving and stone cutting
(D) Weaving and grain milling
(E) Food processing and banking

Your Answer _____

_____

Q–299

A way for a nation to protect itself from cheap foreign imports is to

(A) steal technology from more advanced nations
(B) lower prices on domestic manufactured items
(C) set high tariffs on incoming goods
(D) form economic alliances with powerful nations
(E) limit exports to neighboring countries

Your Answer _____

_____

Correct Answers

A–298

(B) Continental Europe used heavier industry to lay the foundation for its industrialization. The French and Belgians led the way in learning newer metalworking and construction skills. This led to a demand for more engineers from state-sponsored schools. Powered industry was still unevenly spread across central Europe into the 1800s.

A–299

(C) When Britain sold its cheaper textiles successfully to the rest of Europe, nations searched for a way to protect their own industries. One of the most common responses in this case was to tax foreign goods, which artificially raised their prices in the marketplace. Germany began to advocate this policy so it could protect its own young industries against foreign competition.

Q–300

Which of the following was essential to the success of continental European industrialization in the nineteenth century?

(A) Growing empires abroad

(B) The development of joint-stock investment banks

(C) New territory won in wars

(D) Conservative monarchies that favored business interests

(E) Rising labor costs

Your Answer _____

Q–301

Buildings in urban areas during the early industrial era were often blackened by

(A) burning wood used for fuel

(B) fires from local kilns

(C) young gangs who vandalized walls

(D) the burning of coal to heat homes and power factories

(E) acid rain that fell during summer showers

Your Answer _____

Correct Answers

A–300

(B) Continental banks began to grow and use private deposits for industrial investments, making money available for railroad building and ship manufacture. Private investors could buy shares in these new industries and limit their liability to the amount they risked buying the stock. Powerful banks emerged in France, the German Confederation, and Belgium, which helped finance Europe's heavy industry.

A–301

(D) Coal became the cheap fuel that powered the Industrial Revolution. It is a very dirty fuel; it pollutes the air and colors the buildings. The soot from the burning of coal created a considerable health hazard as people breathed the dirty air. Eventually, companies installed filters and scrubbers to reduce the soot output of factories in cities. Throughout the nineteenth century, people in urban areas were accustomed to blackened skies and unclean air.

Q–302

They [the urban poor] eat, drink, breed, work and die; and . . . the richer and more intelligent classes are obliged to guard them with police.

—A. Smyth, 1850

The comment above reveals what about the view held by the upper class of the poor in the middle of the Industrial Revolution?

(A) Many wealthy people were contemptuous of the poor.

(B) The classes mixed comfortably with one another.

(C) The poor depended on the government for protection.

(D) There was a tolerant appreciation of the problems of the poor.

(E) The police sympathized with the urban poor.

Your Answer _____

_____

Correct Answers

A–302

(A)   The quote reveals the superior attitude that some wealthy people felt toward the poor. The separation between rich and poor was considerable: the wealthy lived on the fringes of urban areas and the poor lived in crowded city centers. Many elites feared the uneducated masses, and as the quote depicts, the police were needed to keep them under control.

Q–303

Liberalism in the nineteenth century demanded what kind of government?

(A) Enlightened despotism

(B) Representative government

(C) Totalitarian rule

(D) An oligarchic system

(E) A strong monarchy

Your Answer _____

_____

Q–304

Eighteenth-century mercantilism was challenged in the nineteenth century by the idea of

(A) technological conservatism

(B) democratic republicanism

(C) laissez-faire capitalism

(D) regulatory intervention

(E) rugged individualism

Your Answer _____

_____

Correct Answers

A–303

(B)   The revolutions of the eighteenth century promoted the ideas of liberty and the rights of people. This gave rise to constitutionalism, which sought to create representative governments, with the people being able to choose their leaders. Great Britain was the first to develop representative rule for the landed elites. The French Revolution sought to eliminate all class distinctions and create a national representative assembly. These trends were often slowed by conservative interests that favored the rule of monarchy or sharing power with the people.

A–304

(C)   In the early modern era, it was believed that nations should strive to create self-sufficient economies regulated by their governments. This approach was later criticized by Adam Smith, who said that economies should be left alone to rise and fall. Some early liberals who wanted the government to take a smaller role in overseeing the economy favored this idea of laissez-faire capitalism. Free competition was seen as the "invisible hand" that guided success and failure in the marketplace.

Q–305

The right to vote in the early nineteenth century was largely defined by

(A) familial ties to the monarchy

(B) property ownership and business success

(C) poll taxes, which some could not afford

(D) literacy tests

(E) professional qualifications

Your Answer _____

_____

Q–306

In nineteenth-century Europe, national consciousness was aided by which of the following dynamics?

(A) Various dialects spoken in different regions

(B) Dynasties that ruled an area for centuries

(C) A period of relative peace

(D) Common language and religion

(E) The weak leadership of the church

Your Answer _____

_____

Correct Answers

A–305

(B) The rights of individuals were often defined by class status in the 1800s. Although more people could vote, the right was often tied to property ownership and wealth, and those who could vote included the old aristocratic elites, successful middle-class professionals, and businesspeople. Only qualifying men could vote, and often property taxes were used to determine who could participate in elections.

A–306

(D) After 1700, the idea of the modern nation-state took root. Kingdoms that grew and consolidated their rule over an area started to create a national consciousness among the people. This was a force that challenged the status quo in large empires such as Austria and Ottoman Turkey. Nationalist politicians in central Europe began to frame the idea of a German people who had a common language and culture. War was often used to forge new nations because the threat of an enemy would unite a people in the name of their country.

Q–307

Early socialist thinkers saw capitalism as a system that encouraged

(A) a strong relationship between state and church

(B) national unity

(C) a breakdown in class distinctions

(D) obedience to state authority

(E) selfish individualism

Your Answer _____

_____

Q–308

Early critics of capitalism called into question the idea of

(A) a regulated economy

(B) personal property

(C) the infallibility of religious scripture

(D) state interference in the marketplace

(E) a national currency

Your Answer _____

_____

Correct Answers

A–307

(E) Liberal observers of the many changes during the nineteenth century saw that the commercial revolution was creating new tensions and problems in Europe. There was a widening gap between the rich and poor. Capitalism seemed to appeal only to the selfish interests of humankind. Some liberals saw that the pursuit of individual profit led to abuses when workers were exploited. This also guaranteed that the poor would remain disadvantaged and uncared for.

A–308

(B) Some thinkers, such as Fourier (1768–1830), suggested an alternative to the capitalistic order in western Europe. He imagined utopian groupings where goods were shared by everyone and the state took a role in regulating the economy. Capitalism was seen as unjust because some benefited from the system while others did not. The gap between rich and poor was easily observed in nations such as France and Great Britain. This gave rise to the question of what an alternative to capitalism would look like. Chief among the ideas was the abolition of private property.

Questions

Q–309

The term *proletariat* means which of the following?

(A) The theory of historical evolution posited by Engels

(B) A political party in France after 1870

(C) Opponents of the labor movement

(D) Factory managers who abused workers

(E) The modern working class

Your Answer _____

_____

Q–310

Work days in the early Industrial Revolution ranged from

(A) twelve to sixteen hours

(B) eight to ten hours

(C) fifteen to twenty hours

(D) nine to eleven hours

(E) six to ten hours

Your Answer _____

_____

Correct Answers

A–309

(E) As socialist thinkers began to write about modern economics, they coined new terms to describe the people involved. The term *proletariat* came to mean the modern working class, which included everyone who worked in factories and mills. Philosophers such as Marx saw the proletariat as being exploited by the wealthy elites. Some socialists urged the working class to rise up and take control of the economy that it served.

A–310

(A) Workers in nineteenth-century factories faced long work days in poor conditions. Work days could be as long as sixteen hours, and there were many rules to follow. Managers watched their workers carefully and would fine them if they did not maintain discipline in the workplace. Most workers were on the factory floor six days a week. Temperatures in some textile mills exceeded 100 degrees Fahrenheit.

Questions

Q–311

The patterns of kinship employment during the Industrial Revolution meant that

(A) men migrated from the countryside in search of work

(B) nepotism was disallowed in the workplace

(C) brothers could not work in the same factories

(D) parents and children were often employed together

(E) managers paid their wives for work not done

Your Answer _____

_____

Q–312

The Poor Law Act of 1834 established which of the following in Britain?

(A) Charity funds to feed the hungry

(B) Workhouses where poor people were forced to work to live

(C) Nonprofit agencies to care for the homeless

(D) Immigration programs for the poor to settle in North America

(E) Laws that made it illegal to be in debt

Your Answer _____

_____

Correct Answers

A–311

(D) Before the Industrial Revolution, families often worked together in their homes to create goods for the textile industry. With the advent of factories, some families would apply for work together. Siblings, cousins, and spouses would often work side by side in the factories. Even young children were put to work. Parents often encouraged their children to work because it meant more income for the family.

A–312

(B) In the first half of the nineteenth century, many people believed that the poor were responsible for their own misery. In 1834, the British created a system for the poor where they could be made to live in workhouses and work for the government. The idea was to make these places more like prisons so that people would become motivated to stay out of them. The food was terrible, and sometimes children would be grouped together as a source of cheap labor for nearby factories. Authors of the time period, such as Charles Dickens, wrote about these places, where the poor were virtually imprisoned.

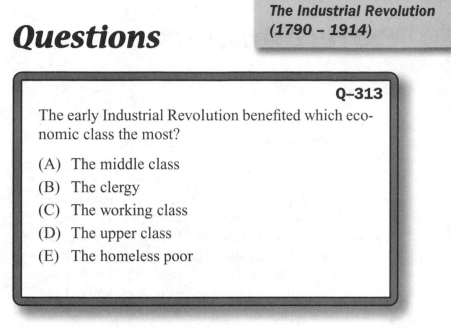

Q–313

The early Industrial Revolution benefited which economic class the most?

(A) The middle class

(B) The clergy

(C) The working class

(D) The upper class

(E) The homeless poor

Your Answer _____

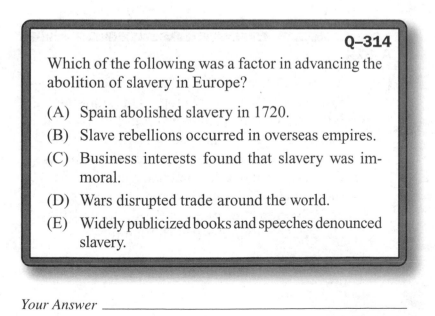

Q–314

Which of the following was a factor in advancing the abolition of slavery in Europe?

(A) Spain abolished slavery in 1720.

(B) Slave rebellions occurred in overseas empires.

(C) Business interests found that slavery was immoral.

(D) Wars disrupted trade around the world.

(E) Widely publicized books and speeches denounced slavery.

Your Answer _____

Correct Answers

A–313

(A) Historians have debated who benefited as western Europe began to industrialize. Certainly some businesspeople became very rich when factories prospered and profits grew. But overall, it was the middle class that gained the most in terms of wages and status. Skilled professionals saw their lifestyles improve and their incomes rise. The middle class consisted of smaller-scale businesspeople, professionals, and middle managers in companies. They also might be farmers with large landholdings. These were people who could afford to live outside the city centers if they wanted to.

A–314

(E) Many different factors helped to end slavery in nineteenth-century Europe. One important influence was the printed word in Europe and America. Slaves who had run away to gain their freedom wrote their life stories, and many thus learned about the inhuman conditions Africans endured. Also, British politicians, such as Wilberforce, worked tirelessly to end the slave trade within the British Empire.

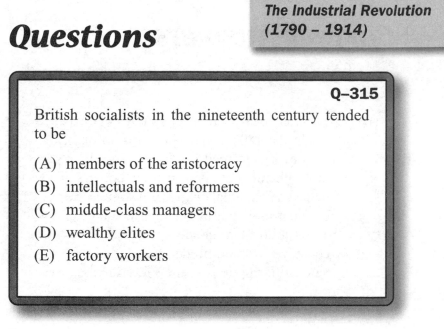

Q–315

British socialists in the nineteenth century tended to be

(A) members of the aristocracy

(B) intellectuals and reformers

(C) middle-class managers

(D) wealthy elites

(E) factory workers

Your Answer _____

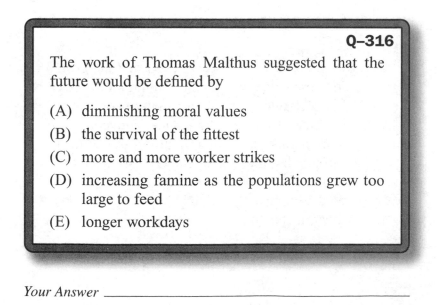

Q–316

The work of Thomas Malthus suggested that the future would be defined by

(A) diminishing moral values

(B) the survival of the fittest

(C) more and more worker strikes

(D) increasing famine as the populations grew too large to feed

(E) longer workdays

Your Answer _____

Correct Answers

A–315

(B) Socialist ideas were not popular in Great Britain in the 1800s. In 1884, a group of British intellectuals formed the Fabian Society to promote liberal socialism in their country. They believed in gradual change but wanted the government to play a larger role in the economy. Their political influence was marginal because conservatives and moderates tended to dominate British politics in the Victorian era.

A–316

(D) Malthus (1766–1834) believed that the growing population would result in the food supply being unable to sustain so many people. This pessimistic forecast did not take into consideration higher yields in agriculture over time as farming became more efficient. Still, Malthus is one of the early demographers who considered the impact of rising populations in the modern era.

Questions

Q–317

The most important duty of middle-class European women in the nineteenth century was to

(A) take on jobs to support their families

(B) obey their mothers-in-law

(C) prepare their sons and daughters for higher education

(D) raise their children at home

(E) enter the professional ranks after having children

Your Answer _____

Q–318

In the early nineteenth century, organizing worker unions was difficult because

(A) workers were apathetic

(B) socialist goals were promoted by many governments

(C) anticombination laws made it illegal to strike

(D) democratic parliaments were dominated by the working classes

(E) they were opposed by anarchists

Your Answer _____

Correct Answers

A–317

(D) During the Victorian era, middle-class women raised their own children and were stay-at-home mothers. They passed on housekeeping skills, such as embroidery and cooking, to their daughters. Most professional careers were difficult for women to enter. Some managed to go to medical school, but they were extraordinary pioneers in their fields.

A–318

(C) Prior to 1848, governments were opposed to labor reforms. Laws in Germany, Britain, France, and other industrial nations banned most union activities such as worker strikes. Only after 1850 were new laws passed that allowed workers to organize. By the end of the century, millions of workers were members of unions in Europe and the United States.

Q–319

All the following are examples of nineteenth-century European nationalism EXCEPT

(A) Zionist plans to settle in Palestine

(B) Danish resistance to Norwegian control

(C) Hungarian independence from Austria

(D) the fight between German states and France in 1871

(E) Italian desire to unify the nation under a monarchy

Your Answer _____

_____

Q–320

The goal of Marxist socialism was the creation of

(A) a single-party dictatorship

(B) a classless society

(C) many worker councils in urban areas

(D) a partnership between capitalists and the workers

(E) agricultural collectives

Your Answer _____

_____

Correct Answers

A–319

(B)   Many expressions of nationalism were evident after the defeat of Napoleon. Some European Jewish nationalists began to promote a homeland in the Middle East. Nations such as Italy and Germany came into being through military campaigns that united the people behind strong nationalist leaders. Large empires such as Austria had difficulty keeping their multiethnic subjects loyal to the monarchy.

A–320

(B)   Some nineteenth-century socialists were more idealistic than others, but Marx set forth a goal of the classless society, which depended on the overthrow of capitalism. Production would then be in the hands of the workers, who would create a new order where goods were shared among the people according to their needs.

Q–321

The British passed the Combination Acts of 1799 and 1800 in reaction to

(A) German industrial successes

(B) Napoleon's continental system

(C) the radicalism of the French Revolution

(D) Marxist agitation among the working class

(E) child-labor protests

Your Answer _____

Q–322

By 1850, wages for the working classes in Europe were

(A) stagnating across the continent

(B) rising for the majority of people

(C) plummeting for most employees

(D) controlled by tight government regulations

(E) no better than after the Napoleonic period

Your Answer _____

Correct Answers

A–321

(C) The rights of the common person were advanced by the French Revolution, and conservative interests in Britain were afraid this idea would spread to England. Business interests were particularly afraid that workers might band together and fight for higher wages. During the Napoleonic period, Parliament passed laws that outlawed combinations or worker associations. This did not succeed in the long run because workers organized themselves into trade unions that gave them more power in dealing with employers.

A–322

(B) By the middle of the nineteenth century, working conditions were improving for many European workers. While the gap between rich and poor remained large, workers earned some concessions from their employers. Shorter workdays were negotiated and wages rose for most workers. This trend continued until World War I, leading to gains in the standards of living for the working classes.

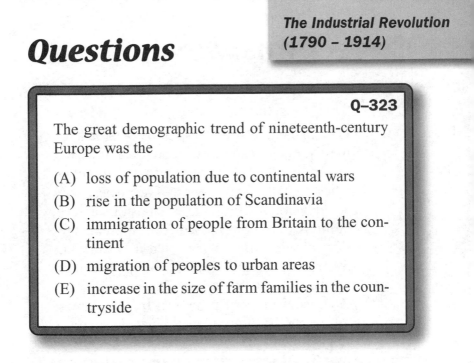

Q–323

The great demographic trend of nineteenth-century Europe was the

(A) loss of population due to continental wars

(B) rise in the population of Scandinavia

(C) immigration of people from Britain to the continent

(D) migration of peoples to urban areas

(E) increase in the size of farm families in the countryside

Your Answer _____

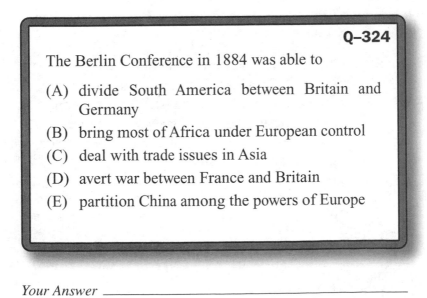

Q–324

The Berlin Conference in 1884 was able to

(A) divide South America between Britain and Germany

(B) bring most of Africa under European control

(C) deal with trade issues in Asia

(D) avert war between France and Britain

(E) partition China among the powers of Europe

Your Answer _____

Correct Answers

A–323

(D) Prior to the Industrial Revolution, people lived mostly in the rural areas and were involved in agriculture. The creation of factory jobs in cities drew the rural poor to cities where they could work. During the nineteenth century, millions of people moved from the country-side into the cities. They could find work but had to live in cramped and often unhealthy apartments. The streets were open sewers, and facilities were very primitive. In some areas, it is likely that more than 100 people shared a single toilet.

A–324

(B) The late 1800s were sometimes called the Scramble for Africa. New powers such as Germany and Italy wanted empires like France and Britain. Germany invited the nations to meet in Berlin to divide up the African continent and avoid imperial conflict among the European powers. All of Africa, except for Ethiopia and Liberia, was taken over by European powers.

Questions

Q–325

The great breakthrough in understanding disease transmission came with

(A) successful inoculations against polio

(B) Curie's experiments with radiation

(C) private rooms in hospitals

(D) confirmation of the miasmatic theory

(E) Pasteur's germ theory in the 1850s

Your Answer _____

Q–326

Early mass transportation in nineteenth-century cities consisted of

(A) steam-powered trains to move people

(B) buses powered by coal

(C) electric trains to move commuters

(D) horse-drawn streetcars

(E) subway systems under the streets

Your Answer _____

Correct Answers

A–325

(E) Medical knowledge of disease and how it spread was limited in the early nineteenth century. The miasmatic theory suggested that people breathed bad odors and became ill afterward. While studying brewing techniques, Louis Pasteur discovered living organisms that were part of the process. The connection between germs and disease led to new ways to avoid contamination and stay healthier. New laws to improve public sanitation led to fewer deaths from communicable diseases.

A–326

(D) Streets in cities were often muddy and filthy in the nineteenth century. As cities began to improve roads, wood and brick were used to provide a smoother surface for people to travel on. Around 1870, cities allowed private companies to lay rails so that horse-drawn streetcars could travel on major urban arteries. These cars would travel slowly down the street and people could hop on and off them, depending on where they were going. Fares were pennies per person.

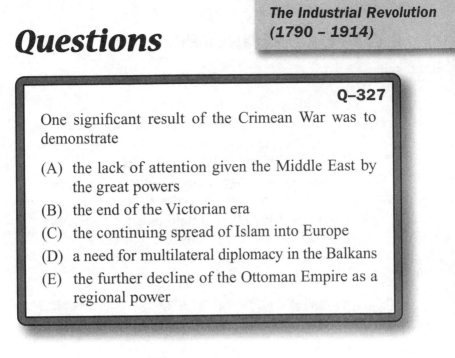

Q–327

One significant result of the Crimean War was to demonstrate

(A) the lack of attention given the Middle East by the great powers

(B) the end of the Victorian era

(C) the continuing spread of Islam into Europe

(D) a need for multilateral diplomacy in the Balkans

(E) the further decline of the Ottoman Empire as a regional power

Your Answer _____

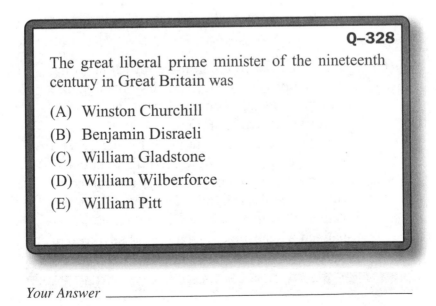

Q–328

The great liberal prime minister of the nineteenth century in Great Britain was

(A) Winston Churchill

(B) Benjamin Disraeli

(C) William Gladstone

(D) William Wilberforce

(E) William Pitt

Your Answer _____

Correct Answers

A–327

(E) The so-called Eastern Question was a way to describe the complex rivalry between the declining Ottoman Empire and Russia's desire for more territory in the Balkans. The British and French supported the Ottoman Empire against Russia to maintain balance and stability in the region. In any case, it showed that the Ottoman Empire was vulnerable to Russian expansion in the region.

A–328

(C) Gladstone was prime minister in 1868, during the time of Queen Victoria. His liberal legacy was considerable because he pushed for reforms in the British military and the legal system. He had a deep sympathy for the general public and put through many bills to alleviate poverty. He tried unsuccessfully to push home rule for the Irish through Parliament. Conservatives thwarted many of his bills, but he remained a determined debater and advocate of the people.

Q–329

Economic depressions in the nineteenth century were most often characterized by

(A) the creation of jobs in large industries

(B) severe deflation

(C) government intervention and price fixing

(D) inflationary forces in the marketplace

(E) rising confidence in the banking industry

Your Answer _____

Q–330

In the late nineteenth century, the upper middle class tended to consist of

(A) small-scale industrialists and professionals

(B) factory workers

(C) successful businesspeople and artisans

(D) skilled craftspeople and union leaders

(E) small-scale merchants and clergy

Your Answer _____

Correct Answers

A–329

(B)   Deflation means the lowering of prices. This happens in an economic depression because money is so scarce. People lose their jobs and consumer spending dries up. This causes prices to go down as demand decreases. Governments in the nineteenth century rarely intervened in the economy because they preferred to wait out the bad times. Price fixing was unheard of in the nineteenth century, and laissez-faire approaches were much more common.

A–330

(A)   The middle class of the nineteenth century was a diverse and multilevel hierarchy. Most middle-class people tended to be service providers or small merchants. The upper middle class consisted of more successful businesspeople and doctors or lawyers with modest practices. They earned a good living but were not particularly wealthy. The upper classes consisted of large-scale manufacturers or entrepreneurs.

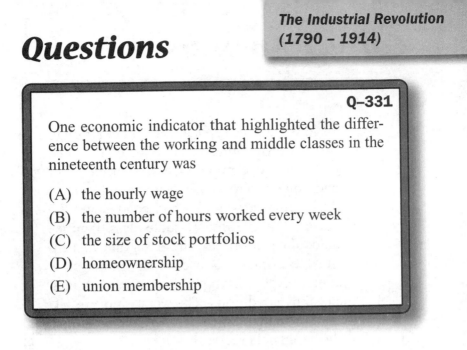

Q–331

One economic indicator that highlighted the difference between the working and middle classes in the nineteenth century was

(A) the hourly wage

(B) the number of hours worked every week

(C) the size of stock portfolios

(D) homeownership

(E) union membership

Your Answer _____

_____

Correct Answers

A–331

(D)   The lower classes typically could not afford to buy their own homes and often lived in rented apartments. The middle classes, on the other hand, could aspire to owning their own homes, which provided stability and equity over the course of a lifetime. Middle-class families could often afford to hire a servant to help with the cleaning and cooking. Lower-class families lived in cramped quarters and often in unhealthy conditions. The worst slums in cities were crammed with working-class families who could not escape their lot.

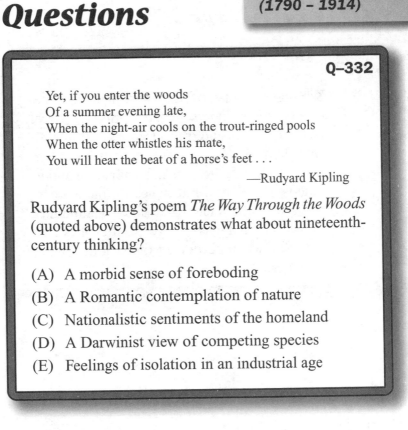

Q–332

Yet, if you enter the woods
Of a summer evening late,
When the night-air cools on the trout-ringed pools
When the otter whistles his mate,
You will hear the beat of a horse's feet . . .

—Rudyard Kipling

Rudyard Kipling's poem *The Way Through the Woods* (quoted above) demonstrates what about nineteenth-century thinking?

(A) A morbid sense of foreboding

(B) A Romantic contemplation of nature

(C) Nationalistic sentiments of the homeland

(D) A Darwinist view of competing species

(E) Feelings of isolation in an industrial age

Your Answer _____

_____

Correct Answers

A–332

(B)   Kipling was one of the most famous nineteenth-century poets in the world. He wrote on many topics and traveled widely. While his most famous poems were of British soldiering and animals, here he talks of nature and its sounds. It is somewhat typical of the Romantic style, which idealized and contemplated nature. The language is rich and evokes how one feels when observing the beauties of the natural world.

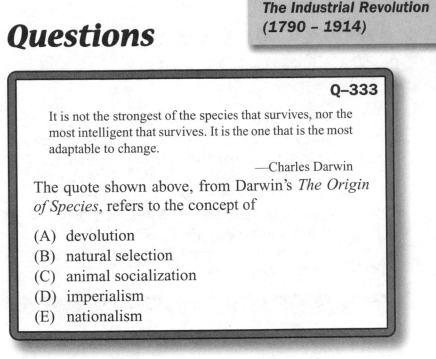

Q–333

It is not the strongest of the species that survives, nor the most intelligent that survives. It is the one that is the most adaptable to change.

—Charles Darwin

The quote shown above, from Darwin's *The Origin of Species*, refers to the concept of

(A) devolution
(B) natural selection
(C) animal socialization
(D) imperialism
(E) nationalism

Your Answer _____

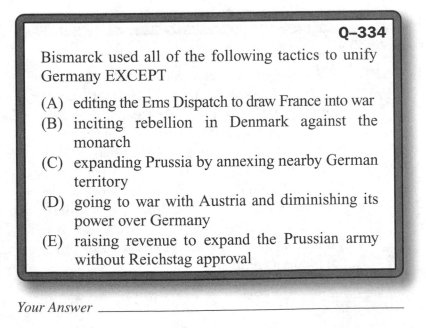

Q–334

Bismarck used all of the following tactics to unify Germany EXCEPT

(A) editing the Ems Dispatch to draw France into war
(B) inciting rebellion in Denmark against the monarch
(C) expanding Prussia by annexing nearby German territory
(D) going to war with Austria and diminishing its power over Germany
(E) raising revenue to expand the Prussian army without Reichstag approval

Your Answer _____

Correct Answers

A–333

(B) Darwin was a British naturalist who argued that all species, from birds to humans, change over time depending on their environment. The idea of natural selection was radical in the late nineteenth century and created much discussion and controversy. Some used Darwin's theories to explain why some nations or races were superior to others, but Darwin was concerned only with the zoological world.

A–334

(B) Bismarck was the chancellor of Prussia after 1860 who sought to unify all German people into a greater Germany. He created a foreign policy of *Realpolitik* and went to war regularly to unite German kingdoms together. He did this with wars against Denmark, Austria, and France. He built up the Prussian army and circumvented democratic control of the military. The final success came with a decisive defeat of France in 1871, when he declared the birth of modern Germany.

Q–335

The Realism movement in the arts in the nineteenth century sought to

(A) show the social and economic conditions that affected humans

(B) portray the lives of the upper classes

(C) romanticize the Industrial Revolution and its effects

(D) advance social harmony among the classes

(E) inspire nationalism among the masses

Your Answer _____

Q–336

What military capability was seen as the key to empire building in the late nineteenth century?

(A) Naval power

(B) Aviation technology

(C) Possessing large ground armies

(D) A modest merchant marine

(E) Intelligence services

Your Answer _____

Correct Answers

A–335

(A)   Realist artists were social observers who used their art to show how average people lived and to criticize the impact of industrialization on people. Both artists and writers tried to record what they actually saw and portray the dilemmas of workers in the industrial world.

A–336

(A)   After 1815, Great Britain became the world model for empire building. It created the greatest empire in human history in part because it had a well-organized and powerful navy. Other industrial nations, such as Germany, France, and the United States, also built navies that could patrol the oceans and protect their interests at home and abroad. Bigger and faster battleships became the pride of leading powers prior to 1914.

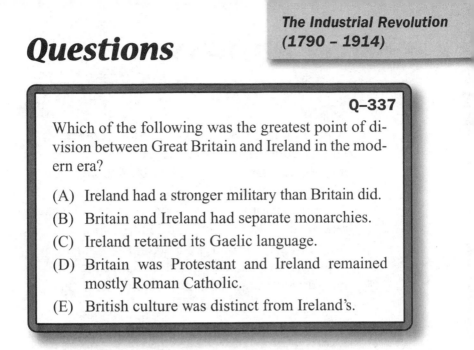

Q–337

Which of the following was the greatest point of division between Great Britain and Ireland in the modern era?

(A) Ireland had a stronger military than Britain did.

(B) Britain and Ireland had separate monarchies.

(C) Ireland retained its Gaelic language.

(D) Britain was Protestant and Ireland remained mostly Roman Catholic.

(E) British culture was distinct from Ireland's.

Your Answer _____

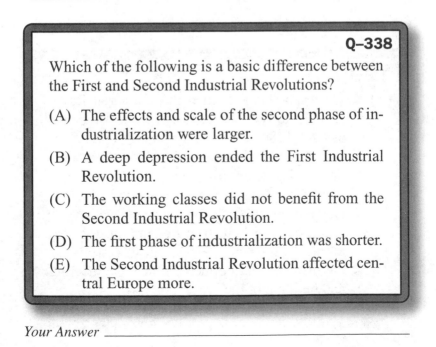

Q–338

Which of the following is a basic difference between the First and Second Industrial Revolutions?

(A) The effects and scale of the second phase of industrialization were larger.

(B) A deep depression ended the First Industrial Revolution.

(C) The working classes did not benefit from the Second Industrial Revolution.

(D) The first phase of industrialization was shorter.

(E) The Second Industrial Revolution affected central Europe more.

Your Answer _____

Correct Answers

A–337

(D) Britain and Ireland have had contentious relations going back to medieval times. In the modern era, British control of Ireland created many conflicts and eventually led to partial independence for the Irish. Religious issues have remained central to their difficult relationship over time. The British sponsored Protestant immigration to Ireland to counterbalance the cultural divide, but most Irish remained staunchly Catholic and saw the British as invaders.

A–338

(A) Historians have divided the Industrial Revolution into two phases. The first phase began around 1780 and went to about 1870. This initial burst of industrial development was defined by steam power and the expansion of factory manufacturing. The second phase is dated from 1870 to the dawn of World War I. The Second Industrial Revolution was also known as the Age of Steel because steel was the material that defined the new engineering and building of the era.

Q–339

Which of the following conflicts tested the alliances of the Concert of Europe?

(A) The Mexican War of 1846

(B) The Franco-Prussian War of 1871

(C) The Irish Rebellion of 1848

(D) The Crimean War of 1853

(E) The Opium War of 1844

Your Answer _____

Q–340

The term *Luddite* refers to which of the following nineteenth-century groups?

(A) Agents who infiltrated union movements

(B) Loyalists who defended monarchy

(C) People who opposed the mechanization of industry

(D) Followers of Marx who believed in a workers' utopia

(E) Middle-class factory workers

Your Answer _____

Correct Answers

A–339

(D) The Crimean War was the most destabilizing European conflict of the mid-nineteenth century. It challenged the alliances that had been created after the defeat of Napoleon in 1814. The Concert of Europe set up Austria, Britain, Prussia, and Russia as guarantors of the peace. When tensions over eastern Europe brought Russia into conflict with Britain and France, the old alliances were broken.

A–340

(C) In the early nineteenth century, some textile workers felt threatened by the new machines that made fabric. These people had previously worked in their own homes with looms. The new machines were transforming manufacturing, and this was frightening to the artisans who had worked with their hands prior to industrialization. Luddites sometimes banded together to destroy machinery that they saw threatening their livelihood.

Questions

Q–341

European military expeditions during the so-called Scramble for Africa were marked by

(A) mixed success because natives fought back in numerous parts of the continent

(B) complete domination over the continent within ten years

(C) German stealing of colonies from the Dutch

(D) unsuccessful searches for precious metals

(E) few Protestant missions being established

Your Answer _____

_____

Q–342

In the nineteenth century, Russia was remarkable for its

(A) dynamic political leadership

(B) robust steel industry that bypassed the steel industry in England

(C) democratic reforms that gave the vote to all men

(D) lack of a middle class

(E) openness to modern ideas from the West

Your Answer _____

_____

Correct Answers

A–341

(A) European military ventures in Africa during the late nineteenth century were ad hoc and sometimes unsuccessful. Natives were sometimes victorious and other times led resistance movements for decades against the Europeans. While the Europeans eventually colonized many parts of the continent, there were continuing frustrations with native resistance.

A–342

(D) Russia attempted some reforms in the nineteenth century but still lagged behind the West in giving rights to its people. The Romanov tsars tended to be conservative and heavy-handed in dealing with dissent. All reforms were top-down, and the large peasant class lived in poverty. There was almost no merchant middle class to give stability to the nation.

Questions

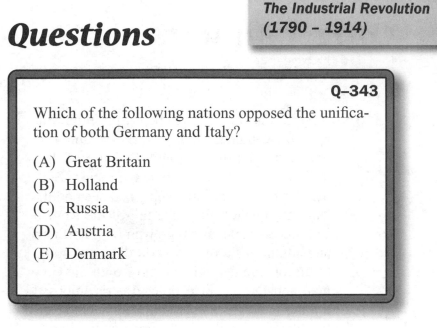

Q–343

Which of the following nations opposed the unification of both Germany and Italy?

(A) Great Britain

(B) Holland

(C) Russia

(D) Austria

(E) Denmark

Your Answer _____

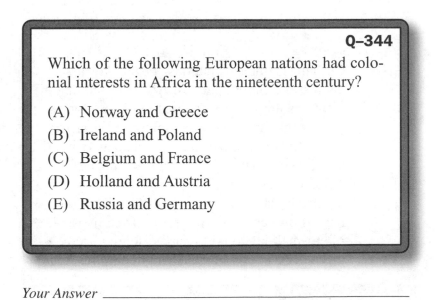

Q–344

Which of the following European nations had colonial interests in Africa in the nineteenth century?

(A) Norway and Greece

(B) Ireland and Poland

(C) Belgium and France

(D) Holland and Austria

(E) Russia and Germany

Your Answer _____

Correct Answers

A–343

(D) Austria was the dominant power in central Europe for centuries. It had territorial interests both to the north and south. Because of this, it did not want a rival state in the region. Both the German and Italian people had been politically fragmented since the fall of the Roman Empire. As nationalism grew in both northern and southern Europe, Austria did all it could to discourage the unification of both the German and the Italian people. Austria imposed treaties and agreements in the nineteenth century that tried to thwart the creation of either a modern Germany or Italy.

A–344

(C) Certain European nations began to assert claims to different parts of Africa in the nineteenth century. The early explorer nations such as Portugal and Spain had interests in Africa, but it was the stronger nations, such as Britain and France, that claimed huge sections of the African continent and attempted to colonize them. The latest colonizer was Germany, who helped broker the partition of Africa in 1884. Even small kingdoms such as Belgium took a piece of Africa and created small empires.

Questions

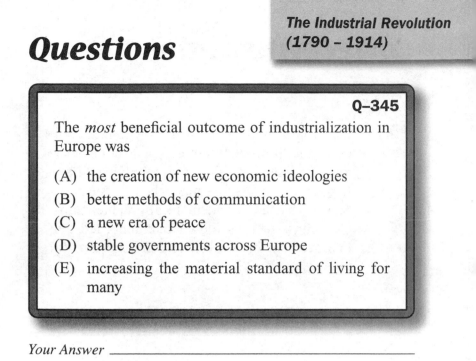

Q–345

The *most* beneficial outcome of industrialization in Europe was

(A) the creation of new economic ideologies

(B) better methods of communication

(C) a new era of peace

(D) stable governments across Europe

(E) increasing the material standard of living for many

Your Answer _____

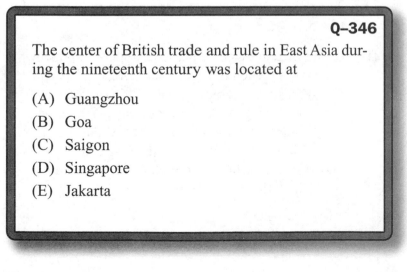

Q–346

The center of British trade and rule in East Asia during the nineteenth century was located at

(A) Guangzhou

(B) Goa

(C) Saigon

(D) Singapore

(E) Jakarta

Your Answer _____

Correct Answers

A–345

(E) Industrialization had many outcomes, but over time, it produced more goods at cheaper rates for many. Middle-class people could afford new products that made their lives easier. Travel was faster and more affordable. Simple things, such as indoor plumbing, led the improvement in comfort and the standard of living.

A–346

(D) The British made impressive imperial gains in East Asia when they took territories in Malaya and Australia. Trading with China required a major port at an Asian crossroads. Singapore is a small island at the tip of the Malay Peninsula; it is well located with a very good harbor. British and Chinese merchants soon made it into a vital center of world trade.

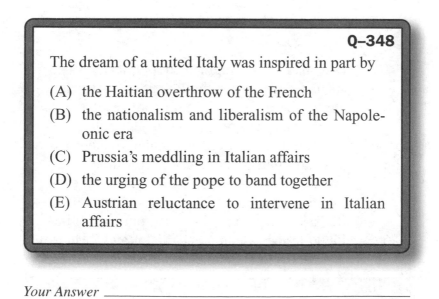

Q–347

All of the following were advancements in shipbuilding in the nineteenth century EXCEPT

(A) steel hulls

(B) propellers for propulsion

(C) diesel engines

(D) coal-fueled steam engines

(E) larger tonnage per ship

Your Answer _____

_____

Q–348

The dream of a united Italy was inspired in part by

(A) the Haitian overthrow of the French

(B) the nationalism and liberalism of the Napoleonic era

(C) Prussia's meddling in Italian affairs

(D) the urging of the pope to band together

(E) Austrian reluctance to intervene in Italian affairs

Your Answer _____

_____

Correct Answers

A–347

(C)   Ships became stronger, heavier, and faster in the 1800s. First wood was replaced with iron, and then steel became the main material for shipbuilding. Paddle wheels were exchanged for propellers, which were more efficient and speedier. The change from wind power to steam power made ships more maneuverable and able to sail in any direction.

A–348

(B)   Italy had been fragmented politically since ancient times. After the Renaissance, foreign powers became more and more involved in dominating parts of the Italian peninsula. Austria and France were particularly interested in controlling parts of southern Europe. The French Revolution inspired many Europeans to consider their national and cultural roots. Italians struggled against Austrian control but found leaders, such as Garibaldi and Cavour, to lead them.

Q–349

Which of the following show Italian *Realpolitik* during unification in the 1860s?

(A) The use of Swiss mercenaries against the French

(B) Pursuing free trade with Greece

(C) Crowning the king of Naples as overall monarch

(D) Negotiating the Treaty of Paris to settle a dispute with Prussia

(E) An alliance with Napoleon III against Austria

Your Answer _____

_____

Q–350

Democratic liberalism in Europe was most evident in which of the following two nations prior to 1910?

(A) Germany and Denmark

(B) France and Britain

(C) Italy and France

(D) Britain and Austria

(E) Russia and Germany

Your Answer _____

_____

Correct Answers

A–349

(E)   Many Italians were inspired to unify their country, but they needed an ally against Austria, which opposed unification. France agreed to help Italian nationalists in exchange for other territorial gains in southern Europe. Cavour arranged the political alliance and lived to see the birth of modern Italy in 1861.

A–350

(B)   Liberal reforms, which gave more political power to average people, took root in France and Britain after the Age of Revolutions. Suffrage and labor reform made the most progress in Britain and France, while other nations clung to conservative monarchies that opposed liberal changes. Russia was the least progressive, while Germany and Italy made modest progress prior to 1910.

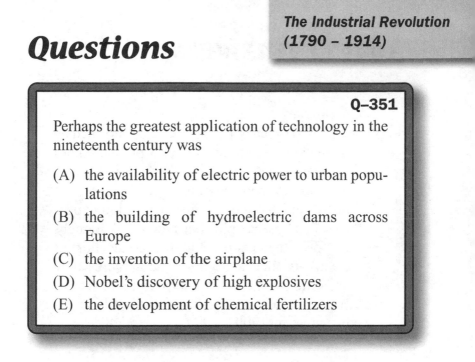

Q–351

Perhaps the greatest application of technology in the nineteenth century was

(A) the availability of electric power to urban populations

(B) the building of hydroelectric dams across Europe

(C) the invention of the airplane

(D) Nobel's discovery of high explosives

(E) the development of chemical fertilizers

Your Answer _____

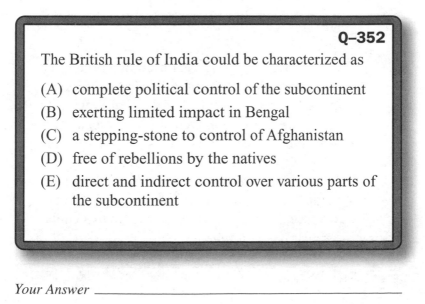

Q–352

The British rule of India could be characterized as

(A) complete political control of the subcontinent

(B) exerting limited impact in Bengal

(C) a stepping-stone to control of Afghanistan

(D) free of rebellions by the natives

(E) direct and indirect control over various parts of the subcontinent

Your Answer _____

Correct Answers

A–351

(A)   The lives of many people were transformed by the generation of electricity to private homes in the nineteenth century. Electricity was most common in the cities and spread much later to the countryside. At first it was too expensive for most people, but new breakthroughs in power generation and the conduction of electricity allowed homes to be lit more safely and efficiently. Electric transportation, such as subways and streetcars, appeared in large urban areas by 1900.

A–352

(E)   British rule of India was a complex tapestry of direct rule and some alliances with Indian princes. Britain connected the region with its railroads and established its educational system in many parts of South Asia. Different arrangements were made with Indian rulers that created indirect protectorates over many subregions. The crown appointed a single British overseer, called the viceroy, who managed the vast British holdings.

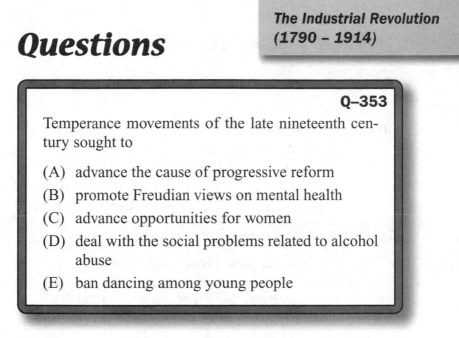

Q–353

Temperance movements of the late nineteenth century sought to

(A) advance the cause of progressive reform

(B) promote Freudian views on mental health

(C) advance opportunities for women

(D) deal with the social problems related to alcohol abuse

(E) ban dancing among young people

Your Answer _____

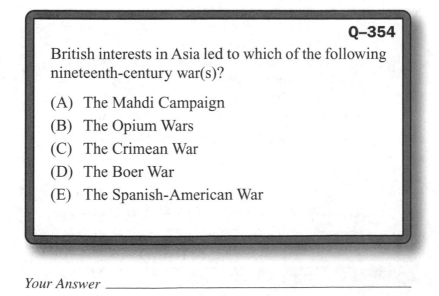

Q–354

British interests in Asia led to which of the following nineteenth-century war(s)?

(A) The Mahdi Campaign

(B) The Opium Wars

(C) The Crimean War

(D) The Boer War

(E) The Spanish-American War

Your Answer _____

Correct Answers

A–353

(D) Reform movements were part of the political landscape of the late nineteenth century. As urban populations grew, social outlets were important to many city dwellers. Drinking wine and beer became a popular mode of socializing, and the price of cheap liquor also declined, making alcohol more available. Church organizations preached against the evils of too much drink, but popular demand for wine, beer, and other types of liquor rose dramatically in the late 1800s. Alcoholism rates rose, and temperance was largely a failed movement in Europe.

A–354

(B) Britain encouraged maritime trade throughout the world, and privateers began doing business in China in the eighteenth century. Although the Chinese resisted the intrusion of westerners, the Qing dynasty was weakening and foreigners took advantage of this reality. When the opium trade became a source of friction, two wars broke out that gave the British an excuse to quickly defeat the Chinese. This defeat led to further trading privileges for Britain and other foreign nations in the Far East.

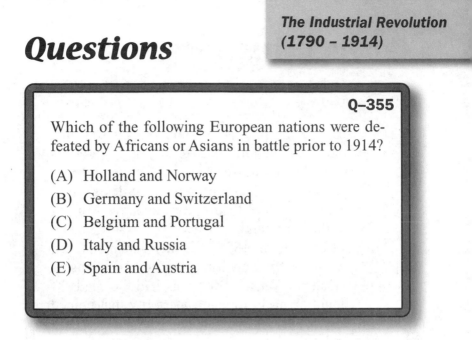

Q–355

Which of the following European nations were defeated by Africans or Asians in battle prior to 1914?

(A) Holland and Norway

(B) Germany and Switzerland

(C) Belgium and Portugal

(D) Italy and Russia

(E) Spain and Austria

Your Answer _____

_____

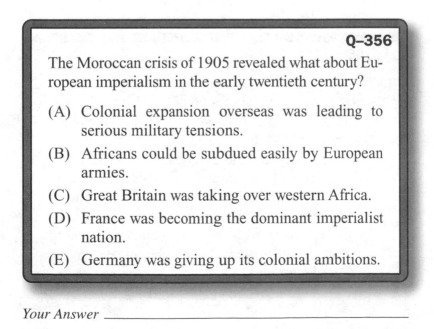

Q–356

The Moroccan crisis of 1905 revealed what about European imperialism in the early twentieth century?

(A) Colonial expansion overseas was leading to serious military tensions.

(B) Africans could be subdued easily by European armies.

(C) Great Britain was taking over western Africa.

(D) France was becoming the dominant imperialist nation.

(E) Germany was giving up its colonial ambitions.

Your Answer _____

_____

Correct Answers

A–355

(D) Part of the premise of imperialism was that European culture and technology were superior to nonwestern ones. This began to be refuted as African and Asian peoples showed they could defeat Europeans in battle, starting in the nineteenth century. Italy was defeated by Ethiopia in 1898, and then Japan shocked the world by defeating Russia in the Russo-Japanese War in 1905. This laid the seeds of doubt about European superiority that helped foster later nationalist movements in Africa and Asia.

A–356

(A) After 1895, European nations began to challenge one another for control of parts of Africa and Asia. The Russians and British squabbled over the Middle East, while Germany and France had to settle differences in northwestern Africa. Colonial boundaries had been vaguely set in the 1800s, but as the twentieth century dawned, some of these boundaries were contested. None of these diplomatic crises led to war, but they showed that imperial rivalry was growing prior to 1914.

Q–357

The term *belle époque* refers to which of the following eras in European history?

(A) The period of tensions before the Crimean War

(B) The early Victorian era

(C) The decades prior to 1914

(D) The pre-Napoleonic period

(E) The interwar period

Your Answer _____

Q–358

What role did Victorian society suggest for women?

(A) Head of the household who disciplined the children

(B) Moral guardians for the husband and children

(C) Political activist

(D) Equal partners in business ventures

(E) Leaders in educational management

Your Answer _____

Correct Answers

A–357

(C) Different eras have been named according to the dynamics of the times. The *belle époque* is a French name for the era just prior to World War I. It celebrates the fashion and culture of the period when the privileged wore colorful fashions and society seemed to be progressing in impressive ways. Many consider it the zenith of European power in the world. Technology was advancing in extraordinary ways; the telephone and airplane were invented and developed. Terms that demark periods in history are varied and often overlap. The Victorian and Edwardian periods in British history coincide with the belle époque in western Europe.

A–358

(B) Historians have continued to debate the gender roles that Victorian society embodied. Women were expected to remain at home as caretakers and moral examples for both their children and their husbands. Men ventured out into the world; women were to keep the home a kind of sanctuary to which their husbands could return. There has been debate about the pedestal that women were placed on. Some suggest they were given a narrow yet crucial function for stabilizing the life of a family. Few women could aspire to professional lives, but this era saw the first female doctors and lawyers break into the workforce.

Q–359

Which of the following was part of the classical liberal agenda?

(A) Constitutional government

(B) Promoting education and literacy

(C) Expansion of suffrage

(D) Guarantees of basic human rights

(E) All of the above

Your Answer _____

_____

Q–360

To mollify the workers of Germany, Bismarck initiated a policy known as

(A) republican reform

(B) middle-class relief

(C) Marxist compromise

(D) state socialism

(E) conservative progress

Your Answer _____

_____

Correct Answers

A–359

(E) The nineteenth century saw the creation of the classical liberal agenda. Those who believed in progressive change saw the inequities and injustices of the political status quo and sought to change it. The battle to abolish slavery took place in the 1800s, and women also began to campaign for their own rights. The key political right was to be able to vote. More and more men were given the right of suffrage; ultimately property qualifications were completely eliminated.

A–360

(D) Bismarck was the great architect of modern Germany after 1871. He was a conservative but had to deal with the socialist agenda of the Social Democratic Party (SPD). Bismarck sought to marginalize the SPD, but it was growing more powerful as a political party. To placate its members, he initiated the first welfare program in European history, which gave workers retirement benefits and unemployment pay during layoffs.

Q–361

Even after the creation of the dual monarchy in 1867, Austria continued to experience

(A) ethnic solidarity

(B) Slavic domination of the Imperial Parliament

(C) political fragmentation along nationalistic and cultural lines

(D) socialist challenges to traditional authority

(E) an economic malaise

Your Answer _____

Q–362

Violent radicals who believed in no governmental power or regulations were called

(A) anarchists

(B) plebeians

(C) progressives

(D) fascists

(E) moderates

Your Answer _____

Correct Answers

A–361

(C)   The Hungarians had won some concessions as the most aggressive non-German minority within the Austrian Empire. They sought to marginalize other Slavic minorities who competed with them for political influence. Over time, Poles, Czechs, and other groups were given some political seats in the Imperial Parliament in exchange for their loyalty to the dynasty. These reforms were opposed by the Germanic elites, and the political system did not function well as the twentieth century dawned.

A–362

(A)   Anarchism is a belief in individuality that denies the right of any authority to have power over people. Thus, anarchists do not believe in governments or politics. They assert that ultimate freedom is found in a world without rules or laws. They do not have a well-developed ideology because they believe in unrestricted freedom. After the failure of some nineteenth-century revolutions, some frustrated radicals resorted to individual terrorism and called themselves anarchists. They believed that any disruption of the state was necessary, and they used violence to achieve their goals.

Questions

Q–363

The application of Darwin's zoological theories to the world of politics became known as

(A) cultural Darwinism

(B) the law of the masses

(C) political selection

(D) survival of the inept

(E) social Darwinism

Your Answer _____

Q–364

Which of the following is the additional dimension suggested by Einstein's new theory of relativity?

(A) Depth in perspective

(B) Linear distance

(C) Space-time

(D) Measured curvature

(E) Atomic mass

Your Answer _____

Correct Answers

A–363

(E) *The Origin of Species* by Charles Darwin in 1859 created a stir because of his observations about the animal world. His belief that species adapted to their environment and competed with one another was a new view of nature. Some thinkers saw parallels with the political world, in which competition yielded winners and losers. Others used Darwin's ideas to explain why some nations seemed dominant over others. Some Europeans suggested that their domination over other parts of the world proved that races and peoples fought and competed with each other just as animals do in nature. These ideas became known as social Darwinism.

A–364

(C) Albert Einstein was the great physicist who transformed the human view of the universe. He believed that time and space were not absolute but instead relative. He added a fourth dimension to our three-dimensional view of the universe. This fourth dimension was space-time. He suggested that in the presence of a massive object, space and time would curve.

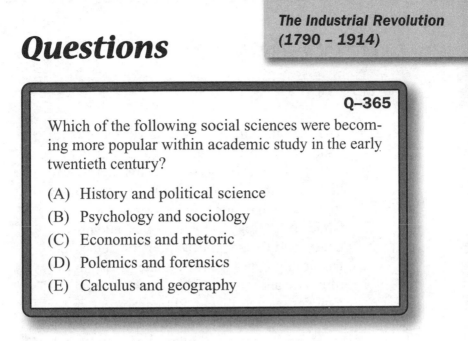

Q–365

Which of the following social sciences were becoming more popular within academic study in the early twentieth century?

(A) History and political science

(B) Psychology and sociology

(C) Economics and rhetoric

(D) Polemics and forensics

(E) Calculus and geography

Your Answer _____

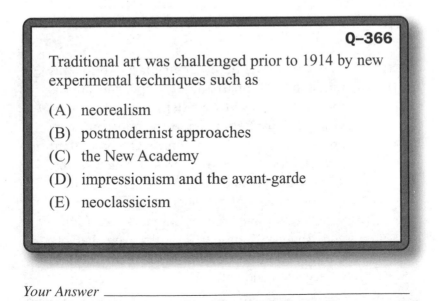

Q–366

Traditional art was challenged prior to 1914 by new experimental techniques such as

(A) neorealism

(B) postmodernist approaches

(C) the New Academy

(D) impressionism and the avant-garde

(E) neoclassicism

Your Answer _____

Correct Answers

A–365

(B) The Enlightenment encouraged the examination of both the natural world and human activity. New schools of investigation looked at how humans behave and live. Sociology looks at social cause and effect in the world, while psychology is a field that attempts to understand deeper motivations of human behavior. Sigmund Freud was the great pioneer of psychoanalysis, which theorized about human desires and fears and their impact on the individual. The fields of anthropology, political science, and criminology also were founded in the late nineteenth and early twentieth centuries.

A–366

(D) The early twentieth-century art world was mired in traditionalism in Europe, and various movements arose to challenge the orthodoxy. Groups of painters began to venture into new areas and created great controversy with their nontraditional ways of expressing themselves. The use of light and visible brushstrokes yielded new schools of art, such as impressionism, which was pioneered by painters like Monet and Renoir. Their early works were harshly criticized, and it took years for their works to be accepted and valued.

Q–367

Which of the following changes in mass ethnic prejudice was observable in the late nineteenth century?

(A) Discrimination and prejudice were increasingly expressed in racial and political terms.

(B) Minorities were protected against discrimination by governments.

(C) Churches spoke out against racism.

(D) Constitutions were amended to prevent public and private racism.

(E) Ethnic groups avoided controversy to avoid attention.

Your Answer _____

Q–368

Which of the following was an aspect of nineteenth-century romanticism in Europe?

(A) The virtues of the hero-artist were extolled.

(B) Art was viewed as an illumination of the world within.

(C) The uniqueness of the individual was promoted.

(D) The emotional impact of art was emphasized.

(E) All of the above

Your Answer _____

Correct Answers

A–367

(A) Various European minority groups suffered discrimination throughout history. Gypsies, Jews, and Armenians are examples of ethnic minorities who struggled to deal with discrimination in the societies they lived in. New trends in thinking suggested that people could be categorized into racial groupings, and ethnic prejudice took on a new racial tone. Political parties were organized that created agendas against various minorities.

A–368

(E) Romanticism was a broad movement that affected many areas of the arts. Romantics included painters, composers, and writers in the nineteenth century. The movement was known for a more emotional style that appealed to the senses. It could combine with the growing nationalism of the era, and artists created music and literature that appealed to one's sense of patriotism. It broke from the more accepted neoclassicism and showed that artists need not be confined to traditional rules when creating their works.

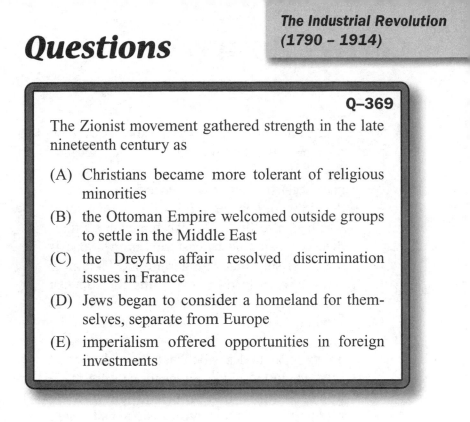

Q–369

The Zionist movement gathered strength in the late nineteenth century as

(A) Christians became more tolerant of religious minorities

(B) the Ottoman Empire welcomed outside groups to settle in the Middle East

(C) the Dreyfus affair resolved discrimination issues in France

(D) Jews began to consider a homeland for themselves, separate from Europe

(E) imperialism offered opportunities in foreign investments

Your Answer _____

_____

Correct Answers

A–369

(D) The Zionist movement was another expression of nineteenth-century nationalism. Because Jewish people were seen more in racial terms and because they experienced considerable discrimination in eastern Europe, a movement was begun to find a Jewish homeland. Prejudice was common in eastern Europe, so it is not surprising that Hungarian and Ukrainian Jews took the lead in advocating for a Jewish nation. Russian persecution of poor Jews had been going on for centuries. By the end of the nineteenth century, various books and pamphlets began to describe what a Jewish-Zionist state would look like. Suggestions were made to colonize part of Africa or to return to the Middle East, where Jewish history had begun in ancient times.

Questions

Which of the following revealed the political fragility of the Russian Empire by 1910?

(A) The collapse of old alliances with France and Italy

(B) War victories in Asia

(C) Popular revolts against the Russian police state

(D) Mass immigration to the Americas

(E) The success of Marxist revolutionaries

Your Answer _____

_____

Correct Answers

A–370

(C) Russia lost a humiliating war to Japan in 1905, and revolution was in the air. Many socialists and Marxists were arrested and imprisoned as a result. While some Russians emigrated to America, it was not a significant number given the nation's large population. In January 1905, a large demonstration took place outside the tsar's winter palace. Organized by discontented workers, the demonstrators sought to petition the monarch about the grievances of the poor in Russia. Palace guards opened fire and killed hundreds while dispersing the crowd. This event helped inspire further cooperation between urban workers and professionals who wanted to liberalize the government. No real success came of this, however, but it revealed the instability of Russia prior to 1914.

Q–371

Revolutionary socialism threatened which of the following classes in Europe prior to 1914?

(A) The middle-class intelligentsia

(B) Professional elites

(C) Urban workers

(D) Rural peasants

(E) Conservative aristocrats

Your Answer _____

Q–372

Migration out of Europe reached its apex in which of the following decades?

(A) 1870–1880

(B) 1900–1910

(C) 1890–1900

(D) 1910–1920

(E) 1860–1870

Your Answer _____

Correct Answers

A–371

(E) Socialism as a political movement gathered strength and support from various groups in Europe prior to 1914. There were still glaring contrasts between the rich and the poor. Socialism sought to bring government into the reform process and provide more advantages for the working classes. Support for these reforms came from various quarters, including liberals from the middle classes. The class that had the most to lose from the gains of socialism was the old landed elites. They feared the masses might rise up and take away some of their traditional privileges and power. They also objected to the international emphasis of the socialists, which contrasted with their conservative nationalism.

A–372

(B) A mass emigration out of Europe occurred after 1860, and this outflow of people reached its greatest point in the first decade of the twentieth century. More than 11 million people emigrated from Europe between 1900 and 1910. The most popular destinations were Canada and the United States, but many also immigrated to Brazil and Australia. Some were induced to leave because of poverty and famine, while others simply heard of better land opportunities elsewhere.

Q–373

Which of the following regions in Europe was the most politically unstable prior to 1914?

(A) Scandinavia

(B) The Low Countries

(C) The Balkans

(D) The Iberian peninsula

(E) The British Isles

Your Answer _____

Q–374

Which of the following nations had surpassed Great Britain in terms of industrial production by 1910?

(A) Austria and Russia

(B) Norway and Sweden

(C) Germany and the United States

(D) France and Holland

(E) Italy and Japan

Your Answer _____

Correct Answers

A–373

(C)　With the continuing waning of the Ottoman Empire, the southeastern part of Europe was being contested by other powerful empires. The Turks had been under attack since the mid-eighteenth century. Russia and Austria tried to expand at the expense of the Ottomans. In 1912–1913, two short wars were fought in the Balkans to rearrange the political map in that part of Europe. Large and small kingdoms were involved in deciding the fate of nations such as Albania and Macedonia. The settlements were unsatisfactory to nations such as Serbia and further worsened relations in the region.

A–374

(C)　After 1830, Great Britain was the great pioneer as an industrial nation. It created a worldwide empire and could manufacture many goods for sale around the world. With the unification of Germany in 1870, Britain had a new rival in terms of industrial capability, and Germany surpassed Britain in steel production by the beginning of the twentieth century. The United States, with its vast territory and resources, also had an industrial sector to rival that of Europe by 1910.

Questions

Q–375

Which of the following statements best expresses European motives for imperialism prior to 1914?

(A) World peace would be enhanced by overseas possessions.

(B) Imperialism would help spread democracy to the rest of the world.

(C) Europeans were altruistic and wanted to help other people.

(D) New living space was needed to relieve the growing homeless population.

(E) Colonies were an economic benefit to the mother country.

Your Answer _____

_____

Correct Answers

A–375

(E) There was more than one motivation for creating overseas colonies by Europeans between 1850 and 1910. Some wanted to spread Christianity and bring Western culture to so-called less civilized peoples. Governments were more interested in economic benefits, however, and overseas colonies were seen as new marketplaces to penetrate and sources of goods that could be sold worldwide. Tea grown in India was imported cheaply back to Europe, and cotton was made into cheap textiles in Britain for sale afterward.

STOP **Take Test-Readiness Quiz 3 on CD**
(to review questions 252–375)

Questions

Which of the following best describes the geopolitical situation prior to 1914 in Europe?

(A) Great Britain was in decline, and this decline inspired aggression in Central Europe.

(B) Russia and France were on the brink of war over the Balkans.

(C) War in Asia was draining the resources of some European powers.

(D) The rise of Germany and the decline of the Ottoman Empire were changing the power relationships within Europe.

(E) Revolts in Africa were causing the collapse of European imperialism.

Your Answer _____

Correct Answers

A–376

(D) After 1860, the Ottoman Empire was referred to as the sick man of Europe, meaning a once-mighty empire was in decline and causing a power vacuum in one part of the continent. At the same time, Germany had become the most powerful continental power, with a large, modern standing army. These two factors created specific regional tensions that would help bring war in 1914.

Q–377

A significant reason for the instability that led to World War I in 1914 was the rise of

(A) Spain as a military force in Europe

(B) Germany as a rival power to Great Britain in Europe

(C) Russia as a new European empire

(D) Great Britain as a military aggressor

(E) Italy as an imperial power

Your Answer _____

Q–378

Which of the following was the *immediate* cause of World War I (1914–1918)?

(A) A Serbian nationalist assassinated Archduke Franz Ferdinand.

(B) Local tensions in Russia escalated into war.

(C) A treaty between Russia and France angered Germany.

(D) A confrontation between France and Italy in Africa led to fighting.

(E) Germany invaded Belgium in an attempt to increase its territory.

Your Answer _____

Correct Answers

A–377

(B) New nations were created and rose in power after the old balance of power fashioned after the Napoleonic era was disrupted. After 1870, Germany built both a powerful industrial capability and an impressive land army. This led to competition between Germany and Great Britain, the established power in Europe. Britain's navy was a foil to Germany's land army. Germany also aspired to have a world-class navy and embarked on a plan to build many warships.

A–378

(A) World War I was initially started by an assassination in Sarajevo in 1914. A Serbian nationalist who wanted to incite his people to revolt against the Austrians shot the heir to the Austria-Hungarian throne. This led to a declaration of war on Serbia by Austria, which in turn led to other nations joining to help their allies. Immediate causes of war are differentiated from the long-term causes of war, which usually exist many years beforehand.

Questions

Q–379

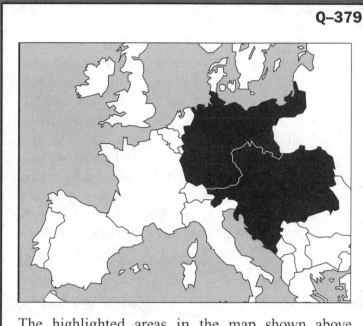

The highlighted areas in the map shown above represent the

(A) site of the Franco-Prussian War in 1870

(B) Scandinavian alliance after the Balkan crisis

(C) Rhineland Confederation of 1856

(D) Hanseatic League in the early modern period

(E) Austro-German alliance prior to World War I

Your Answer _____

_____

Correct Answers

A–379

(E) Prior to World War I, Europe was divided into two camps. The Germans and Austrians were allied in central Europe, while Russia and France were combined. Austria had difficulties dealing with the Slavic minorities in its empire and feared that Russia, as a Slav nation, would help its fellow Slavs. The Germans were keenly aware that they faced enemies on both sides of their country, so they prepared for the possibility of a two-front war. Germany had the best trained and largest reserve force in Europe, and it was confident that it could face both France and Russia successfully.

Questions

Q–380

Which of the following was NOT a long-term cause of the World War I?

(A) Imperialistic competition for foreign territories

(B) Defensive alliances between European powers

(C) Military buildup of navies and armies

(D) Socialistic influences on governments

(E) Preplanned war movements

Your Answer _____

_____

Q–381

Which of the following regions was NOT the site of military battles in World War I?

(A) The Atlantic Ocean

(B) Asia

(C) Africa

(D) South America

(E) Europe

Your Answer _____

_____

Correct Answers

A–380

(D) While socialism was making inroads in some nations, it did not create the atmosphere before 1914 that led to war. Powerful nations such as France, Britain, Germany, and Italy were building up their militaries in anticipation of a conflict. Generals created multiple war plans to be put into action should war come. Alliances were created that bound certain nations to one another should one of them be attacked. During the summer of 1914, these pieces played a role in turning a regional conflict in the Balkans into a global war.

A–381

(D) World War I was the largest war to take place in so many different parts of the globe. While the main battles took place in western and eastern Europe, there were also colonial battles taking place in the Middle East, Africa, and the Far East. Navies fought on the high seas, and new submarine technology meant that ships were vulnerable around the world. The North Atlantic was the scene of many attacks by German submarines on shipping headed for France and Britain. South America was the only region that did not see military action during World War I.

Questions

Q–382

The military situation during most of World War I can best be described as which of the following?

(A) Defensive tactics were useless against automatic weapons.

(B) Airplanes played a crucial role in winning battles.

(C) Brilliant generals commanded on both sides of the conflict.

(D) The Allies moved rapidly and won quick victories.

(E) Both sides experienced frustrating stalemate and high casualty rates.

Your Answer _____

Q–383

Which of the following military technologies made their debut in World War I?

(A) Battleships and automatic rifles

(B) Rockets and pistols

(C) Rifle grenades and steel helmets

(D) Tanks and airplanes

(E) Mobile cavalry and jeeps

Your Answer _____

Correct Answers

A–382

(E) World War I was a new kind of conflict with automatic weapons, such as the machine gun, which caused extraordinarily high death rates. Massive frontal assaults into rapidly firing guns led to many deaths but little military advantage. Defensive works were built so soldiers lived underground to protect them from artillery and bombings. The airplane was introduced as a weapon, but it had little impact on so vast a land war. Until the breakouts of 1918, there was a basic stalemate in which neither side could gain much territory from the other side.

A–383

(D) World War I saw the introduction of many new weapons. The airplane had been invented 10 years before the war began and was used during the war for reconnaissance and shooting down observation balloons. Tanks were a new machine to gain advantage in the trench warfare that characterized World War I. Flamethrowers could also be used in attacking the defensive works of the enemy. The use of portable bombs or grenades also was perfected in World War I. The most deadly weapon of the war was the machine gun, which was not a new technology because it was invented in the previous century.

Q–384

How did European nations pay for World War I while
the fighting was going on?

(A) Issuing national bonds

(B) Borrowing from Asian nations

(C) Cutting government spending

(D) Taxing the rich

(E) Raising poll fees

Your Answer _____

_____

Q–385

What was the political impact of World War I on
party politics in European nations in the beginning
of the war?

(A) Right-wing regimes often took over the governments.

(B) Coalition governments created instability.

(C) Socialists often attacked the decision to go to war.

(D) Parliaments were divided when it came to supporting the fighting.

(E) War patriotism subverted political differences.

Your Answer _____

_____

Correct Answers

A–384

(A) In both world wars, nations would appeal to the public to buy war bonds, which would be paid back after the war. This was a mechanism for short-term borrowing that allowed nations to buy the weapons and pay the soldiers. Bond issues were promoted by huge rallies in which famous people would travel across the nation, urging citizens to tighten their belts and lend their money to the cause. These were patriotic appeals that were mostly successful. Citizens lent millions of pounds, francs, and marks to their nations, believing that they were participating in the eventual victory of their respective countries.

A–385

(E) The mood in most nations as the war began in 1914 was optimism that the war would be short and victorious. Political parties that were critical of the government fell in line and supported the war effort. Socialists toned down their agendas and became partners in promoting the war goals of their nations. In France, parties pledged a sacred union as long as the war would last. All in all, the early phase of the war was one of general political unity in European nations.

Q–386

Which of the following best describes the situation of working women during World War I?

(A) Women took over many managerial positions.

(B) More jobs were available to women but at lower pay than that earned by men.

(C) Working conditions improved markedly for women.

(D) Wages rose and commodities became cheaper.

(E) Households received special allowances for food.

Your Answer _____

_____

Q–387

Which World War I weapon was banned after the war because of its horrible impact on the soldiers?

(A) High-powered rifles

(B) Bayonets

(C) Automatic machine guns

(D) Poison gas

(E) Booby traps

Your Answer _____

_____

Correct Answers

A–386

(B) After 1914, women did take many jobs that had once belonged to men now in uniform. World War I was a so-called total war, so governments called on their citizens to pitch in and sacrifice for the nation. Women did their part but were paid less than men. This allowed companies to benefit, and their profits increased as a result. Working conditions were often poor, and some women did protest and even strike to demand a safer work environment.

A–387

(D) World War I was the first testing ground for chemical weapons in world history. France first used tear gas during World War I, and later Germany tried phosgene, or mustard gas, against the Allies. Soon both sides were using this poison gas with mixed results. The gas would often wound instead of kill, but its effects were so gruesome that after the war the international community moved to ban its use in any future war. This was formalized in the 1920s when nations signed the Geneva Protocol banning gas and biological weapons. All the major powers agreed not to use chemical weapons in time of war.

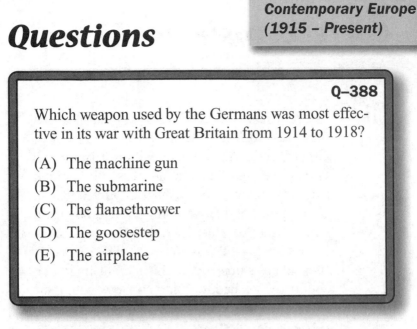

Q–388

Which weapon used by the Germans was most effective in its war with Great Britain from 1914 to 1918?

(A) The machine gun

(B) The submarine

(C) The flamethrower

(D) The goosestep

(E) The airplane

Your Answer _____

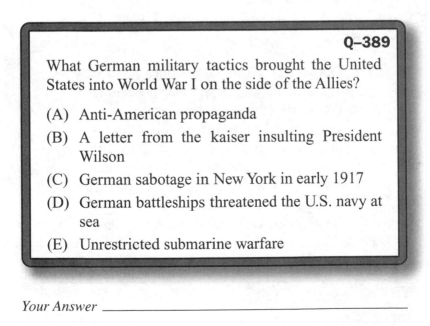

Q–389

What German military tactics brought the United States into World War I on the side of the Allies?

(A) Anti-American propaganda

(B) A letter from the kaiser insulting President Wilson

(C) German sabotage in New York in early 1917

(D) German battleships threatened the U.S. navy at sea

(E) Unrestricted submarine warfare

Your Answer _____

Correct Answers

A–388

(B)   The Germans built a fleet of submarines that they used to interrupt shipping in and out of Great Britain. As an island nation, Britain was vulnerable and had to aggressively defend shipping against the U-boat (*Unterseeboot*). Both France and Britain imported goods from North America and depended on an uninterrupted supply of war materiel. The Germans sunk many ships (up to 25 percent in 1917), and the Allies had to guard convoys with their surface navies.

A–389

(E)   Germany used its submarines to great effect against shipping in the North Atlantic. When the *Lusitania*, a civilian liner, was sunk in 1915, over 100 Americans died. Protests from the American government led to Germany's promise to curtail its submarine campaign. As the war went on, Germany resumed unrestricted submarine attacks on all ships headed for Britain. They gambled that Britain would conclude a peace agreement before the United States could enter the war.

Questions

Q–390

Which of the following treaties formalized the Russian exit from the war in 1917?

(A) Versailles

(B) Coblenz

(C) Paris

(D) Brest-Litovsk

(E) Konstance

Your Answer _____

Q–391

Which of the following European nations were members of the Big Four at the Versailles Peace Conference in 1919?

(A) Belgium, France, and Holland

(B) Norway, Switzerland, and Germany

(C) Spain, Great Britain, and Austria

(D) France, Great Britain, and Italy

(E) Italy, Poland, and Denmark

Your Answer _____

Correct Answers

A–390

(D) Russia suffered terrible casualties fighting Germany after 1914. As the war dragged on, Russian morale plummeted and starving Russian soldiers refused to fight. The tsar abdicated in early 1917 as the nation began to fall apart. A provisional government tried to continue the war effort, but the military could no longer function on the front. Radical socialists took over the government and promised the people food and peace. This new government settled quickly with the Germans and pulled out of the war. The treaty was signed at Brest-Litovsk in March 1918, ending war on the Eastern Front.

A–391

(D) Many nations and peoples sent delegates to the Peace Conference of 1919 to voice their opinions about the postwar order. All the major belligerents, winners and losers, had lost a lot in the war. The conference was mainly for the victors, and the heads of government of the four major Allied nations were de facto leaders in the process. The Big Four were the United States, Great Britain, France, and Italy. These leaders headed the committees that drew up the very long treaty that hoped to settle the war.

Questions

Q–392

We shall insist on the imposition of penalties on the authors of the abominable crimes committed during the war. Has anyone any question to ask in regard to this? If not, I would again remind you that every delegation should devote itself to the study of this first question, which has been made the subject of reports by eminent jurists, and of a report, which will be sent to you, entitled, "An Inquiry into the Criminal Responsibility of the Emperor William II."

—Georges Clemençeau, 1919

The statement shown above, by the president of France, has to do with which of the following political agendas after World War I?

(A) Finding war criminals who fought on either side

(B) Creating legal frameworks for surrender documents

(C) Granting self-determination to the Polish people

(D) Attempting to blame Germany for crimes during the war

(E) Studying the question of neutrality in future wars

Your Answer _____

_____

Correct Answers

A–392

(D) President Wilson of the United States suggested that the war end without a victor. The French, however, had a different agenda at the Peace Conference that took place outside Paris in 1919. France had experienced an incredible amount of devastation because the war was fought on its soil. The German attack had come across its borders, and millions of French soldiers died defending their nation. President Clemençeau was chosen to be the presiding officer of the Peace Conference, and he insisted that Germany pay for war damages and even accept guilt for starting the conflict. In the end, European revenge was more powerful than American largesse.

Q–393

In Russian history, the term *soviet* means which of the following?

(A) The Russian parliament

(B) A council of local workers

(C) A socialist party that took over the government

(D) The Red Army

(E) The Provisional Assembly

Your Answer _____

Q–394

The Bolshevik Revolution of 1917 succeeded because

(A) Lenin was arrested by the Mensheviks

(B) the military situation at the front started to improve for Russia

(C) the Allies were in support of the takeover

(D) it was supported by certain members of the aristocracy

(E) core revolutionaries were disciplined and opportunistic

Your Answer _____

Correct Answers

A–393

(B) After the attempted revolution in Russia in 1905, some workers began to form councils to discuss their grievances. The socialist radicals saw this as a grassroots, local practicing of democracy. It also gave the workers an outlet for their energies and prepared some for the more successful revolution later on. The creation of the soviets was also a practical way to put Marxist theory into practice.

A–394

(E) The political situation in Russia in 1917 was very chaotic. The provisional government that was in charge after the tsar abdicated insisted on staying in the war. The Bolsheviks were a minority in the government, but they were determined to take charge of the situation. As the war bled the military and the government, the Bolsheviks prepared for the right time to strike. While they were unsuccessful in July, by October certain Bolsheviks believed the time was right. Under the leadership of V. I. Lenin, they took over the government in a remarkably short time. Discontented soldiers and sailors, as well as workers who were fed up with the provisional regime, aided the Bolsheviks.

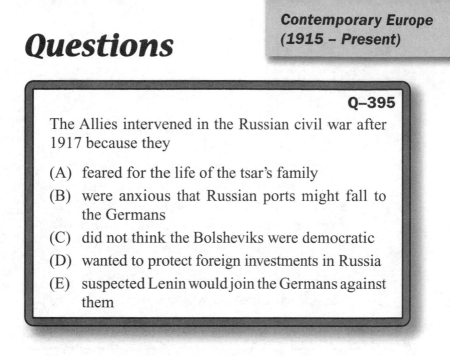

Q–395

The Allies intervened in the Russian civil war after 1917 because they

(A) feared for the life of the tsar's family

(B) were anxious that Russian ports might fall to the Germans

(C) did not think the Bolsheviks were democratic

(D) wanted to protect foreign investments in Russia

(E) suspected Lenin would join the Germans against them

Your Answer _____

_____

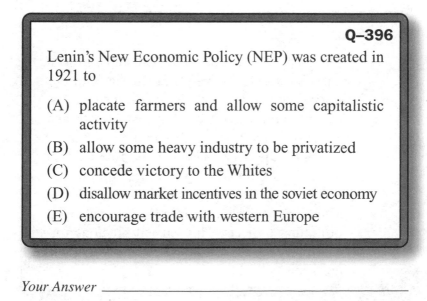

Q–396

Lenin's New Economic Policy (NEP) was created in 1921 to

(A) placate farmers and allow some capitalistic activity

(B) allow some heavy industry to be privatized

(C) concede victory to the Whites

(D) disallow market incentives in the soviet economy

(E) encourage trade with western Europe

Your Answer _____

_____

Correct Answers

A–395

(B) Allied intervention in the Russian civil war of 1918 has been hotly debated by historians. As the first Marxist state in history, Russia had taken a new path. Many in the West feared the spreading of the revolution to other countries. The war situation was still fluid, and Russian ports needed protection from German control. The intervention had little impact on the outcome of the civil war, but it did lead to suspicion that the West was antagonistic toward Bolshevism.

A–396

(A) The civil war was won by the Bolsheviks but at a terrible cost to the people of Russia. Millions starved and the economy was in shambles. Lenin compromised his Marxist beliefs and allowed farmers some freedom to sell their goods on the open market. It was hoped that this would stimulate agricultural production and the mass famine would be lessened. Lenin also allowed foreigners to come in and invest in mining projects. This earned precious foreign currency for the government, which had no credit.

Questions

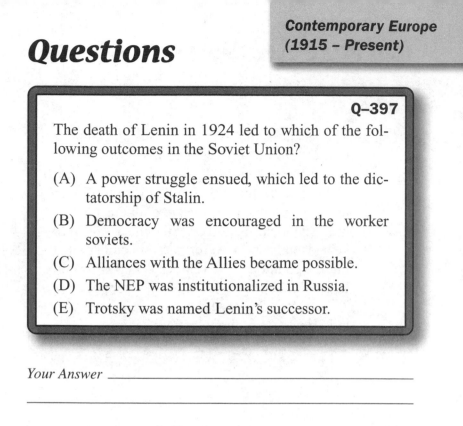

Q–397

The death of Lenin in 1924 led to which of the following outcomes in the Soviet Union?

(A) A power struggle ensued, which led to the dictatorship of Stalin.

(B) Democracy was encouraged in the worker soviets.

(C) Alliances with the Allies became possible.

(D) The NEP was institutionalized in Russia.

(E) Trotsky was named Lenin's successor.

Your Answer _____

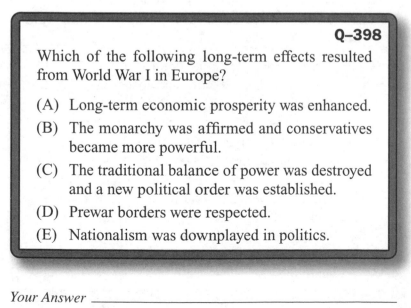

Q–398

Which of the following long-term effects resulted from World War I in Europe?

(A) Long-term economic prosperity was enhanced.

(B) The monarchy was affirmed and conservatives became more powerful.

(C) The traditional balance of power was destroyed and a new political order was established.

(D) Prewar borders were respected.

(E) Nationalism was downplayed in politics.

Your Answer _____

Correct Answers

A–397

(A)   The sickness and eventual death of Lenin allowed Stalin to consolidate his power in the young Soviet Union. In the role of party general secretary, Stalin was able to control high-level appointments in the government. One by one, Stalin eliminated or exiled his rivals until he had total control of the party machinery that ran the country. A vast police state was established that ruthlessly eliminated all opposition. This created the largest and longest-lasting totalitarian state in the twentieth century.

A–398

(C)   World War I brought significant changes to Europe. It bled victors and losers alike. Both Britain and France borrowed heavily to win the war and never regained the power they had before it. Germany was punished and forced to pay reparations. Little was left of the old order because principal monarchies collapsed at the end of the war. The war created a spirit of pessimism. Countries counted their casualties in the millions, which left the political leadership timid and afraid to make a mistake that might lead to another war.

Q–399

The main liberal agenda of the Versailles Peace Conference was

(A) punishing Germany for starting the war
(B) marginalizing Russia for leaving the war so early
(C) land reform for all of Europe
(D) self-determination for peoples around the world
(E) a new domination of Europe by Italy

Your Answer _____

Q–400

What was the League of Nations supposed to achieve for Europe?

(A) Enhanced economic relations
(B) Continental control by France
(C) Tax revenue for Switzerland
(D) An economic boost for Germany and Russia
(E) Collective security for peace-loving nations

Your Answer _____

Correct Answers

A–399

(D) President Wilson of the United States was a key figure at the peace conference in 1919. He and other liberals hoped for a just peace that all nations could live with and would guarantee that war would not break out again. As in the nineteenth century, liberals believed that the common people deserved more power and that democracy was the answer. While Britain, France, and the United States were all democracies, they did not always agree on granting power to all people. Britain and France, after all, had vast empires of subject peoples. In the end, the peace conference was a long series of deals and compromises that the major powers agreed to.

A–400

(E) The final mechanism of the Versailles peace treaty was the League of Nations, which was supposed to help keep the peace. Collective security was a new approach to avoiding war and held that many nations could discourage belligerent action by any nation if they reacted together. If Nation A invaded a neighbor, then the international community would join together and denounce the offending nation. Economic and even military action could result to stop a small crisis from becoming a large one. This strategy was designed to avoid a repeat of the events such as those following the assassination in Sarajevo in 1914.

Questions

Q–401

Which of the following was NOT a cause of the Russian Revolution of 1917?

(A) A long war had exhausted the military.

(B) The death of the tsar weakened the government.

(C) Germans helped Lenin return to Russia.

(D) Charismatic leadership was spurred on by the radical revolutionaries.

(E) Widespread famine destabilized the nation.

Your Answer _____

_____

Q–402

Britain maintained a protectorate in Egypt primarily to

(A) oversee the gold mines there

(B) guard the Suez Canal

(C) steal antiquities for the British Museum

(D) sponsor democracy in the region

(E) thwart Spanish interest in the area

Your Answer _____

_____

Correct Answers

A–401

(B) World War I brought about the downfall of the tsarist regime in Russia. Losses on the battle-field left the army in shambles, and famine was common across the nation. The tsar abdicated and turned the government over to moderate socialists, who took charge briefly. The radical Bolsheviks then took over and placed the tsar under house arrest. To end the monarchy, the entire royal family was eventually killed.

A–402

(B) Great Britain's twentieth-century empire spanned the globe, and India was regarded as the "jewel in the crown." The key shipping route to India was via the Suez Canal in Egypt. This shortcut through the Mediterranean was vitally important to the British crown, so it maintained a presence in North Africa. The French also were involved in overseeing the canal because they had interests in Southeast Asia.

Questions

Q–403

Which of the following is NOT a reason for the Allied victory in 1918?

(A) Mutinies took place in the German navy.

(B) Germany went back to unrestricted submarine tactics in the North Atlantic.

(C) American troops were bolstering the Allied army.

(D) Russia stopped fighting after the 1917 revolution.

(E) The long war had exhausted Germany and Austria.

Your Answer _____

Q–404

The 1920s were seen as the "heroic age of physics" because of the discovery of

(A) radium as a chemical element

(B) subatomic particles, such as neutrons

(C) Newtonian principles

(D) the theory of relativity

(E) existential science

Your Answer _____

Correct Answers

A–403

(B)   The war in Europe had many unintended consequences, such as the Russian Revolution in 1917. The Bolsheviks took power in Russia and promised to end the war. This was an advantage for the Germans because they could now concentrate their armies in the West and hope for a breakthrough in that stalemated campaign. But after four years of high losses, morale was very low on both sides. Some French and German units refused to fight or follow orders. When the United States entered the war, American troops began to replace many exhausted French, British, and Canadian divisions. This allowed for an Allied breakthrough in the fall of 1918, which led to a cease-fire agreement in November.

A–404

(B)   Einstein and Curie both made important contributions to the field of physics before the war. After 1918, other physicists made breakthroughs in the field of subatomic particles. The understanding of nuclei and neutrons added to the understanding of the universe and previewed the field of atomic energy and weaponry later in the century.

Q–405

By Marxism I understand a doctrine which in principle rejects the idea of the worth of personality, which replaces individual energy by the masses and thereby works the destruction of our whole cultural life. This movement has utilized monstrously effective methods and exercised tremendous influence on the masses, which in the course of three or four decades could have no other result than that the individual has become his own brother's foe, while at the same time calling a Frenchman, an Englishman, or a Zulu his brother. This movement is distinguished by incredible terror, which is based on a knowledge of mass psychology.

—Adolf Hitler, 1923

The courtroom speech by Hitler excerpted above highlights what part of his ideology?

(A) The anticommunist agenda of Nazism

(B) The internationalist emphasis he believed in

(C) The use of mass psychology

(D) A belief in the brotherhood of man

(E) An anti-French bias

Your Answer _____

_____

Correct Answers

A–405

(A) Adolf Hitler was one of many disaffected veterans after World War I in Germany. He was frustrated by the onerous Treaty of Versailles that punished Germany for starting the war. The revolutionary success of Marxism in Russia also created a reaction in German conservative politics. Hitler saw Marxism as a great threat to Europe and thought of it as a Jewish plot to subvert civilization. After an unsuccessful attempt to overthrow the Weimar government, Hitler was tried for treason and gave the speech from which the excerpt is taken. In it he preached how Marxist communism was an attack on individualism and German nationalism.

Q–406

Twentieth-century literature responded to totalitarianism with dystopic novels such as

(A) *All Quiet on the Western Front*

(B) *Who's Afraid of Virginia Wolf?*

(C) *The Great Gatsby*

(D) *Brave New World*

(E) *Pride and Prejudice*

Your Answer _____

Q–407

Which of the following were "successor states" to the Austro-Hungarian empire after 1919?

(A) Yugoslavia and Dalmatia

(B) Czechoslovakia and Romania

(C) Albania and Turkey

(D) Corsica and Serbia

(E) Bulgaria and Moldova

Your Answer _____

Correct Answers

A–406

(D) Some writers, alarmed by the mass political movements in the Soviet Union and Italy after World War I, wrote fictional accounts of anti-utopian worlds where the individual struggles to survive. Huxley's *Brave New World* and Orwell's *1984* are examples of dystopian novels that criticized statist ideologies. In his short stories, Kafka also envisioned a totalitarian world that terrorized the individual.

A–407

(B) One of the great challenges at Versailles was the redrawing of the map of Europe. The Austro-Hungarian empire was dismantled and a number of new nations resulted. Slavic nationalism was one of the reasons for the war in 1914, and after the war, Slavic nations, such as Yugoslavia, Czechoslovakia, Bulgaria, and others, were created. The Poles and Hungarians also became nations. This transformed the political landscape of eastern Europe but also created some of the tensions that led to the next world war.

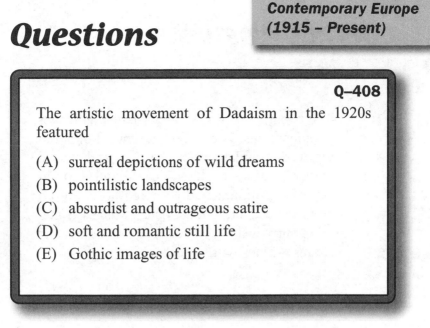

Q–408

The artistic movement of Dadaism in the 1920s featured

(A) surreal depictions of wild dreams

(B) pointilistic landscapes

(C) absurdist and outrageous satire

(D) soft and romantic still life

(E) Gothic images of life

Your Answer _____

_____

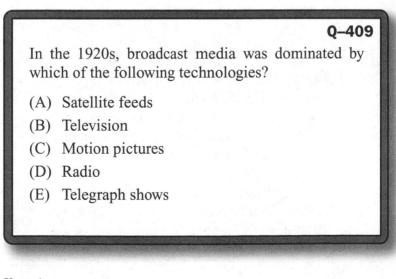

Q–409

In the 1920s, broadcast media was dominated by which of the following technologies?

(A) Satellite feeds

(B) Television

(C) Motion pictures

(D) Radio

(E) Telegraph shows

Your Answer _____

_____

Correct Answers

A–408

(C)   The twentieth century saw artistic challenges to older forms. The orthodox schools of painting were scandalized by the wild and surreal works of artists such as Picasso and Kandinsky. Dadaism attacked accepted norms in art and created outrageous visual images. Likewise, surrealism represented wild dreams and strange scenes with alien backdrops.

A–409

(D)   Wireless broadcast became possible with Marconi's work around the turn of the century. Music and voice could be transmitted after the vacuum tube was invented in 1904. Radios, as consumer items, were not common until after World War I. For the first time, political speeches, news, and sporting events could be broadcast over the airwaves. National broadcast companies, such as the BBC in Great Britain, were founded by many nations.

Questions

Q–410

The post–World War I economic order in Europe was destabilized by

(A) low tariffs that hindered trade

(B) the pacifism of governments in France and Spain

(C) American interference in international affairs

(D) harsh reparations that crippled the German economy

(E) threats from the Soviet Union

Your Answer _____

Q–411

The multinational agreement of the 1920s that renounced war as national policy was the

(A) Locarno Treaty

(B) Stresemann Pact

(C) Kellogg-Briand Pact

(D) Dawes Plan

(E) Weimar Agreement

Your Answer _____

Correct Answers

A–410

(D) The Versailles Treaty blamed Germany for the war and imposed large indemnities on the new Weimar government. This created great difficulties for the young democracy and also led to hyperinflation in the early 1920s. Germany needed loans to cover the war reparations that were to be paid to Great Britain and France. As time went on, British and American critics of the Versailles Treaty urged a revision of its harsh features, which had already tainted relations with both Weimar and later Nazi Germany.

A–411

(C) The period following World War I saw a profound desire for peace among many people. Pacifism as a political movement was evident in many parts of Europe. The prospect of another war was unthinkable. The spirit of internationalism and peace led to the Kellogg-Briand Pact, which many nations signed in 1928. Sponsored by the French and the Americans, this agreement was a pledge not to resort to war in the future. The late 1920s were an optimistic time and many hoped that humanity had learned the terrible lessons of World War I.

Questions

Q–412

His Majesty's Government view with favour of the establishment in Palestine of a national home for the Jewish
people, and will use their best endeavours to facilitate the
achievement of this object, it being clearly understood
that nothing shall be done which may prejudice the civil
and religious rights of existing non-Jewish communities
in Palestine, or the rights and political status enjoyed by
Jews in any other country.

—Lord Balfour, letter, 1917

The excerpt shown above fulfills the desires of which
of the following twentieth-century movements?

(A) Pan-Slavism in the Balkans

(B) Zionism in Europe

(C) Pan-Arabism in the Middle East

(D) National Socialism in Germany

(E) Syrian nationalism in Asia Minor

Your Answer _____

_____

Correct Answers

A–412

(B) The letter, written in 1917, expressed some support by the British government for the Zionist movement that developed in the late nineteenth century in Europe. Nationalism took root in certain Jewish circles that sought a homeland for Jewish people. The Ottoman Empire dominated the former geography of ancient Israel but tolerated some Jewish settlement after 1880. Influential Jewish leaders sought support for the idea of a Jewish state from important nations such as Britain. A steady stream of European Jews began to relocate in Palestine through the early twentieth century.

Questions

Q–413

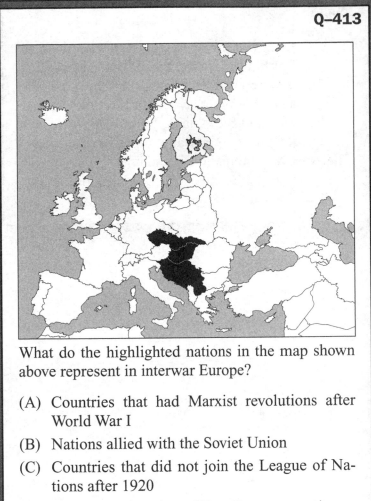

What do the highlighted nations in the map shown above represent in interwar Europe?

(A) Countries that had Marxist revolutions after World War I

(B) Nations allied with the Soviet Union

(C) Countries that did not join the League of Nations after 1920

(D) An economic union of East European nations

(E) New nations created out of the old Austrian Empire

Your Answer _____

_____

Correct Answers

A–413

(E)   The map of Europe was drastically redrawn after World War I. Old empires like Austria-Hungary were chopped up and new nations were created. Former Slav minorities, such as the Czechs and Slovakians, were given their own nations in the postwar settlement. Yugoslavia was a combination of southern Slav people such as the Bosnians, Serbs, and Slovenians.

Q–414

The twentieth-century counterbalance to democratic liberalism in Europe was

(A) conservative authoritarianism

(B) radical socialism

(C) moderate conservatism

(D) libertarian regimes

(E) Marxist communism

Your Answer _____

Q–415

All of the following are features of twentieth-century fascism EXCEPT

(A) pro-Marxist policies

(B) support of conservative business interests

(C) single-party rule

(D) ultranationalist themes used to inspire patriotism

(E) the buildup and promotion of militaries

Your Answer _____

Correct Answers

A–414

(A) The interwar period saw some advances in democracy, but over time, authoritarian and totalitarian governments took control in many European nations. Strong central regimes were basically antidemocratic and ruled severely. Conservative governments on the right fostered the support of business but eliminated many civil liberties. Radical leftist regimes marshaled national energies to achieve socialist goals but also brutally suppressed human rights in the process.

A–415

(A) Fascism was a reaction to the Marxist revolution after World War I. After 1920, fascist movements were successful in gaining power in Europe and Latin America. Capitalist interests supported fascist leaders as long as communism and unionism were thwarted. Nationalism and militarism are central features of fascism, which helps to keep people prepared to fight for their country. Flags were used extensively to stimulate patriotism in the population and gather support for the government.

Questions

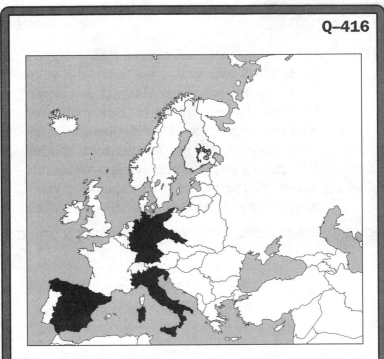

Q–416

In the map shown above, what did the highlighted nations have in common politically in the interwar period?

(A) They had communist revolutions after World War I.

(B) All opposed the League of Nations.

(C) These nations concluded alliances with the United States.

(D) All became repressive fascist regimes.

(E) Marxist regimes gained control through popular elections.

Your Answer _____

Correct Answers

A–416

(D)   The establishment of radical right-wing regimes in Italy, Germany, and Spain was a political reaction to radical Marxism in Europe.
This new ideology known as fascism opposed
communism and democratic liberalism. All
three nations had powerful dictators who led
their parties and nations as nationalists and
militarists. The armies were expanded, which
helped lead to World War II.

Questions

Q–417

What political and social trends were apparent in eastern European nations after World War I?

(A) Nations experienced widespread harmony among ethnic groups.

(B) Traditional conservatives took control of many nations.

(C) Socialism was opposed in many capitals.

(D) Military dictatorships proliferated.

(E) Labor unions were strengthened and social legislation was advanced.

Your Answer _____

Q–418

In establishing modern Turkey, all of the following were accomplished by Kemal EXCEPT

(A) suppressing Muslim courts

(B) banning women from wearing veils

(C) introducing European laws

(D) retaining the Arabic alphabet

(E) declaring Turkey a secular republic

Your Answer _____

Correct Answers

A–417

(E) After 1918, there was a brief period when eastern Europe tended toward liberal democracy. New nations, such as Czechoslovakia and Hungary, were born out of the old Austrian Empire and established popular governments elected by the people. Eastern Europe was still an ethnic patchwork quilt with many different cultures and subcultures. Many of these fledgling democracies did not survive the economic depression and the test of time.

A–418

(D) Mustafa Kemal, also known as Ataturk, is the father of modern Turkey and radically remade the country after its defeat in World War I. He was a military hero and father figure who wanted to make Turkey into a modern European nation. To do this, he reformed education and took power away from Muslim clerics. He did away with the Arabic alphabet and replaced it with a Romanized Latin writing system still used today.

Questions

Q–419

We want to glorify war, the world's only hygiene-militarism, pure in deed, destroyer of anarchisms, . . .

—Filippo Marinetti, 1920

The slogan shown above relates to which twentieth-century political phenomenon?

(A) Trade unionism

(B) Marxist revolutionary movements

(C) Italian fascism in the interwar period

(D) Wilsonian democracy

(E) Liberal positivism

Your Answer _____

Q–420

Five-Year Plans initiated by Hitler, Stalin, and Mussolini were evidence of which trend in governmental management?

(A) Mass production in government-owned factories

(B) Fascist control of manufacturing

(C) Marxist oversight of industry

(D) Liberal democratic approaches to ending the Great Depression

(E) Centrally planned economies under single-party dictatorships

Your Answer _____

Correct Answers

A–419

(C)   After the Treaty of Versailles, many nations, including Italy, were dissatisfied with the settlement provided in the treaty. Some Italian nationalists dreamed of a strong nation led by military men who glorified war and masculine struggle. Benito Mussolini became the spokesperson for this new political ideology and took power in Italy after 1922. These fascists believed that war was the great endeavor of powerful nations, so they built up their armies to fight and expand their territories.

A–420

(E)   Powerful dictators took control of Germany, Russia, and Italy in the twentieth century. Some were fascist and others were socialist, but they all sought to control their nations. While Germany and Italy allowed private investment, the Soviet Union became communistic, with complete government control of the economy. Dictators on the right and left tried to plan, develop, and grow their national economies while maintaining their power over the populations they led.

Q–421

The term *collectivization* can best be described as which of the following?

(A) The consolidation of small farms into a large state enterprise

(B) Acquisition of overseas territories

(C) Internationalism on a global scale

(D) Building of labor organizations in different countries

(E) Promoting of land reform for peasants in Latin America

Your Answer _____

Q–422

Economic depression is characterized by all of the following EXCEPT

(A) bank failures

(B) rampant inflation

(C) high unemployment

(D) collapse of the equity markets

(E) declining prices

Your Answer _____

Correct Answers

A–421

(A) After the Russian Revolution, Stalin began to create large-scale agricultural enterprises in an attempt to control national farming and the people who worked the land. Many resisted and were starved or imprisoned by the Soviet dictator. Machinery and mass production modernized farming in the Soviet Union. Only obedient farmers survived the transition, and land was brought under government control by the 1930s.

A–422

(B) Economic depression is defined as a long-term shrinking of the economy. Depressions tend to occur periodically throughout history, and the most severe world depression took place in the 1930s. Depressions are evidenced by the closing of both companies and banks. Panic results in large-scale selling of stocks and plummeting share prices. Prices for goods fall as demand decreases and money is scarce. Workers are laid off and joblessness increases dramatically. Inflation, the rising of consumer prices, cannot occur during a depression.

Q–423

Which of the following was NOT a factor in the rise of Nazism in Germany?

(A) The Treaty of Versailles was seen as unjust.

(B) Germans were drawn to western liberalism.

(C) Fear of communism began taking root.

(D) The Great Depression caused political instability.

(E) Adolf Hitler appealed to German pride by promising a stronger nation.

Your Answer _____

_____

Q–424

Which of the following was a challenge to Yugoslav unity after 1920?

(A) Soviet domination in Yugoslav politics

(B) Ethnic Germans' desire to secede

(C) Italian invasion, which led to war

(D) Serb-Croat rivalry and other ethnic tensions

(E) League of Nations condemnation of the government for aggression

Your Answer _____

_____

Correct Answers

A–423

(B) Germany was saddled with large war debts after World War I. The economy suffered rampant inflation, followed by the devastation of the global depression in the 1930s. The success of communism in the nearby Soviet Union also caused anxiety in the middle and upper classes. Hitler crafted an appealing message of returning Germany to greatness. He promised to tear up the Treaty of Versailles and rebuild the military.

A–424

(D) Serbs were the dominant ethnic group in the newly formed nation of Yugoslavia, and the capital of Belgrade became the political center of greater Yugoslavia. The Serbs shared some power with the Croats, who also were a significant part of the population. In addition, other ethnic groups, such as Hungarians, Greeks, and Bulgarians, struggled to have a voice in the new nation.

Questions

Q–425

All of the following destabilized international relations in the 1930s EXCEPT

(A) the Munich Agreement of 1938

(B) Japan's invasion of Manchuria

(C) Hitler's annexation of Austria

(D) Italy's invasion of Ethiopia

(E) Lenin's death in Russia

Your Answer _____

Q–426

The creation of the British Commonwealth in 1926 recognized the basic independence of

(A) select African colonies

(B) India and Pakistan

(C) Ireland and Scotland

(D) former colonies such as Canada and Australia

(E) Anglo domains in the southern hemisphere

Your Answer _____

Correct Answers

A–425

(E) Strong and aggressive military regimes came to power in Japan, Germany, and Italy in the 1930s. Each nation used military force to expand its power. Germany absorbed Austria and took Czechoslovakia with the Munich accord in 1938. Japan took northern China, and Italy invaded East Africa. All these acts of aggression weakened the liberal powers in the West and made war more likely. The death of Lenin in 1924 led to the rise of Stalin in the Soviet Union.

A–426

(D) World War I weakened the British Empire and forced it to rely on its colonies in defeating Germany. The former colonies of Canada, Australia, and New Zealand contributed to the war effort and lost many men in the conflict. Britain recognized this contribution in the 1920s by giving these colonies de facto independence, with the proviso that they maintain a loose connection to the crown in London. This traditional relationship has endured ever since.

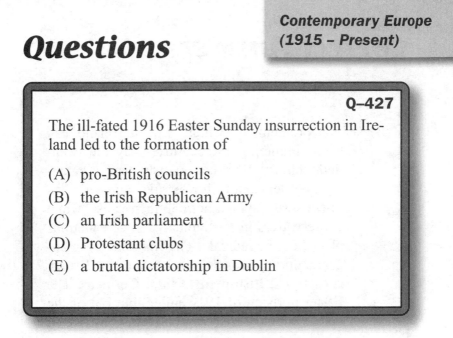

Q–427

The ill-fated 1916 Easter Sunday insurrection in Ireland led to the formation of

(A) pro-British councils

(B) the Irish Republican Army

(C) an Irish parliament

(D) Protestant clubs

(E) a brutal dictatorship in Dublin

Your Answer _____

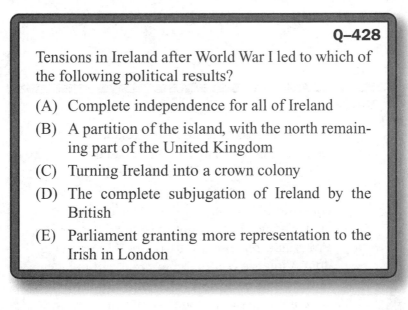

Q–428

Tensions in Ireland after World War I led to which of the following political results?

(A) Complete independence for all of Ireland

(B) A partition of the island, with the north remaining part of the United Kingdom

(C) Turning Ireland into a crown colony

(D) The complete subjugation of Ireland by the British

(E) Parliament granting more representation to the Irish in London

Your Answer _____

Correct Answers

A–427

(B) The problem of British rule in Ireland had been simmering for centuries. By the twentieth century, Irish nationalists were organizing and demanding home rule. Some British liberals were sympathetic to their cause, while conservatives in Parliament wanted sanctions placed on the radicals. The Irish had been angered during World War I when the British conscripted Irish men to fight Germany. The Easter uprising of 1916 failed, but out of the defeat came the Irish Republican Army (IRA), which dedicated itself to the violent expulsion of the British. From 1920 to 1922, there was an ongoing guerilla war between the IRA and British troops and police.

A–428

(B) After continued violence in Ireland in 1919–1920, the British Parliament debated the issue of home rule for the Irish. In the end, a compromise was reached and the Irish Free State, consisting of the majority of the island, was created. The northern counties, which were partly Protestant, remained part of the United Kingdom. Violence continued to break out in Ulster in the north because Protestants and Catholics were not able to live together in peace.

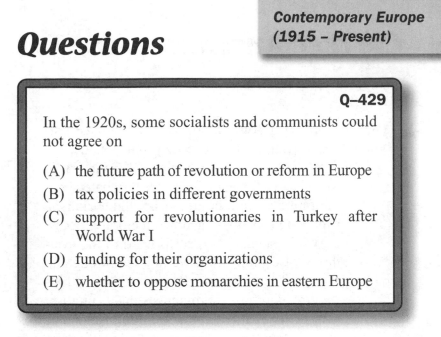

Q–429

In the 1920s, some socialists and communists could not agree on

(A) the future path of revolution or reform in Europe

(B) tax policies in different governments

(C) support for revolutionaries in Turkey after World War I

(D) funding for their organizations

(E) whether to oppose monarchies in eastern Europe

Your Answer _____

_____

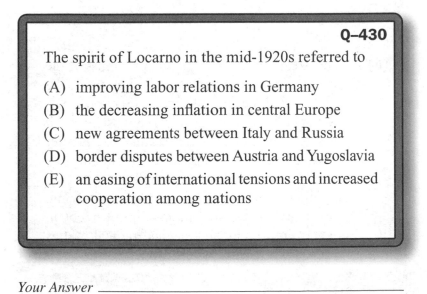

Q–430

The spirit of Locarno in the mid-1920s referred to

(A) improving labor relations in Germany

(B) the decreasing inflation in central Europe

(C) new agreements between Italy and Russia

(D) border disputes between Austria and Yugoslavia

(E) an easing of international tensions and increased cooperation among nations

Your Answer _____

_____

Correct Answers

A–429

(A)   World War I was a setback for socialist parties in Europe because they put country before ideology. The surprising 1917 victory of Marxism in Russia caused great debate about the future of both communism and socialism. Moderate socialists favored electoral processes, while radicals looked forward to the overthrow of capitalistic governments throughout Europe. The economic downturns of the 1920s suggested to some communists that capitalism was in its final decline. Communism made gains in Germany and France while in Britain, the party remained relatively small.

A–430

(E)   The Treaty of Locarno, signed by most of the major powers of Europe, settled some of the territorial issues in the west. Germany participated in the treaty, which suggested that it was returning to the international arena after its defeat in 1918. Only seven years after the war, Locarno created some confidence that the diplomatic mood of Europe was improving. The late 1920s also saw an improvement in the economy, which weakened radical parties in most of the nations of Europe.

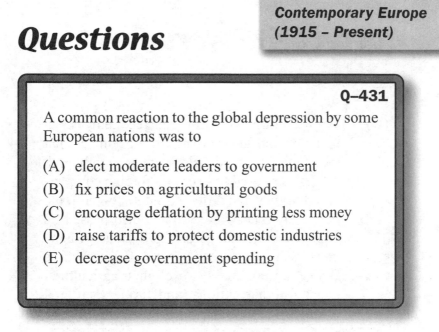

Q–431

A common reaction to the global depression by some European nations was to

(A) elect moderate leaders to government

(B) fix prices on agricultural goods

(C) encourage deflation by printing less money

(D) raise tariffs to protect domestic industries

(E) decrease government spending

Your Answer _____

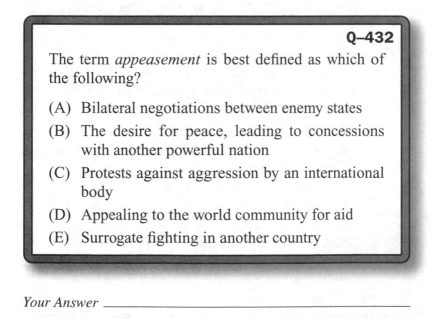

Q–432

The term *appeasement* is best defined as which of the following?

(A) Bilateral negotiations between enemy states

(B) The desire for peace, leading to concessions with another powerful nation

(C) Protests against aggression by an international body

(D) Appealing to the world community for aid

(E) Surrogate fighting in another country

Your Answer _____

Correct Answers

A–431

(D) The downturn in the European economy began in 1928, and governments tried policies that they thought would help businesses rebound. Tariffs were used to keep out foreign competition, but they also affected international trade negatively. The United States also passed its highest tariff, which further discouraged the movement of goods. Poorer nations, such as Bulgaria, were unable to sell their agricultural goods to other nations, and farmers suffered greatly.

A–432

(B) The term *appeasement* is often used to describe the events of 1938, when Germany demanded territorial adjustments in central Europe. Hitler, believing that the Treaty of Versailles did not take ethnic Germans into consideration, demanded control over the border region of Czechoslovakia. Britain and France negotiated a settlement that allowed Germany to take parts of Czechoslovakia in return for a promise that Hitler would keep the peace. That agreement has been criticized as a precursor to World War II because Hitler was not satisfied with the Czech settlement and later invaded Poland.

Q–433

Compared with nations in the West, eastern European nations had

(A) higher gross domestic products

(B) more stable governments

(C) the same incomes per capita

(D) smaller middle classes and poorer, agriculturally based economies

(E) stronger parliamentary traditions

Your Answer _____

_____

Q–434

The National Socialists in Germany were able to gain some support from the industrial class because

(A) big business did not favor parliamentary government

(B) they controlled the Reichstag deputies

(C) the communists cooperated with them

(D) business elites were antifascist

(E) militarization was not part of the Nazi platform

Your Answer _____

_____

Correct Answers

A–433

(D) Except for Czechoslovakia, most nations in eastern Europe were poorer and more agricultural, and their populations were less educated. Most of the population worked the land and struggled to provide for their families. Illiteracy was high; schools were poorly funded and not always available to the general population. Unlike western nations, such as France and Britain, eastern Europe did not have experience with either liberal democracy or parliamentary mechanisms. As the economy worsened in the late 1920s, most of these nations turned into authoritarian regimes.

A–434

(A) Most of the business elites in Germany were conservatives who lamented the end of the old monarchy. They were uncomfortable with the new democracy, and the economic ups and downs of the 1920s did not help them embrace the Weimar government. National Socialism reached out to industrialists for support and promised that they would bring order to Germany and protect their profits. In addition, the Nazis promised to help businesses by rearming Germany and abolishing organized labor.

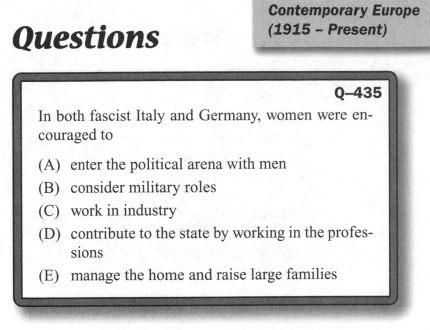

Q–435

In both fascist Italy and Germany, women were encouraged to

(A) enter the political arena with men

(B) consider military roles

(C) work in industry

(D) contribute to the state by working in the professions

(E) manage the home and raise large families

Your Answer _____

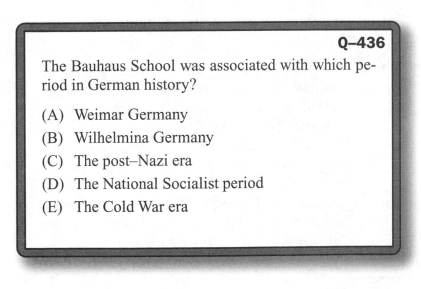

Q–436

The Bauhaus School was associated with which period in German history?

(A) Weimar Germany

(B) Wilhelmina Germany

(C) The post–Nazi era

(D) The National Socialist period

(E) The Cold War era

Your Answer _____

Correct Answers

A–435

(E) The fascist states glorified martial values and war. Having large armies depended on having large populations, so women were encouraged to bear many children. Special awards and incentives were given to families with more than five children. Mothers wore medals that celebrated their fertility and service to the state. In Germany, women were excluded from teaching and other traditionally female jobs.

A–436

(A) In 1919, architect Walter Gropius founded the Bauhaus School, a school of design that combined art and simple style. *Bauhaus* means "house for building." Gropius created an approach that was without ornamentation. The Bauhaus School was part of a larger artistic atmosphere in Weimar Germany between the world wars. Although Germany was somewhat unstable economically and politically, this period was a creative one for the arts.

Questions

Q–437

Hitler shocked the diplomatic world in 1939 by signing a nonaggression pact with

(A) Denmark

(B) Hungary

(C) the Soviet Union

(D) Great Britain

(E) Ireland

Your Answer _____

Q–438

All of the following were new technologies adapted to warfare in World War II EXCEPT

(A) armored tanks

(B) long-range missiles

(C) nuclear bombs

(D) jet aircraft

(E) radar

Your Answer _____

Correct Answers

A–437

(C)   Hitler made a career of opposing communism as he rose politically in Germany. He believed that Marxist communism was the great threat to Western civilization. The Nazis also criticized the Treaty of Versailles, which had taken so much territory from Germany. To pave the way for a move into Poland, Germany negotiated a nonaggression pact with the Soviet Union. This confounded the international community because it was common knowledge that Hitler and Stalin were ideological opposites.

A–438

(A)   World War II saw the advent of many new technologies used by both sides to fight the war. The Germans made impressive advances in rocketry and launched the first long-range missiles that delivered explosives to foreign cities. They also produced the first jet aircraft used in war. The British developed radar to detect aircraft from afar, and the Americans developed the atomic bomb, which was dropped on Japan in the last month of the war. Tanks had been produced a generation earlier, during World War I.

Q–439

Which of the following proved advantageous for the Allies in their victory over the Axis in World War II?

(A) New technologies such as rockets

(B) Stronger navies at the start of the conflict

(C) Abundant natural resources and large populations

(D) Shorter supply lines

(E) Support from African nations

Your Answer _____

Q–440

The nation that experienced the most casualties (dead and wounded) during World War II was

(A) the Soviet Union

(B) Germany

(C) the United States

(D) Japan

(E) France

Your Answer _____

Correct Answers

A–439

(C) After the Soviet Union and the United States entered the war in 1941, the Axis faced two very large and resourceful nations. The United States was already the most productive industrial nation in the world and could manufacture large quantities of materiel for the war effort. The Soviet Union had a large population to contribute and was able to design weaponry to counter the German assault on their nation. The advantage of natural resources, which Japan and Germany lacked, was a decisive advantage in a long, protracted war.

A–440

(A) It is estimated that over 50 million people died in World War II. Battles between Germany and the Soviet Union were particularly gruesome and hard fought, which left as many as 20 million dead in the Soviet Union. Both sides set aside the conventional rules of combat and fought one another without mercy. While many more Soviets died in the battles, the Germans were eventually invaded by the Allied army led by the Soviet Union and defeated in 1945.

Q–441

The Axis powers of World War II consisted of which of the following?

(A) Spain, Switzerland, and Sweden

(B) Germany, Italy, and Japan

(C) Portugal, Hungary, and Romania

(D) Great Britain, France, and Italy

(E) Ireland, Great Britain, and Norway

Your Answer _____

Q–442

An important military advantage for Great Britain during World War II was its success in

(A) invading North Africa in 1943

(B) trading with neutral Sweden

(C) sinking German shipping in the North Sea

(D) bombing train routes in France

(E) decoding military communications

Your Answer _____

Correct Answers

A–441

(B) Militaristic regimes grew in power during the 1930s. European fascism established itself in Germany, Italy, and Spain. In Asia, Japan was dominated by its military and began to expand into China. As Japan absorbed European colonies in Asia, it drew closer to Germany diplomatically. In 1940, the three expansionist military powers concluded a defensive alliance and were known at the Axis powers as the war began.

A–442

(E) The intelligence war was a crucial piece of the fighting in World War II. Each side tried to discover the movements of the other and anticipate the fighting. The Allies scored important breakthroughs when they were able to decode both German and Japanese messages between 1940 and 1943. In the Pacific theater, the Allies used codetalkers, speaking the traditionally unwritten language of the Navajo tribe, to confound the Japanese. This helped them turn the tide because the Axis countries were clearly winning the war before that.

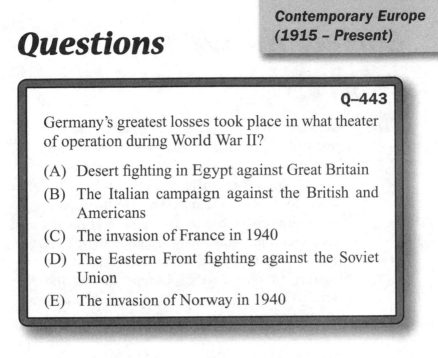

Q–443

Germany's greatest losses took place in what theater of operation during World War II?

(A) Desert fighting in Egypt against Great Britain

(B) The Italian campaign against the British and Americans

(C) The invasion of France in 1940

(D) The Eastern Front fighting against the Soviet Union

(E) The invasion of Norway in 1940

Your Answer _____

_____

Q–444

Which of the following was the declared Allied war goal by 1943?

(A) The demilitarization of the Rhineland

(B) Unconditional surrender of the Axis powers

(C) The revival of the League of Nations

(D) American hegemony in Europe

(E) The joint occupation of Japan

Your Answer _____

_____

Correct Answers

A–443

(D) Germany had impressive military success when it invaded Poland, Scandinavia, and France in the first year of the war. Fighting in North Africa was difficult, but it did not involve so many divisions. The German decision to invade the Soviet Union in 1941 meant a huge commitment of men and materiel. At first, it seemed destined for success, but the weather in northeastern Europe helped the Soviet Union as much as anything. The war turned into a marathon death struggle for the Soviets, who finally turned the invasion back and began to win victories by late 1942.

A–444

(B) The outcome of World War I had been so unsatisfactory for most nations that a new strategy was applied as the Allies met in World War II. In 1918, World War I ended with a ceasefire and the promise that a settlement would be made afterward. The 1919 settlement was so anti-German that it encouraged the rise of the Nazi party afterward. World War II was to end with the clear defeat of the Axis powers and a reestablishment of international law and order, with the organization of the United Nations.

Questions

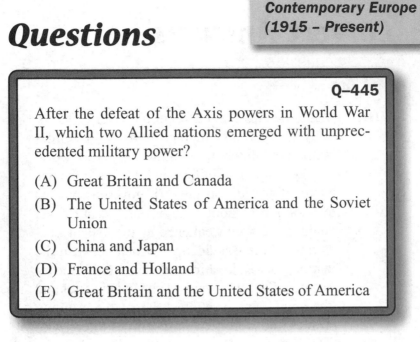

Q–445

After the defeat of the Axis powers in World War II, which two Allied nations emerged with unprecedented military power?

(A) Great Britain and Canada

(B) The United States of America and the Soviet Union

(C) China and Japan

(D) France and Holland

(E) Great Britain and the United States of America

Your Answer _____

_____

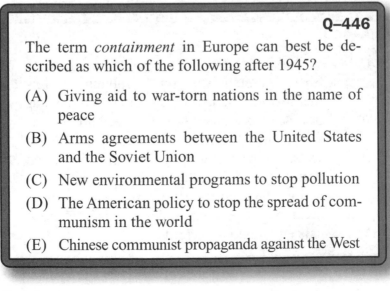

Q–446

The term *containment* in Europe can best be described as which of the following after 1945?

(A) Giving aid to war-torn nations in the name of peace

(B) Arms agreements between the United States and the Soviet Union

(C) New environmental programs to stop pollution

(D) The American policy to stop the spread of communism in the world

(E) Chinese communist propaganda against the West

Your Answer _____

_____

Correct Answers

A–445

(B) After the massive destruction of World War II, only two nations emerged with the resources and populations to continue as true world powers. Japan and Germany, utterly defeated, were left to reconstitute their governments and economies. Although victorious, Great Britain and France were weakened by their spent treasuries. China was deeply divided between the nationalist leadership and communist movements in the countryside. The United States and the Soviet Union retained their large standing armies and were rich in resources after 1945. The term *superpower* was coined to describe the United States and the Soviet Union in the postwar period.

A–446

(D) In 1945, American attitudes with regard to Soviet communism were evolving. A former World War II ally, the Soviet Union was now seen as a threat to democracy around the world. George Kennan, a top expert on the Soviets, wrote a paper suggesting that the United States seek to limit the influence of the Soviet Union. This policy would become an overarching goal to contain communism where it existed around the world.

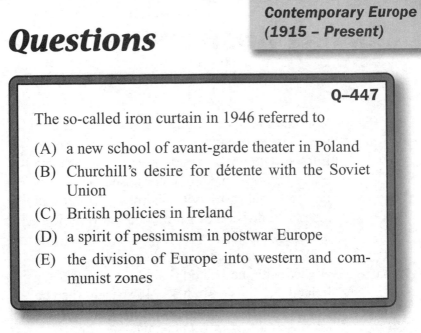

Q–447

The so-called iron curtain in 1946 referred to

(A) a new school of avant-garde theater in Poland

(B) Churchill's desire for détente with the Soviet Union

(C) British policies in Ireland

(D) a spirit of pessimism in postwar Europe

(E) the division of Europe into western and communist zones

Your Answer _____

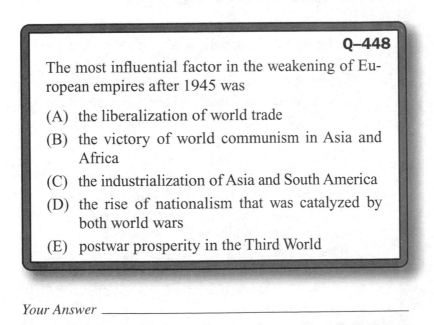

Q–448

The most influential factor in the weakening of European empires after 1945 was

(A) the liberalization of world trade

(B) the victory of world communism in Asia and Africa

(C) the industrialization of Asia and South America

(D) the rise of nationalism that was catalyzed by both world wars

(E) postwar prosperity in the Third World

Your Answer _____

Correct Answers

A–447

(E) With the end of the war, the great Allied armies were left to occupy the former Nazi areas of Europe. The Soviet Union's army had overrun eastern Europe, and the Soviets used this advantage to establish friendly regimes. This created a de facto division of Europe into governments aligned with the Soviet Union and those that were democratic and capitalistic, and therefore aligned with the United States. Churchill highlighted this division in his 1946 speech when he described the Soviet zone as creating an iron curtain that now separated the East and the West.

A–448

(D) The Age of Imperialism was at its peak prior to World War I, when European nations competed for foreign territories in Asia and Africa. Both World War I and World War II dealt severe blows to European powers, whose weakened status encouraged Asian and African nationalism. Even victorious powers such as Britain and France suffered greatly in fighting the long and costly wars of the twentieth century. After 1945, they tried unsuccessfully to retain their empires but no longer had the will or resources to do so. One by one, Asian and African nations fought for and won their independence. By 1970, little was left of European power in the southern and eastern hemispheres.

Q–449

The Allied powers held war tribunals after World War II to establish the principle of

(A) collective security

(B) moral rectitude

(C) total war

(D) international justice

(E) neutral alliances

Your Answer _____

_____

Correct Answers

A–449

(D)   As the Allies planned the postwar era in Europe, they started to create a legal mechanism in which those who started the war would be held accountable to the international community. They organized an international court with multiple judges from the Allied nations and began the European trials in Nuremberg, Germany, in 1946. Similar trials were held in Tokyo for the Japanese militarists blamed for starting the war and committing atrocities in Asia. In 1948, following the Nuremberg and Tokyo tribunals, the United Nations General Assembly recognized the need for a permanent international court to deal with atrocities of the kind committed during World War II. At the request of the General Assembly, the International Law Commission drafted two statutes by the early 1950s, but these were shelved because the Cold War made the establishment of an international criminal court politically unlikely. The idea was revived in 1989 when the prime minister of Trinidad and Tobago proposed the creation of a permanent international court to deal with the illegal drug trade. While work began on a draft statute, the international community established ad hoc tribunals to try war crimes in the former Yugoslavia and Rwanda, further highlighting the need for a permanent international criminal court. Today, The Hague in the Netherlands is the permanent seat of the International Criminal Court.

Q–450

Which of the following are examples of the work of the United Nations since 1945?

I. Promoting cultural and educational programs worldwide

II. Helping newly independent nations establish themselves

III. Dealing with crises that lead to war

IV. Promoting human rights around the world

(A) I, II, and IV

(B) I and II

(C) III and IV

(D) I, II, III, and IV

(E) I and IV

Your Answer _____

_____

Correct Answers

A–450

(D) The United Nations (UN) was founded in 1945 as a peace organization in the aftermath of the worst war in human history. The five Allied victors of the war, the United States, the Soviet Union, China, Great Britain, and France, were charter members. The United Nations has grown to over 190 nations, as former colonies became new countries. The UN has multiple organs that deal with economic issues, security problems, and international law. It has promoted an international understanding of basic human rights around the world.

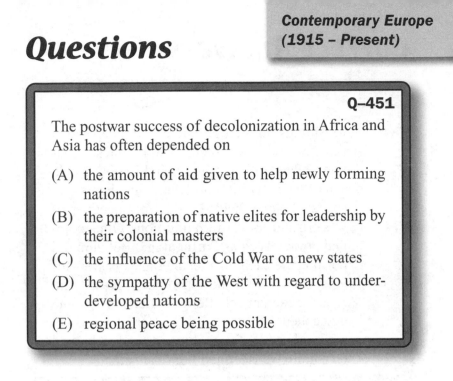

Q–451

The postwar success of decolonization in Africa and Asia has often depended on

(A) the amount of aid given to help newly forming nations

(B) the preparation of native elites for leadership by their colonial masters

(C) the influence of the Cold War on new states

(D) the sympathy of the West with regard to under-developed nations

(E) regional peace being possible

Your Answer _____

_____

Q–452

Which of the following European nations are permanent members of the United Nations Security Council?

(A) Italy, France, and Germany

(B) Great Britain, France, and the Soviet Union

(C) Spain, France, and Poland

(D) France, Great Britain, and Holland

(E) Great Britain, Ireland, and France

Your Answer _____

_____

Correct Answers

A–451

(B) Most transitions from colonial to independent rule have been overseen by well-educated native leaders such as Gandhi and Ho Chi Minh. Educated in British and French schools, respectively, they held the dual perspectives of western and nonwestern traditions. Other colonial powers such as Portugal and Belgium did not prepare their former colonies as well for independence. All new nations in Africa and Asia faced many challenges after 1950. Some descended into civil war and great violence, while others wrote constitutions and embarked on a more well-defined political path.

A–452

(B) The larger Allied nations that had led the fight against the Axis nations were the founding members of the United Nations after World War II. They invited all peace-loving nations to join the new international association but kept some special powers for themselves. As the leading military powers of the postwar world, five Allied nations made up the Big Five, and they had permanent membership in the Security Council. These five Allied nations were the United States, China, the Soviet Union, Britain, and France.

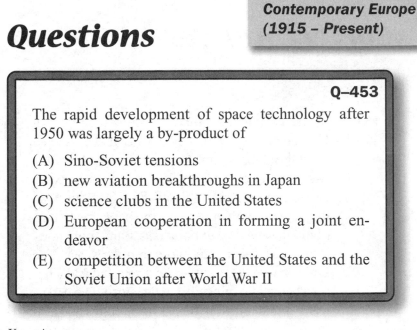

Q–453

The rapid development of space technology after 1950 was largely a by-product of

(A) Sino-Soviet tensions

(B) new aviation breakthroughs in Japan

(C) science clubs in the United States

(D) European cooperation in forming a joint endeavor

(E) competition between the United States and the Soviet Union after World War II

Your Answer _____

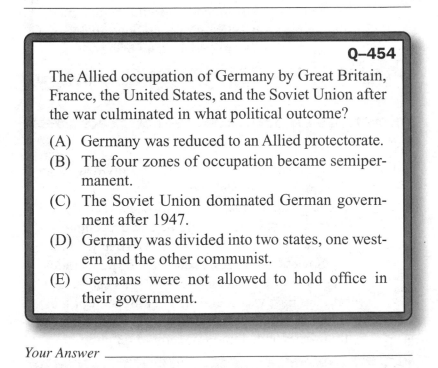

Q–454

The Allied occupation of Germany by Great Britain, France, the United States, and the Soviet Union after the war culminated in what political outcome?

(A) Germany was reduced to an Allied protectorate.

(B) The four zones of occupation became semipermanent.

(C) The Soviet Union dominated German government after 1947.

(D) Germany was divided into two states, one western and the other communist.

(E) Germans were not allowed to hold office in their government.

Your Answer _____

Correct Answers

A–453

(E)   In the twentieth century, before World War II, Germany was the first nation to make marked breakthroughs in missile technology. After the war, the American and Soviet armies raced to capture top German scientists to find out what they knew. Both superpowers spent great sums of money and time to build better and more powerful rockets that could go into outer space. The Soviets were the first to send a satellite and a human being into orbit around the earth. The Americans countered with their own satellites and also sent men into orbit. By the 1960s, a competition was under way to send rockets and even people to the moon. The United States put the first men on the moon in 1969, after spending billions of dollars to overtake the Soviet lead in space.

A–454

(D)   The end of the war saw Germany divided into four military zones overseen by the British, French, Americans, and the Soviets. The three western zones were combined and eventually became the Federal Republic of Germany, while the Soviet Union's zone became the Democratic Republic of Germany. The West was capitalist, and the East was socialist. This division of the German people lasted until 1989, when the nation was reunited into one federal republic.

Q–455

The North Atlantic Treaty Organization (NATO) was formed in 1949 to

(A) stop fascist militarism

(B) defend Europe against communist aggression

(C) create a free-trade zone in western Europe

(D) formalize the postwar treaties with Germany

(E) ensure socialist security in northern Europe

Your Answer _____

_____

Q–456

The communists expanded their presence in eastern Europe in 1948 with a coup d'état in

(A) Poland

(B) Romania

(C) Czechoslovakia

(D) Moldova

(E) Hungary

Your Answer _____

_____

Correct Answers

A–455

(B) Although the United Nations was founded to stop aggression that threatened world peace, other mechanisms were organized to respond to regional needs. The nations of western and northern Europe joined the United States and Canada to form the North Atlantic Treaty Organization (NATO) after World War II. This was a further sign that relations with the former Soviet ally were deteriorating. NATO was a purely military alliance that promised to come to the aid of any nation threatened by the communists in the East. Headquartered first in Paris and later in Brussels, NATO has continued to be involved in military actions in Europe when fighting has broken out.

A–456

(C) Before the war, Czechoslovakia was the most liberal and developed of the eastern European nations. It was the only one not to turn into a dictatorship prior to the outbreak of the war. The United States offered financial assistance to European nations, and the Czech government made a move to accept it. At this point, the communists overthrew the government in a successful coup d'état.

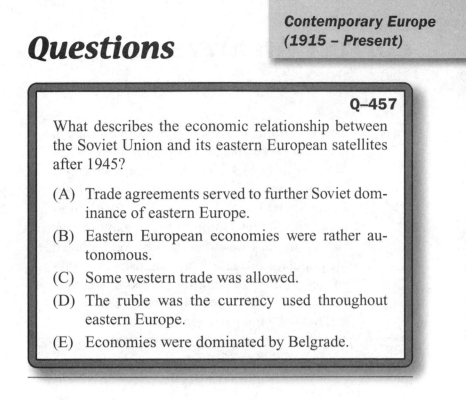

Q–457

What describes the economic relationship between the Soviet Union and its eastern European satellites after 1945?

(A) Trade agreements served to further Soviet dominance of eastern Europe.

(B) Eastern European economies were rather autonomous.

(C) Some western trade was allowed.

(D) The ruble was the currency used throughout eastern Europe.

(E) Economies were dominated by Belgrade.

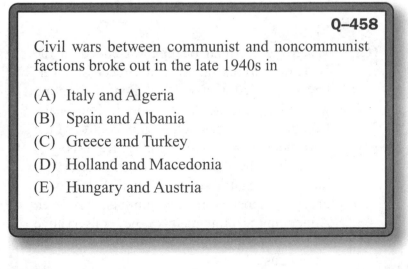

Q–458

Civil wars between communist and noncommunist factions broke out in the late 1940s in

(A) Italy and Algeria

(B) Spain and Albania

(C) Greece and Turkey

(D) Holland and Macedonia

(E) Hungary and Austria

Your Answer _____

_____

Correct Answers

A–457

(A)   The economic interests of eastern European countries were subservient to the interests of Moscow after 1945. The communist bloc was also an economic union of sorts. The satellites of the Soviet Union had Five-Year Plans similar to the Soviet Union, and agriculture was collectivized. Consumer goods were denied the populace because heavy industry was given top priority. Economies tended to stagnate because economic decisions were centralized and made by the party leaders.

A–458

(C)   When the German occupation ended in the Balkans, various factions in Greece and Turkey contended for political power. Fighting was bloody and lasted for three to four years. Communist groups tried to gain control of the governments, and some assistance was given to them by the Soviet Union. After 1947, the United States sent millions of dollars to groups opposing the communist takeover. Anticommunists tended to be conservative monarchists, and they were able to defeat the communists by 1949.

Q–459

The 1948 Marshall Plan provided postwar assistance to

(A) Allied nations

(B) eastern European nations

(C) Belgium, which had suffered the most during the fighting

(D) recovering western European economies

(E) Scandinavian nations that had been occupied by the Nazis

Your Answer _____

Q–460

Which of the following best describes the role of socialism in postwar Europe?

(A) Conservative governments banned socialist political parties.

(B) Capitalists marginalized socialist political power.

(C) Socialists and labor unions paralyzed many economies.

(D) Socialists were unable to appeal to populations.

(E) Socialist policies created welfare states throughout Europe.

Your Answer _____

Correct Answers

A–459

(D) Europe was in ruins in 1945, and the Allies laid out plans for the postwar recovery as the war was ending. The wealthiest nation in the world was the United States, and it took the lead in helping Europe reestablish its economic vitality. President Truman proposed that billions of dollars be earmarked for European nations that applied. Originally offered to any European nation, in the end the aid went to West Germany and nations in western and southern Europe.

A–460

(E) The mixing of market capitalism and socialistic policies is one of the most significant political features of postwar Europe. The Labor Party in Britain pushed through broad socialized programs in medicine and education. Almost all European nations embraced socialized features in their economies. The central planning of the war led to greater expectations by people with regard to their governments. Some nations such as Sweden developed comprehensive welfare systems that provided for many basic needs for their people.

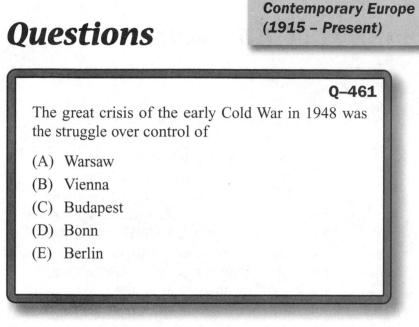

Q–461

The great crisis of the early Cold War in 1948 was the struggle over control of

(A) Warsaw

(B) Vienna

(C) Budapest

(D) Bonn

(E) Berlin

Your Answer _____

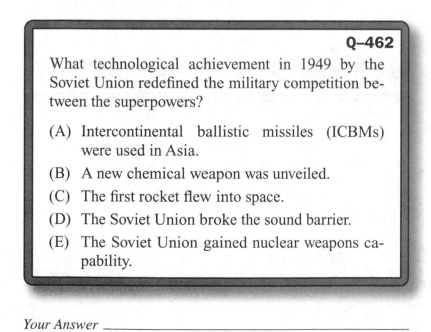

Q–462

What technological achievement in 1949 by the Soviet Union redefined the military competition between the superpowers?

(A) Intercontinental ballistic missiles (ICBMs) were used in Asia.

(B) A new chemical weapon was unveiled.

(C) The first rocket flew into space.

(D) The Soviet Union broke the sound barrier.

(E) The Soviet Union gained nuclear weapons capability.

Your Answer _____

Correct Answers

A–461

(E)   The occupation of postwar Germany by four Allied powers was a complex geographical mechanism. The capital, Berlin, was divided into four sections, each occupied by one of the Allied armies. This setup presented a problem because Berlin was located within the Soviet zone of occupation, the East. Hoping to bully the French, British, and Americans to abandon the former German capital, the Soviets sealed Berlin off from the rest of occupied Germany. This standoff between the Soviet Union and the rest of the Allies was the tensest confrontation in the immediate postwar period that began to frame the Cold War in Europe. The airlift to supply West Berlin finally forced the Soviets to recognize that the West was not going to give up the city.

A–462

(E)   At the end of the war, only the United States possessed the knowledge of the making and delivering of atomic weapons. This gave the United States a great advantage in dealing with the Soviet Union as a new political rival. But it took the Soviet Union only four years to acquire the same technology, which gave it some parity with the United States. This started a long weapons race and buildup by both superpowers that lasted for decades, into the 1980s.

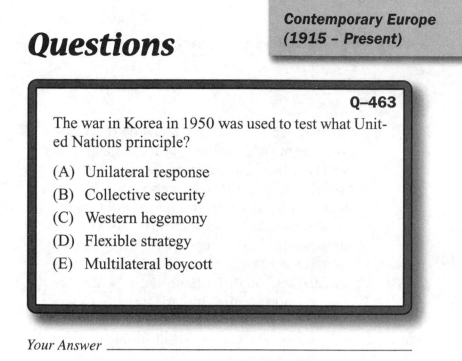

Q–463

The war in Korea in 1950 was used to test what United Nations principle?

(A) Unilateral response

(B) Collective security

(C) Western hegemony

(D) Flexible strategy

(E) Multilateral boycott

Your Answer _____

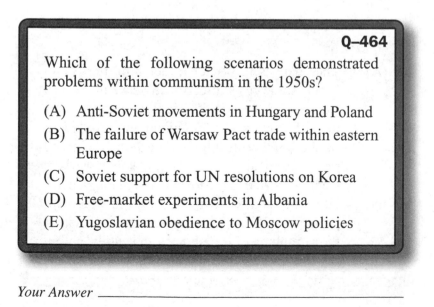

Q–464

Which of the following scenarios demonstrated problems within communism in the 1950s?

(A) Anti-Soviet movements in Hungary and Poland

(B) The failure of Warsaw Pact trade within eastern Europe

(C) Soviet support for UN resolutions on Korea

(D) Free-market experiments in Albania

(E) Yugoslavian obedience to Moscow policies

Your Answer _____

Correct Answers

A–463

(B) As with the League of Nations before World War II, an international peace organization was supposed to organize responses to crises. Military aggression was supposed to be met with quick pressure from the international community. Although tried in 1936 with the invasion of Ethiopia, collective security failed to make Italy back down. When North Korea invaded the South in 1950, the UN Security Council organized a military force from sixteen nations. The application of collective security sought to stop small problems from becoming large wars.

A–464

(A) The changes in Soviet leadership after Stalin led to some resistance to Moscow in eastern Europe. The year 1956 saw liberal movements in both Hungary and Poland that sought to weaken Soviet influence. The Polish released many political prisoners, and some workers went on strike. Dissidents in Hungary actually fought back with weapons and were suppressed by the Soviet army. The tensions within the communist bloc showed that unity within the Soviet-led governments was elusive.

Questions

Q–465

France experienced humiliating military defeat in which of its colonies in 1954?

(A) Mozambique

(B) Morocco

(C) Indochina

(D) East Timor

(E) Algeria

Your Answer _____

Q–466

What technological achievement in 1957 demonstrated communist prowess to the world?

(A) Deploying nuclear aircraft carriers

(B) Launching of super submarines

(C) Building SU-Tropalov bombers

(D) Putting the first satellite in space

(E) The explosion of the hydrogen bomb

Your Answer _____

Correct Answers

A–465

(C) France had been proud of its global empire before World War II, but after the war, it experienced native resistance movements in Asia and Africa. From 1946 to 1954, the Viet Minh fought the French for control of Indochina, which was composed of present-day Vietnam, Laos, and Cambodia. These nationalist movements formed alliances with the People's Republic of China, which was building a communist state. The United States supported the French because Europe's economy had been devastated by the war. The battle of Dien Bien Phu showed France's inability to defeat the Vietnamese and led to the end of French colonial power in Asia.

A–466

(D) The launch of *Sputnik* in 1957 gave the Soviet Union the chance to show its lead in space technology. The satellite had a small transmitter inside that sent out beeps for people on Earth to receive and listen to. It was part of the larger technological competition between the Soviet Union and the United States. Hydrogen bombs were developed earlier and also showed how the weapons race was producing more powerful means of destroying large population centers. The United States responded to the launch of *Sputnik* by reorganizing its space program and did what it could to catch up.

Questions

Q–467

Which of the following European countries granted independence to their colonial possessions in the 1950s?

(A) Norway, Belgium, and Poland

(B) Spain, France, and Austria

(C) Portugal, Great Britain, and Switzerland

(D) Holland, Great Britain and France

(E) France, Albania, and Greece

Your Answer _____

Q–468

The Suez crisis of 1956 revealed European frustrations with

(A) Israeli aggression in the Sinai

(B) rising Arab nationalism in Egypt

(C) Algerian radicals in North Africa

(D) Balkan revolutionaries

(E) Islamic fundamentalists in Arabia

Your Answer _____

Correct Answers

A–467

(D) Decolonization became a global trend in the 1950s as postwar European nations struggled to maintain their older empires. Africans and Asians had begun pressing for more freedom before the war. After the war, European power was considerably lessened, and native peoples organized and fought for their independence. Holland relinquished power in Indonesia, while Great Britain granted freedom to Ghana. France had to agree to leave Southeast Asia after its defeat in Vietnam.

A–468

(B) Great Britain and France had been given oversight of sections of the Middle East after World War I. Oil companies had taken advantage of this and found large reserves of petroleum in Arabia and Persia. The Suez Canal was owned by British and French stockholders and was of vital interest to the two European powers. In the early 1950s, Egyptian army officers took over the government and later threatened to nationalize the canal. This led to an unusual alliance among Britain, France, and Israel and a short war against Egypt in 1956. Egypt was defeated quickly, and the Israelis took the Sinai Peninsula. The United Nations and the international community, excluding Britain and France, intervened and the territory was returned to Egypt.

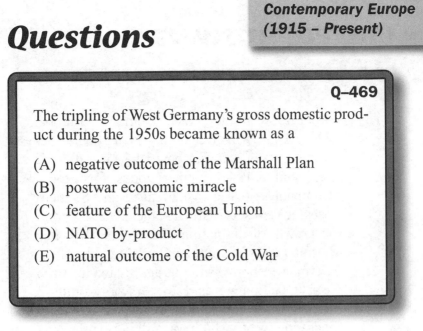

Q–469

The tripling of West Germany's gross domestic product during the 1950s became known as a

(A) negative outcome of the Marshall Plan

(B) postwar economic miracle

(C) feature of the European Union

(D) NATO by-product

(E) natural outcome of the Cold War

Your Answer _____

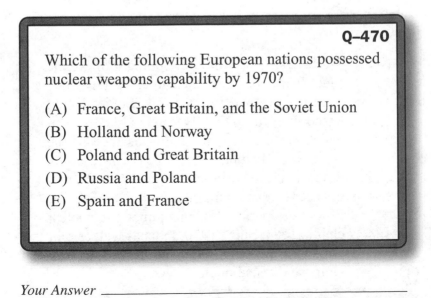

Q–470

Which of the following European nations possessed nuclear weapons capability by 1970?

(A) France, Great Britain, and the Soviet Union

(B) Holland and Norway

(C) Poland and Great Britain

(D) Russia and Poland

(E) Spain and France

Your Answer _____

Correct Answers

A–469

(B) After 1950, foreign trade boomed in Europe. The West German economy in particular became a manufacturing power because it made cars and other consumer goods for export. Companies such as Volkswagen and Siemens became very successful and fueled the economic growth of the nation. The Korean War had been a powerful stimulant to the growth of the German economy. After its aggression in World War II, Germany was restricted from forming a military so it could invest mainly in its manufacturing sector, which was still intact after having sustained minimal damage during the war.

A–470

(A) World War II saw the development of atomic (nuclear) weapons by the United States which were used to end the war. The Soviet Union tested its own nuclear weapons after the war, which set the pace for the arms race of the Cold War. Britain and France successfully tested nuclear weapons in the 1950s to join the nations that could deploy "the bomb." The People's Republic of China joined the nuclear club in 1964. Since 1970, India as well as other nations have created nuclear weapons programs and tested nuclear devices.

Q–471

Which of the following European nations were the most prosperous by the end of the 1960s?

(A) Ireland and Great Britain

(B) Romania and Italy

(C) Sweden and West Germany

(D) Hungary and Austria

(E) Greece and Spain

Your Answer _____

Q–472

The foundation for the European Economic Community (EEC) was formed by

(A) the North Atlantic Treaty Alliance in 1949

(B) the Dunbarton Oaks Conference

(C) agreements at Yalta in 1945

(D) the Concordat of 1953

(E) the Treaty of Rome in 1957

Your Answer _____

Correct Answers

A–471

(C) Industrial development continued to be uneven in Europe in the generation after World War II. Prewar powers such as Britain and France made modest gains, while West Germany and Sweden created industrial export economies that led Europe in business volume. The poorest nations in western Europe were Spain and Ireland, while the eastern European nations of Romania, Albania, and Bulgaria languished.

A–472

(E) After World War II, European nations began to discuss a customs union, or trade association, designed to help the economy of Europe and prevent future war by integrating its members. In 1956, European leaders met at the Intergovernmental Conference on the Common Market and Euratom. The conference led to the signature, on March 25, 1957, of the Treaty of Rome, establishing a European Economic Community. Tariffs were lowered and standardized to encourage the movement of goods from country to country in Europe. Wages were equalized so that workers could become more mobile within Europe. In the beginning, most members were central and southern nations such as Italy, West Germany, and the Netherlands. Other nations joined one by one until most of the western European nations belonged to the EEC, or the Common Market, which is what it came to be called.

Q–473

The possibility of a workers' revolution in Europe after 1950 was greatly discouraged as

(A) labor unions became less powerful

(B) governments favored the business class

(C) the Common Market levied higher taxes

(D) standards of living rose for western industrial employees

(E) managers' salaries declined

Your Answer _____

Q–474

The term *détente* can best be described as which of the following?

(A) Heightening tensions in Europe after 1961

(B) Free-trade agreements between allies after a war

(C) A cultivation of economic partnerships between regions

(D) A warming of relations between two antagonistic rivals

(E) Cultural exchanges between peoples from different regions

Your Answer _____

Correct Answers

A–473

(D) The European economic recovery, fueled by the Marshall Plan after World War II, was more rapid than many imagined. Nations such as West Germany, Sweden, and Switzerland enjoyed economic expansion and higher wages for their workers. This rising standard of living made many employees more comfortable and less likely to organize against the capitalist order. Trade unions lost some of their political power, and strikes were less common.

A–474

(D) The Cold War saw rising and falling tensions between the United States and the Soviet Union over time. Disagreements over Germany and Cuba almost brought about world war in the 1940s and 1960s, respectively. In the 1970s, relations had improved so that arms agreements and technological exchanges were possible. Joint space missions were carried out, and some began to discuss the end of the traditional enmity between communism and capitalism. Détente ended with the invasion of Afghanistan in 1979 by the Soviet Union, after which the United States boycotted the Moscow Olympics and cut off grain exports to the Soviet Union.

Questions

Q–475

Postwar French philosophers developed existential-ism as a

(A) means to inspire nationalism among the people

(B) response to Algerian terrorism

(C) way to encourage world peace

(D) a new political direction

(E) cynical and pessimistic reaction to the destruction of the 1940s

Your Answer _____

Q–476

Dramatic works that shocked audiences with unconventional themes after 1949 in Paris were part of

(A) a rebirth of European arts after the war

(B) the theater of the absurd

(C) new optimistic philosophical trends

(D) French neo-nationalism

(E) anti-imperialistic movements

Your Answer _____

Correct Answers

A–475

(E) The unprecedented destruction of World War II left Europe exhausted and dispirited. With the Cold War tensions and the new nuclear reality, some saw little reason to be hopeful about the future. The senseless loss of life of the 1940s made some intellectuals despair about the future. A new school of philosophy called existentialism denied the existence of God and considered the absurdity of life.

A–476

(B) In addition to the existential pessimism of the postwar period, the arts also expressed the absurdity of the human condition in the nuclear world. Samuel Beckett wrote plays that kept audiences off balance with unrelated events and plot twists. Characters were strange and clownish, creating a bizarre experience. This was a commentary on the strangeness and randomness of life itself.

Q–477

Which of the following was a by-product of rising wages and living standards in postwar Europe?

(A) Europe's percentage of the world population increased.

(B) Europeans paid lower medical costs.

(C) Fewer children finished school and illiteracy rose.

(D) A baby boom occurred.

(E) There were fewer white-collar jobs.

Your Answer ⎯⎯⎯⎯⎯⎯⎯⎯⎯⎯⎯⎯⎯⎯⎯⎯

Q–478

Large-scale commercial agriculture was part of the postwar

(A) green revolution

(B) Marshall Plan

(C) shortage of food in eastern Europe

(D) need for more farmers

(E) reorganization of labor organizations

Your Answer ⎯⎯⎯⎯⎯⎯⎯⎯⎯⎯⎯⎯⎯⎯⎯⎯

Correct Answers

A–477

(D) Workers saw their paychecks increase and living standards improve throughout the 1950s and 1960s. This encouraged families to have more children, which led to a baby boom. There were more managerial jobs created, which lifted some workers into higher positions, also with more pay. By the 1970s, Europe's population topped 320 million. This meant more money was needed for schools in many European nations.

A–478

(A) Immediately following World War II, the United States espoused a policy that would convert Germany into a pastoral and agricultural country that could never go to war again, but the Marshal Plan moved to industrialize agriculture. European agriculture recovered quickly after 1945, and large farm operations became more efficient and productive. In West Germany alone, agricultural production rose almost 300 percent between 1950 and 1965. Farming became more mechanized, and fertilizers boosted harvests across the continent. This made many northern European nations large-scale exporters of food through the 1970s and 1980s.

Questions

Q–479

The new urban sprawl of European cities saw the movement of many people to

(A) rural areas

(B) the outlying suburbs

(C) industrial zones

(D) the inner cities

(E) planned communities in the countryside

Your Answer _____

Q–480

Which of the following transportation technology breakthroughs made Europeans more mobile than ever before?

(A) Hydro-ferries between the continent and Scandinavia

(B) Maglev tracking for trains

(C) Autobahns without speed limits

(D) Jumbo jets and *trés grande vitesse* (TGV) trains

(E) Turbo cars

Your Answer _____

Correct Answers

A–479

(B) In countries from Great Britain to the Soviet Union, urban populations boomed. Many people moved to satellite communities that encircled the cities. Moscow grew to almost 5 million people by 1960. The population of France concentrated itself so that almost 20 percent of the people lived in the greater Paris area by the 1980s. This growth was tied to the industrial economy and the growing economies. After some deterioration of the inner cities, local governments began to plan urban growth more thoughtfully.

A–480

(D) The transition from propeller planes to jets in the 1950s made commercial travel faster and cheaper. Europeans could fly to North America in eight hours. Charter flights also made vacations to the sunny parts of Europe more common for northerners who had more wealth. Train technology also took a leap forward with the introduction of high-speed (*trés grande vitesse*) trains, which transported people faster than ever before, at speeds of over 200 kilometers an hour. Tourism boomed in Europe as Americans and Asians flew on cheap flights to Britain, France, Italy, and Germany.

Q–481

The growing prosperity of Europe was contrasted in the late 1960s with

(A) political upheaval and student demonstrations

(B) rising Cold War tensions

(C) support for American foreign policy

(D) violent evidence of racism

(E) the failure of large Swiss banks

Your Answer _____

_____

Q–482

The 1970s saw a warming of relations between

(A) France and Israel

(B) Germany and Poland

(C) the Soviet Union and the West

(D) Yugoslavia and Moscow

(E) Spain and Portugal

Your Answer _____

_____

Correct Answers

A–481

(A)   Throughout the West, the late 1960s were a turbulent time of student activism and large demonstrations. Paris was the scene of mass student rallies in 1968 that mirrored the unrest in the United States in the same year. A mood of anti-authoritarianism was prevalent among young people as they protested government policies in education and domestic affairs. Many young people felt repelled by the materialism of their World War II-era parents.

A–482

(C)   The Cold War division of Europe and the world was altered in the 1970s as new agreements were signed that led to more cooperation between the East and West. This period of détente led to joint space flights between the United States and the Soviet Union. Summit meetings between the superpowers became more common, and breakthroughs were made in arms control.

Questions

Q–483

Which of the following agreements led to symbolic gains in limiting nuclear arms by the superpowers in the 1970s?

(A) The Stockholm Agreements

(B) The Belgrade Accords

(C) The Nuclear Test Ban Treaty

(D) SALT

(E) The Geneva Convention

Your Answer _____

Q–484

The actions of which cartel caused the rapid rise of fuel costs in Europe in the 1970s?

(A) The EEU

(B) OPEC

(C) The Warsaw Pact

(D) The North Atlantic Consortium

(E) NAFTA

Your Answer _____

Correct Answers

A–483

(D) The relationship between Moscow and Washington changed in the 1970s as the United States established new contacts with China and negotiated with the Soviet Union to reduce nuclear arms. President Nixon traveled to both Beijing and Moscow to sign new agreements with the large communist nations. The Strategic Arms Limitation Treaty (SALT) was signed in 1972 in Moscow. Specific missile technologies were limited in the treaty, and earlier anxiety about war between the superpowers was decreased.

A–484

(B) Tensions in the Middle East led to war between Israel and its Arab neighbors. When Europe and the United States continued to support Israel, oil producers used their economic power to limit production, which caused fuel prices to rise. The Organization of Petroleum Exporting Countries (OPEC) was led by Saudi Arabia, which had the largest petroleum reserves in the world at that time. The rise in the cost of petroleum worldwide caused an inflationary trend as prices rose in Europe and the United States. It prompted governments to initiate conservation of their oil reserves and urge people to adjust their thermostats to save energy.

Questions

Q–485

Wide-ranging international agreements were concluded in the 1970s in

(A) Bruges, Belgium

(B) Bonn, West Germany

(C) Lisbon, Portugal

(D) Kent, England

(E) Helsinki, Finland

Your Answer _____

Q–486

The Prague Spring of 1968 refers to a time of

(A) communist orthodoxy in Hungary

(B) rapprochement between Moscow and Poland

(C) neo-Marxist orthodoxy

(D) political liberalization in Czechoslovakia

(E) solidarity among the members of the Warsaw Pact

Your Answer _____

Correct Answers

A–485

(E) The Conference on Security and Cooperation in Europe (CSCE) was a consortium of 33 European states, Canada, and the United States. A range of issues between the Soviets and the West was discussed in Helsinki, Finland, in 1975. The Soviets wanted the West to formalize the postwar boundaries in Europe, while the West pushed for more freedom to travel and for the liberalization of human rights.

A–486

(D) Czechoslovakia had the most liberal and democratic government in eastern Europe before the war. After the communists took over in 1948, liberals continued to hope for more self-rule in the country. In the mid-1960s, a progressive communist leader, Alexander Dubcek, emerged. In 1968, he became the first secretary and made popular reforms within the party. He talked of a national communism that would improve the lives of the citizens. His reforms were not favored by Moscow; in August, Soviet tanks invaded the country and Dubcek was replaced.

Q–487

What is the main message of the 1962 cartoon shown above?

(A) The Soviet Union is suspicious of western economic combinations.

(B) Capitalism is losing ground to communism in the 1960s.

(C) Europe has not recovered from World War II.

(D) Polish resistance to socialism is growing.

(E) The Common Market is becoming a failed experiment.

Your Answer _____

_____

Correct Answers

A–487

(A)   In the late 1950s, western Europe moved closer to establishing an economic union. This Common Market was part of the backdrop of the Cold War, which had Europe divided into two economic zones. The capitalistic West, led by six nations, began to discuss trade agreements in 1957, which became the Common Market. This development was viewed with suspicion by the Soviet Union, which dominated eastern Europe. The 1962 cartoon shows the Soviet premier, Khrushchev, watching the formation of the Common Market with a disapproving look.

Q–488

The world energy crisis of the early 1970s was caused in part by

(A) the assassination of Prime Minister Meir in Israel

(B) tensions in the Middle East and increasing fuel consumption in the West

(C) the Vietnam War

(D) pan-Arab nationalism promoted by Nassar

(E) American support for a Palestinian state

Your Answer _____

Q–489

All of the following are features of the modern European welfare state EXCEPT

(A) retirement pensions

(B) unemployment benefits

(C) travel stipends

(D) neonatal care

(E) socialized medical care

Your Answer _____

Correct Answers

A–488

(B) Global consumption of petroleum rose steadily in the industrial West throughout the twentieth century. After World War II, major oil corporations searched for and found large petroleum reserves in the Middle East and South America. The creation of the state of Israel provoked tensions between Zionist Israel and neighboring Arab nations. Because the largest oil producer was also Arab Saudi Arabia, this set the stage for the use of petroleum as an economic weapon. Even with the discovery of more oil in Alaska, the United States needed to import large quantities of Middle Eastern petroleum. After four wars in four decades between Israel and Arab nations, Saudi Arabia cut back on oil production, which led to a rise in crude petroleum prices worldwide.

A–489

(C) After World War II, both eastern and western European nations greatly expanded welfare benefits for their citizens. These socialist policies provided for the poor, cared for the elderly, paid unemployment benefits to the jobless, and provided help for young mothers. These benefits are expensive for governments to provide, so taxes have also risen in step with the expansion of the welfare state. Health care for all people, rich or poor, is a hallmark of the modern European state.

Q–490

THE MAN WHO CAME TO DINNER

The primary message in the cartoon above is to show the Soviet Union's

(A) benevolent leadership in the Baltics

(B) blatant commandeering of Estonian resources

(C) displays of socialist solidarity with its satellites

(D) beneficial agricultural programs in eastern Europe

(E) Cold War blunders

Your Answer _____

_____

Correct Answers

A–490

(B)   The 1979 cartoon above suggests that the Soviet Union is the unwanted dinner guest that eats the hosts out of house and home. An elderly farm family represents the Estonians. The Soviet is dressed in uniform to symbolize the military might of the Soviet Union. The size of the Soviet soldier may also stand for the large military presence in the Baltic countries. The plates of the Estonians are empty while the Russian is gorging himself on the national farm production.

Q–491

A new emphasis on environmental issues in Europe after 1970 led to

(A) the fall of governments that had polluted their rivers

(B) the first interior ministries in some countries

(C) new political alliances between liberals and moderates

(D) breakthroughs in nuclear technology

(E) the organization of green parties in major European states

Your Answer _____

_____

Q–492

The breakup of the Soviet Union after 1989 can be attributed in part to

(A) Cold War success in Afghanistan

(B) arms agreements with the United States

(C) new nationalist movements within the Soviet Union

(D) oppressive Politburo policies

(E) pressure from the United Nations to liberalize immigration policies

Your Answer _____

_____

Correct Answers

A–491

(E) As a political force, environmentalism dates back to the late 1960s. The space programs gave humans new perspectives on planet Earth, and some began to preach against the industrial production that degraded the environment. By the 1970s, interest groups began to organize, and eventually political parties developed green agendas and began to win seats in national assemblies. The Green Party in Germany was one of the early successes, and similar parties appeared across Europe by 1985.

A–492

(C) The Soviet Union had always been a diverse mix of people in Europe and Asia. The totalitarian dictatorship of Stalin kept it together before and after World War II. As the Politburo liberalized certain policies in the 1980s, satellite nations and ethnic groups within the Soviet Union began to speak out for more freedom. Pieces of the Soviet Union quickly broke away to create new nations such as Kazakhstan, Ukraine, and Moldova.

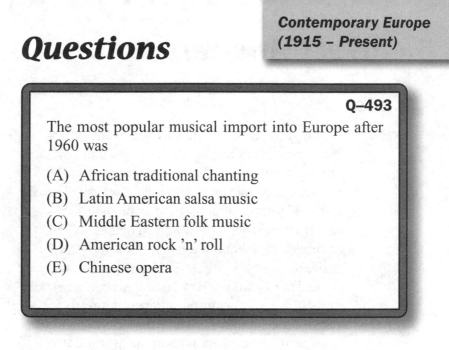

Q–493

The most popular musical import into Europe after 1960 was

(A) African traditional chanting

(B) Latin American salsa music

(C) Middle Eastern folk music

(D) American rock 'n' roll

(E) Chinese opera

Your Answer _____

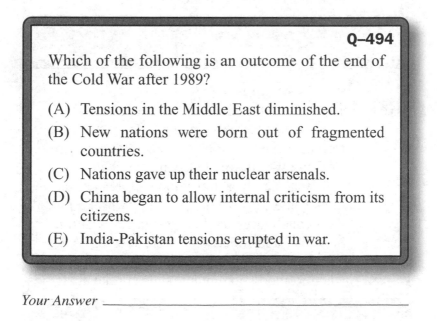

Q–494

Which of the following is an outcome of the end of the Cold War after 1989?

(A) Tensions in the Middle East diminished.

(B) New nations were born out of fragmented countries.

(C) Nations gave up their nuclear arsenals.

(D) China began to allow internal criticism from its citizens.

(E) India-Pakistan tensions erupted in war.

Your Answer _____

Correct Answers

A–493

(D)   Although rock 'n' roll has African roots stemming from blues music, white artists like Elvis Presley popularized the new sound first in the United States and then around the world. The so-called youth culture started in the late 1950s and continued into the 1960s. Themes of this culture were rebellion against authority and a desire to live more freely. This genre was transplanted to England, and in the mid-sixties, a new wave of rock 'n' roll music swept Great Britain and the rest of Europe. The British sound became its own phenomenon spearheaded by immensely popular artists such as the Beatles, the Rolling Stones, and the Who. These groups toured Europe and the rest of the world, and their music reached millions of fans.

A–494

(B)   The end of the Cold War came quickly and resulted in nations breaking into pieces. The former Soviet Union became known as the Commonwealth of Independent States, but this was merely a transition before new nations came into being. Yugoslavia broke into numerous pieces, and nations such as Serbia, Slovenia, and Macedonia were created. After 1990, more than 10 new nations were created when formerly communist states broke apart.

Questions

Q–495

Northern Europe solved its shortage of workers in the 1960s and afterward by

(A) giving mothers tax incentives to have more babies

(B) offering jobs to immigrants from southern Europe and Turkey

(C) exporting jobs to South Asia

(D) manufacturing goods in Latin America

(E) hiring teenagers to work in factories

Your Answer _____

Q–496

A rejection of scientific objectivity and absolutist ideologies led to which of the following intellectual movements in Europe after World War II?

(A) Neo-existentialism

(B) Contemporary fatalism

(C) Absurdist theater

(D) Authentic progressivism

(E) Postmodernism

Your Answer _____

Correct Answers

A–495

(B) As the export economies of Germany and Scandinavia grew, they had difficulty finding enough workers for the manufacturing and service industries. Foreign workers often took jobs that locals would not do, so they tended to be paid less and to receive fewer benefits. Guest workers (*Gastarbeiter* in German) often were not offered citizenship and tended to make up the lower classes. As economies stagnated in the economic malaise of the 1970s, there was some antiforeign sentiment in Germany and France, where large populations of Middle Easterners lived.

A–496

(E) The term *modern* has been used to describe the post-Renaissance world, but after World War II, intellectuals began to discuss a postmodern view of history and literature. Postmodernists emphasized the subjective, rather than the objective, in life. Science and technology were criticized and even blamed for the abuses and carnage of centralized states such as Nazi Germany and Stalinist Russia. After 1960, postmodernists created new approaches to writing, art, and film in Europe and North America.

Questions

Q–497

Religious reform and liberalism was represented in postwar Europe by

(A) secular approaches by church leaders

(B) a new schism in the Christian church

(C) the leadership of Pope Paul XXII

(D) the Second Vatican Council

(E) the exodus of Jewish intellectuals from the eastern bloc

Your Answer _____

Q–498

Which of the following goals was paramount for postwar feminists in Europe?

(A) Suffrage rights in all nations

(B) Environmental reforms in governmental policy

(C) Availability of birth control for poor women

(D) Fighting for equity in the workplace and gaining political power

(E) Liberalizing marriage laws

Your Answer _____

Correct Answers

A–497

(D) Although church attendance declined in postwar Europe, millions were still faithful believers of Christianity, Judaism, and Islam. The pope in Rome continued to guide Catholics, and John XXIII used his influence to modernize the church in the early 1960s. The Second Vatican Council updated the liturgy and allowed Catholics to use their own languages instead of the traditional Latin. New dialogues were opened with Protestants, Jews, and Orthodox faiths.

A–498

(D) After women won the right to vote in western democracies, they gained increasing influence in those nations. After 1960, a new phase of female activism began to seek equality in other spheres. More women took leadership roles in companies, and many more were elected to political office. Scandinavia took the lead in electing more women to its parliament, and Great Britain chose its first female head of government in 1979. A chief goal was to pass legislation that would grant women parity in the workplace. Equal pay for equal work was the common logic that framed desired economic opportunities for women.

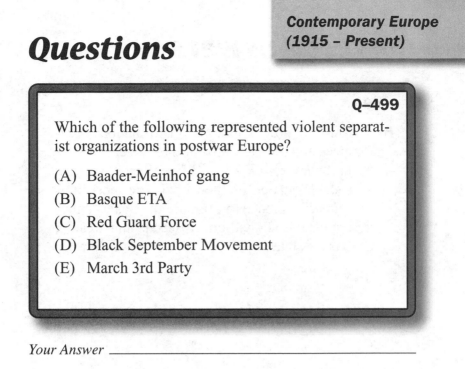

Q–499

Which of the following represented violent separatist organizations in postwar Europe?

(A) Baader-Meinhof gang

(B) Basque ETA

(C) Red Guard Force

(D) Black September Movement

(E) March 3rd Party

Your Answer _____

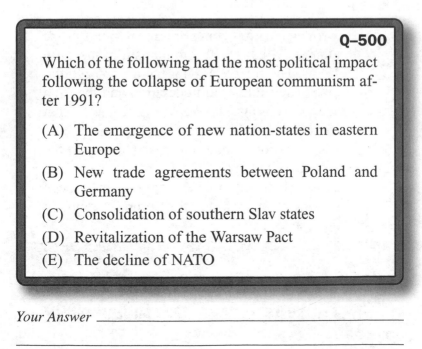

Q–500

Which of the following had the most political impact following the collapse of European communism after 1991?

(A) The emergence of new nation-states in eastern Europe

(B) New trade agreements between Poland and Germany

(C) Consolidation of southern Slav states

(D) Revitalization of the Warsaw Pact

(E) The decline of NATO

Your Answer _____

Correct Answers

A–499

(B) Minority groups in some major nations organized and tried to fight for their independence. In Spain and France, some Basque people sought a nation of their own. The most radical used violence to pressure the Spanish government to allow them to secede and create a Basque state.

A–500

(A) Two large nation-states fragmented in Europe after the collapse of communism in the early 1990s. The former Soviet Union first reorganized itself into a confederation and then fell apart. Yugoslavia broke into five pieces that led to the reappearance of Serbia, Croatia, Slovenia, and other new nations. This led to the second redrawing of the European map since 1940. Many of the new nations have been seeking membership in the European Union in the last decade.

 Take Test-Readiness Quiz 4 on CD
(to review questions 376–500)

Blank Cards for *Your Own Questions*

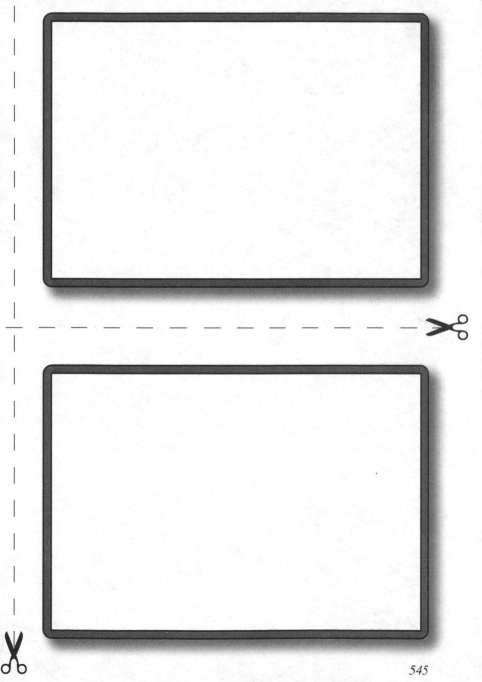

Correct Answers

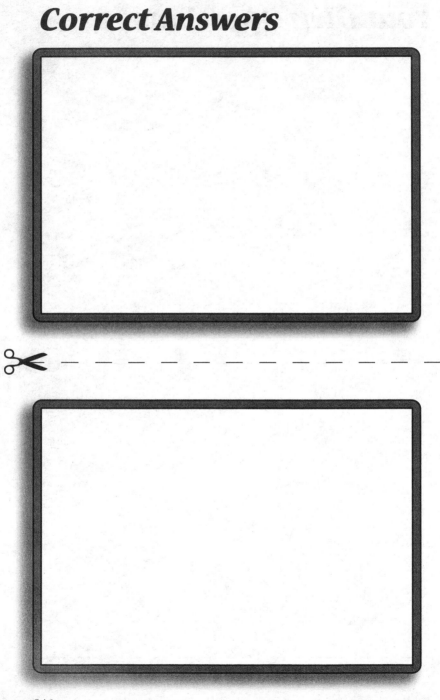

Blank Cards for *Your Own Questions*

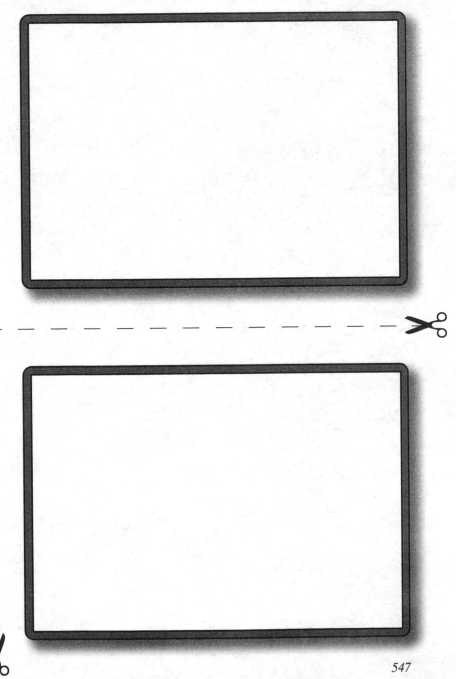

Correct Answers

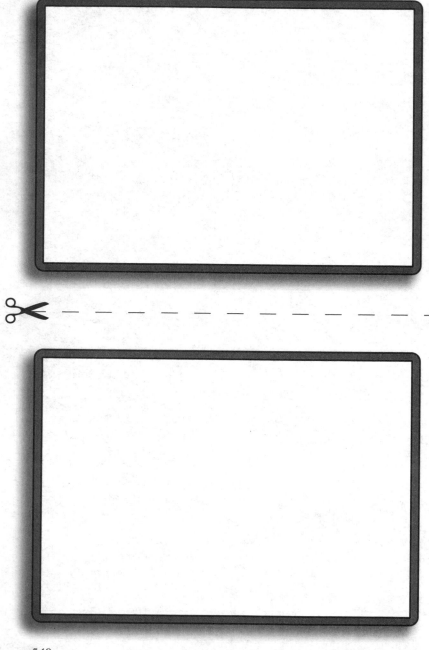

Blank Cards for
Your Own Questions

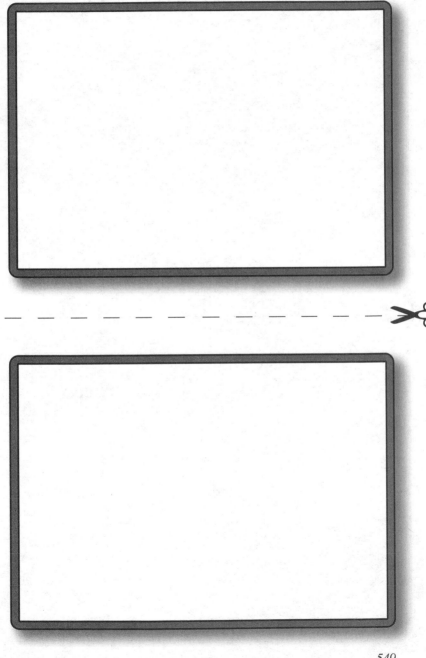

Correct Answers

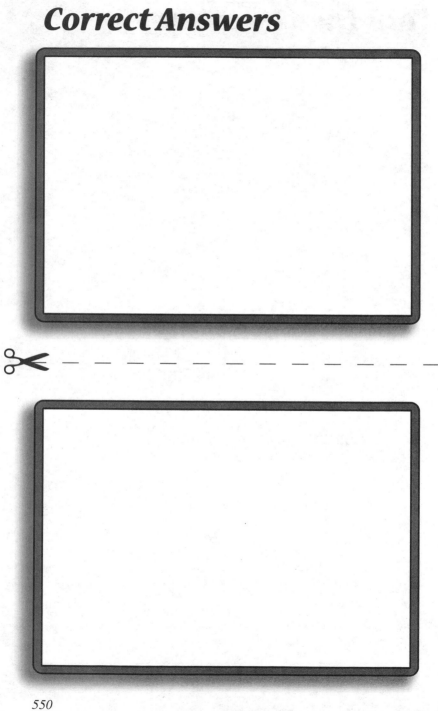

Index

REA's Test Preps

The Best in Test Preparation

- REA "Test Preps" are **far more** comprehensive than any other test preparation series
- Each book contains full-length practice tests based on the most recent exams
- **Every** type of question likely to be given on the exams is included
- Answers are accompanied by **full** and **detailed** explanations

REA publishes hundreds of test prep books. Some of our titles include:

Advanced Placement Exams (APs)
Art History
Biology
Calculus AB & BC
Chemistry
Economics
English Language & Composition
English Literature & Composition
European History
French Language
Government & Politics
Latin Vergil
Physics B & C
Psychology
Spanish Language
Statistics
United States History
World History

College-Level Examination Program (CLEP)
American Government
College Algebra
General Examinations
History of the United States I
History of the United States II
Introduction to Educational Psychology
Human Growth and Development
Introductory Psychology
Introductory Sociology
Principles of Management
Principles of Marketing
Spanish
Western Civilization I
Western Civilization II

SAT Subject Tests
Biology E/M
Chemistry
French
German
Literature
Mathematics Level 1, 2
Physics
Spanish
United States History

Graduate Record Exams (GREs)
Biology
Chemistry
Computer Science
General
Literature in English
Mathematics
Physics
Psychology

ACT - ACT Assessment

ASVAB - Armed Services Vocational Aptitude Battery

CBEST - California Basic Educational Skills Test

CDL - Commercial Driver License Exam

CLAST - College Level Academic Skills Test

COOP, HSPT & TACHS - Catholic High School Admission Tests

FE (EIT) - Fundamentals of Engineering Exams

FTCE - Florida Teacher Certification Examinations

GED

GMAT - Graduate Management Admission Test

LSAT - Law School Admission Test

MAT - Miller Analogies Test

MCAT - Medical College Admission Test

MTEL - Massachusetts Tests for Educator Licensure

NJ HSPA - New Jersey High School Proficiency Assessment

NYSTCE - New York State Teacher Certification Examinations

PRAXIS PLT - Principles of Learning & Teaching Tests

PRAXIS PPST - Pre-Professional Skills Tests

PSAT/NMSQT

SAT

TExES - Texas Examinations of Educator Standards

THEA - Texas Higher Education Assessment

TOEFL - Test of English as a Foreign Language

USMLE Steps 1,2,3 - U.S. Medical Licensing Exams

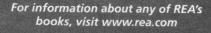

For information about any of REA's books, visit www.rea.com

Research & Education Association
61 Ethel Road W., Piscataway, NJ 08854
Phone: (732) 819-8880